THE LEAP
OUT OF TIME

and into the infinite, out of the difficult concrete into the easy universal, represents, Father Lynch tells us, the decisive temptation of the modern writer. Jean-Paul Sartre, Graham Greene, T. S. Eliot, Eugene O'Neill—each of these has at times fled from the Word-made flesh (which is the essential work of the imagination) to embrace facile absolutes.

What errors of vision bring about this flight from the real? What posture of the soul can give us the courage to end the flight and, instead, to move resolutely through the finite and definite realities that constitute our human task?

In answering these questions, the author turns once again to literature. Offering us examples from artists as varied as Dostoyevsky and Joyce Cary, from characters as seemingly contradictory as Oedipus and Falstaff, he defines, in a way at once traditional and startlingly new, the meaning of human life.

Father Lynch has written on subjects ranging from the metaphysics of Plato to the place of imagination in the popular arts. He has most recently written a series of programs on the imagination for "The Catholic Hour." He is currently developing a book on the mental sciences for the Mentor-Omega Series.

"This is a wise book, and the hours spent with it are spent well."

—Yale Review

Other MENTOR OMEGA Books

Christ
and
Apollo

THE DIMENSIONS OF
THE LITERARY IMAGINATION

by *William F. Lynch, S. J.*

KANSAS SCHOOL OF RELIGION
UNIVERSITY OF KANSAS
1300 OREAD AVENUE
LAWRENCE, KANSAS 66044

A MENTOR-OMEGA BOOK
Published by THE NEW AMERICAN LIBRARY

> *From twenty centuries of literature and scholarship, Mentor-Omega Books present a treasury of Catholic thought for the modern reader.*

religion in literature
Creation (literary, artistic, etc)

Published as a MENTOR-OMEGA BOOK by arrangement with Sheed and Ward, Inc., who have authorized this softcover edition. A hardcover edition is available from Sheed and Ward, Inc., 64 University Place, New York 3, New York.

First Printing, April, 1963

Imprimi Potest:
    John M. Daley, S. J.
    Praep. Prov. Marylandiae

Nihil Obstat:
    Thomas J. McHugh, LL.D.
    Censor Librorum
    February 12, 1960

Imprimatur:
    ✠ Jerome D. Hannan
    Bishop of Scranton
    February 16, 1960

MENTOR TRADEMARK REG. U.S. PAT. OFF. AND FOREIGN COUNTRIES
REGISTERED TRADEMARK—MARCA REGISTRADA
HECHO EN CHICAGO, U.S.A.

MENTOR-OMEGA BOOKS are published *in the United States* by The New American Library of World Literature, Inc., 501 Madison Avenue, New York 22, New York, *in Canada* by The New American Library of Canada Limited, 156 Front Street West, Toronto 1, Ontario

PRINTED IN THE UNITED STATES OF AMERICA

CONTENTS

CONTENTS

ACKNOWLEDGMENTS

THE AUTHOR gratefully acknowledges the kindness of the publishers and authors who have granted him permission to quote from the following material:

La Renaissance du XIIe Siècle by G. Paré, A. Bruner and P. Tremblay, copyright 1933 by Librairie Philosophique J. Vrin.

Esquisse D'Une Histoire De L'Exégèse Latin au Moyen Age by C. Spicq, copyright 1944 by Librairie Philosophique J. Vrin.

The Latin Works of Dante, copyright 1934 by J. M. Dent and Sons, Ltd.

Boccaccio on Poetry, translated by Charles G. Osgood, copyright 1930 by Princeton University Press.

"On Early Christian Exegesis" by Walter J. Burghardt, S. J., from *Theological Studies,* XI (1950).

The Book of the Beasts, translated by T. H. White, copyright 1954 by T. H. White. Published by A. Watkins, Inc.

"Stephen Langton and the Four Senses of Scripture" by Beryl Smalley, from *Speculum* VI (1931).

Mimesis: The Representation of Reality in Western Literature by Erich Auerbach, translated by Willard Trask, copyright 1953 by Princeton University Press.

The Study of the Bible in the Middle Ages by Beryl Smalley, copyright 1952 by Basil Blackwell.

"Myth, Method and the Future" by William Troy, from *Chimera* IV (Spring 1946).

"Historical Criticism" by D. W. Robertson, from *English Institute Essays 1950,* copyright 1951 by Columbia University Press.

The Business of Criticism by Helen Gardner, copyright 1959 by Clarendon Press.

"Symbolism in Medieval Literature" by M. W. Bloomfield, copyright 1958 by the University of Chicago.

"Dante's Ten Terms for the Treatment of the Treatise" by R. P. Blackmur from *Kenyon Review* XIV (Spring 1952).

Gothic Architecture and Scholasticism by Erwin Panofsky, copyright 1957 by St. Vincent Archabbey. Published by Meridian Books 1957.

Poetics of Music in Six Lessons by Igor Stravinsky, copyright 1956 by Harvard University Press.

The Meaning of Art by Herbert Read, copyright 1951 by Faber and Faber.

Letters of W. B. Yeats ed. by Allan Wade, copyright 1955 by The Macmillan Company.

"Time and François Mauriac" by Michael F. Maloney, from *Blackfriars* (April 1957).

Christ and Time by Oscar Cullman, copyright 1950 by W. L. Jenkins. Published by Westminster Press.

"La Pensée Hébraique" from *Essai sur la Pensée biblique* by Claude Tresmontant, copyright 1953 by Les Editions du Cerf.

The Epistle to the Romans by Karl Barth, copyright 1950 by Oxford University Press.

Proust: Portrait of a Genius by André Maurois, copyright 1950 by André Maurois. Published by Harper and Brothers.

Lectures in America by Gertrude Stein, copyright 1957 by Beacon Press.

A Grammar of Assent by John Henry Newman, by permission of Doubleday and Company.

The Anathemata by David Jones, copyright 1952 by Faber and Faber.

"The Emperor Jones" from *The Emperor Jones, Anna Christie and The Hairy Ape*, copyright 1921 by Horace Liveright, Inc. Renewed 1948 by Eugene O'Neill. "Lazarus Laughed" from *Nine Plays by Eugene O'Neill*. Copyright 1926 and renewed 1953 by Eugene O'Neill. Reprinted by permission of Random House, Inc. "Mourning Becomes Electra" from *Nine Plays by Eugene O'Neill*. Copyright 1931 and renewed 1958 by Carlotta Monterey O'Neill. Reprinted by permission of Random House.

Theory of Literature by Austin Warren and René Wellek, copyright 1956 by Harcourt, Brace and Co.

The Modern Temper by Joseph Wood Krutch, copyright 1956 by Harcourt, Brace and Co.

"The Wasteland" by T. S. Eliot, from *Complete Poems and Plays 1909-1935*, copyright 1936 by Harcourt, Brace and Co.

"Four Quartets" by T. S. Eliot, copyright 1943 by T. S. Eliot. Reprinted by permission of Harcourt, Brace and Co.

"Paradise Lost" from *Six Plays* by Clifford Odets, copyright 1939 by Clifford Odets. Reprinted by permission of Random House.

"Riders to the Sea" by John M. Synge, from *Five Great Modern Irish Plays,* by permission of Random House.

Doctor Faustus by Thomas Mann, copyright 1948 by Alfred A. Knopf.

The Plague by Albert Camus, copyright 1948 by Alfred A. Knopf.

"Winterset" by Maxwell Anderson, copyright 1935 by Anderson House and Maxwell Anderson.

Acknowledgments

"Riders to the Sea," by John M. Synge, from *Five Great Modern Irish Plays* by permission of Random House.

Doctor Faustus by Thomas Mann, copyright 1948 by Alfred A. Knopf.

The Trial by Albert Camus, copyright 1944 by Alfred A. Knopf.

Winesburg, Ohio by Sherwood Anderson, copyright 1931 by Sherwood Anderson and Sherwood Anderson.

INTRODUCTION

IN WRITING this book I have been guided by the general assumption that any effort to keep literature in its rightful relation with the human and the real is a service, no matter how meagre, to the truth and to civilization. Every effort to combat the view which makes literature an esoteric and isolated phenomenon in human history is a service to literature itself. This is especially important in the case of those younger people who stand on the first brink of a literary training. They are simply not attracted if and when we tell them that literature is literature and nothing else, that it stands on its own inward feet as a new reality over against every other reality, that it is absolutely autonomous, that the imagination is a special and isolated faculty of man meant to put a relatively few in touch with a special and isolated field of reality.

It would really be quite difficult to count the number of forms of aesthetic theory or of actual criticism which thus give literature a basically strange character. I can only suggest a few in a single paragraph. There is the theory that the literary imagination is absolutely "creative" and productive of altogether new and self-contained realities. There is another which says that if the world is pretty bad the imagination can supply a better substitute. Or literature is a Platonic tool (poor Plato) which puts us in touch with absolutes. Or it is a religion, and the writer a new high-priest who alone can put us in touch with the "sacred." Or we are told that the literary vision is made possible by achieving a "psychic distance" from the actual. Then there are all the non-cognitive theories of poetry which locate it in a world of sensibility without sense. Or there are the various equations of poetry with prayer, and of the artistic process with the inner life of the mystics. Far worse, of course, for the good of literature are all those half doctrines which reduce its life to a life of "taste" in the least important sense of that word or which implicitly tell us that there are bound to be terrible hours in the life of the hyperactive American when he will have nothing better to do than to read good books. He is told that *a gentleman* should read and he submits with as much grace as he can. He goes to college and takes courses in literature on pretty much the same premise. The premise is that literature is wonderful, has nothing to do with anything, and has a place in the American economy.

Those who preach and teach the absolute autonomy of literature are contributors to and causes of this situation. They mean well, but their absolute professionalism and unionism is now not only old-fashioned but is doing more harm than good. Northrop Frye in *The Anatomy of Criticism* tells us insistently that the literary imagination is altogether professional and autonomous and is not science or politics or metaphysics or theology. F. R. Leavis and a number of others give the same kind of warning. But the thought occurs to me that this particular battle, important though it was, has been won, and if we keep fighting it, we will push literary studies into an increasingly remote position where the "people"—who can be pretty sensible—will decide that it is relevant to nothing. As a matter of fact this position already has its sophisticated defenders. But it involves the paying of a price, not the least element of which is solitude.

There is, of course, another refuge in the teaching of literature. It is to declare that literature *is* relevant and to begin to find in it a treasure house of philosophy or theology or politics or sociology. I do not know which taking of refuge is more baleful in our day, but the two attacks, the attack on the absolute purity, autonomy and "irrelevancy" of literature and the attack on the superficial and artificial relevancies of literature to various other fields, can both be used as masks to avoid the question of that true and fundamental relevancy of the literary organism to reality without which the student is perfectly entitled to his boredom or lack of orientation.

It is with this question of fundamental relevancy that this book deals. Its principal point is simple, but it is a simplicity, I hope, which takes on all the complications of the central literary modes and questions without losing simplicity. It holds that the literary process is a highly cognitive passage through the finite and definite realities of man and the world. It is indeed a literary and not a sociological or theological passage (but that I take for granted). I also take for granted, but do not leave the matter without evidence, that the finite and the definite are not flat but have dimensions, and these dimensions can include even the theological. Of course, these dimensions must all be contained within the literary organisms, and must, therefore, be properly literary facts. But again we can also take this for granted as a proviso that must be consistently respected. The counter proviso, however, must always be that the definition of the autonomy of a literary fact should never become absurd.

The test of the validity of an idea must lie in whether or no it is fruitful as it meets the exigencies of the different questions held up against it. If the idea of this book is that literary insight comes from the penetration of the finite and the definite concrete in all its interior dimensions and according to all its real lines, then we must successively ask whether this idea makes sense for the problems of time, of tragedy, of comedy, of creativity. Can it explain what is wrong with the univocal imagination and what is right with the analogical? Can it throw a little light on our contemporary discussion of romanticism and angelism? Does it keep the exploratory task of the imagination properly and endlessly open? Can it give a proper place to a "theological imagination"? Can it add to the discussion which centers around the possibility of a Christic imagination? Does it give a healthy but not self-defeating explanation for the autonomy of the imagination? Or is it a supposition that is here and there effective and illuminating but must constantly be abandoned at critical moments in the face of central literary questions.

I have, therefore, written a book which is an exploration. It nowhere speaks its final mind at any one point and cannot (or should not) be judged with finality at any one point. On the other hand it is the kind of exploration which leaves itself vulnerable and open to approval or disapproval on every page. The method, then, is the Platonic use of the hypothesis: either it succeeds and marches to the tested status of a real Idea and what Newman would call a real assent; or it starts limping, breaks down too often, and must finally be discarded or given a trivial place. The trained reader, and my betters in literature, philosophy, theology, must decide what is the case. I will be happy if it finds *a* place.

As for the title, *Christ and Apollo.* Nietzsche and Spengler have accustomed us to the contrariety and the pairing of Dionysus and Apollo: energy and form, infinite and finite, enthusiasm and control, romantic and classic. Because I think that in our time we need a new movement toward the definite and away from the dream, I take even the symbol of Apollo as a kind of infinite dream over against Christ who was full of definiteness and actuality—and was on that account rejected by every gnostic system since, even up to now. Even if a little unjustly, let Apollo stand for everything that is weak and pejorative in the "aesthetic man" of Kierkegaard and for that kind of fantasy beauty which is a sort of infinite, which is easily gotten everywhere, but which will not abide the straitened gates of limitation that leads to stronger beauty. Let him also stand for a kind of autonomous and facile intellectualism, a Cartesianism, that thinks form can be given to the world by the top of the head alone, without contact with the world, without contact with the rest of the self.

On the other hand I mean Christ to stand for the completely definite, for the Man who, in taking on our human nature (as the artist must) took on every inch of it (save sin) in all its density, and Who so obviously did not march too quickly or too glibly to beauty, the infinite, the dream. I take Him, secondly, as the model and source of that energy and courage we again need to enter the finite as the only creative and generative source of beauty. Finally, but only at the end of this book and in a provisional chapter, I raise certain ontological questions about Christ as the creator and the actuality behind a new imagination and a new creation. And I keep before my mind the remark of W. H. Auden that no one cares much who were the cousins and the sisters and the aunts of Apollo whereas we are completely interested in every detail of the life and being of Christ. Erich Auerbach, in his *Mimesis,* has clarified for us what this has meant for the development of the literary imagination in the West, for the development of "a new heart and a new spirit."

"A new heart and a new spirit." This would indeed seem once more to be the great desideratum. What we need is the restoration of a confidence in the fundamental power of the finite and limited concretions of our human life. But not a cheap confidence.

As I finish this introduction I have by happy accident been reading the work of a psychologist who proclaims the discovery of the "fourth narcissistic hurt" to the greatness of man. He alludes to the famous statement by Freud that mankind has been the subject of three fairly recent narcissistic mortifications: there was Copernicus, who proved that the earth is not the center of the universe: there was Darwin's demonstration that man is not the special crown of creation; there was Freud's own revelation that man is not the master of his own limited house. And finally there is this fourth discovery: that man has a principle in him under the drive of which he is intent on destroying himself.

Perhaps these men have done us an inestimable service by pushing us back on ourselves, our true selves and the true size of our own concrete limitations. For there lies the real power. Not a romantic power which avoids the concretions in the name of unrooted dreams but the power of real being outside of and real self-identity inside the human person. These are the two pearls without price. They are the two things which I have proposed as the relevant objects of the literary imagination.

The supplements, quite extensive on some subjects, have been inserted for several reasons. The first reason was to provide a convenience for many teachers who might be helped by the type of documentation they find there. The supplements will support many a judgment that emerges in the body of the book. The second reason is this. I take great consolation out of thinking that the central judgments that lie ahead are not personal in any narrow sense but are a reflection, in a new generation, of insights that have been the property of a long and creative tradition.

Special attention should be called to the fact that the supplement on the nature of medieval biblical exegesis is the work of Dr. John McCall of the English department of Georgetown University. I cannot thank Dr. McCall sufficiently for so fine an answer to a request that he gather such materials as a background to the type of contemporary literary speculation contained in this book. Both of us would be concerned that the purpose of the supplement be not misunderstood. Certainly there is a strong strain of conviction behind the major part of its documentation, a conviction that no spiritual penetration of the meaning of texts, natural or supernatural, is forthcoming unless the literal and earthly level of texts and facts is thoroughly explored. But in the presentation we intend no appeal for a return to medievalism and we offer many facets of this particular area of human thought, document sometimes contradicting document, in order that students and scholars might have the wherewithal to continue this discussion.

As I bring my own critical work to the temporary conclusion that is meant by any book, I am pleased by the close parallelism of the problems and the conclusions that are open to the literary critic and the biblical theologian. My own final chapter on these matters is only a first thrust at the problems involved and I would recommend to the reader, if he is interested in the total human biblical environment of these literary questions, the brilliant book of the Benedictine scholar Dom Célestin Charlier, *The Christian Approach to the Bible*. We have both independently arrived (he in the analysis of Hebraic and biblical thought and I in the order of current literary problems) at the same conclusions and the same points of appeal.

When one turns to thanking people he is reminded of a salutary truth. Often when a writer tries to say something it is already in the air or much of it has already been said or the germs have been given him by innumerable friends. My own great abiding "friends" and givers have been Plato, St. Ignatius and Cardinal Newman. My contemporary helpers and friends have been as many as the people I have met or have read: but especially writers like Francis Fergusson and Allen Tate, Father Martin C. D'Arcy, S.J., and Father John Courtney Murray, S.J. For various forms of editorial assistance I am deeply indebted to Catherine Carter and above all to Philip Scharper, editor of Sheed and Ward, whose wisdom and friendship have been indispensable. I should also like to thank the editor of *Thought* for his permission to use here certain materials which, in a considerably different form, first appeared in its pages.

Christ
and
Apollo

1 The Definite

This is a book about the dimensions of the literary image. It is certain that, as in the case of every form of professionalism, literature has its own autonomy. It is not psychology or metaphysics or theology or anything else save itself. But it can possess all these things as intrinsic dimensions of its own images and not as artificial appendages or alien invaders. The first and basic image of the literary imagination is the definite or the finite, and not the infinite, the endless, the dream. Beginning with the first battle between the gnostic and Hebraic imaginations, there has been a long war between the two forms of the imagination, between the men of the finite and the men of the infinite. This book takes up the case for the men of the finite and for the power of the definite.

This image of the definite must never be abandoned, but must be continually explored. An extended case in point is taken from Dostoevski and a supplement of parallel materials from other writers has been added. Every subsequent chapter (on time, tragedy, comedy, freedom, the univocal, analogy, the theological imagination, the Christian imagination) will simply be a further and further exploration into the dimensions, the inner dimensions, of this basic literary image of the finite.

HUMAN LIFE, as our own intuitions and our greatest writers have always told us, is simple and limited. It is a process in which one simple moment follows another, in which we take one limited step after another, draw one small breath after another. We can do but one thing at a time. Even our loves are limited; they leave us or die. We are born in helplessness and end in it. The human race is not a great complex entity called man, but many individual men, each leading his own separate, concrete life, each life having its own limited, separate identity.

The human imagination responds in various ways to the vision that is borne in upon it of universal limitation, or particularity. It may, like the great writers of tragedy, see the everlasting particularity of human life as an abyss; the highest dramatic moments of Oedipus and Lear are expressions of this tragic vision, when each of these characters finds himself confronting the abyss of limitation. But the imagination may, on the other hand, as in the case of writers of comedy, see human particularity in the rough and unvarnished guise of a homely, everyday reality; out of this comic vision is created a fat and unpretentious character like Falstaff. No matter what form the vision takes, however, or what its final goal—whether that be beauty, or insight, or peace, or tranquillity, or God—the heart, substance, and center of the human imagination, as of human life, must lie in the particular and limited image or thing.*

In this world there are generalities about things, but there are no generalities. If people and things were themselves

---

*In a world of generalities even our crimes would not bother us. I am using the word "particularity" here in a quite different sense from the narrow technical interpretation put on it by some literary critics in their discussions of particularity as a back-and-forth or cyclic phenomenon in the history of literature. For example, in René Wellek and Austin Warren's *Theory of Literature* (New York: Harcourt, 1956) occurs the following: *The typicality of literature or the particularity: literary theory and apologetics may stress one or the other; for literature, one may say, is more generalized than history or biography but more particularized than psychology or sociology. But not only are there shifts in the stress of literary theory. In literary practice, the specific degree of generality or particularity shifts from work to work and period to period. Pilgrim and Everyman undertake to be mankind. But Morose, the "humorist" of Johnson's Epicoene, is a very special and idiosyncratic person. The principle of characterization in literature has always been defined as that of combining the "type" with the "individual"—showing the type in the individual or the individual in the type* (pp. 20-21). Or, in *Literary Criticism: A Short History*, by W. K. Wimsatt, Jr., and Cleanth Brooks (New York: Knopf, 1957), I find an (justifiably) isolated discussion of "the doctrine of particularity" that grew up during the latter half of the eighteenth century, and found its special champion in Joseph Wharton (pp. 314-316). The use of "particularity" as a name for one doctrine among dozens of others practiced by literary people is of course far from my use of the term.

generalities, they would be far more tractable than they are.

This first situation of the imagination, the confrontation of particularity, is so fundamental, so sure and so obvious that I hesitate to dress it in any of its several possible metaphysical costumes. For that may make it seem a kind of recondite truth, somewhat beyond the reach of the ordinary mind, which it most certainly is not. To use familiar examples, however, the finite is given metaphysical form in the concept of *haecceitas,* the pure and absolute *thisness*-and-not-thatness which the great Scotus saw in all things; in the "inscape" which Hopkins, following in Scotus' footsteps, saw in everything; in the single farthing of the Gospel, which was the key to salvation; and in the little, sensible things which were the source of insight for St. Thomas.[1] It also appears, less familiarly, in Newman, whose extraordinarily concrete metaphysics seemed so revolutionary to many theologians and philosophers, but who said he was confident that he could make all his thought consonant with that of St. Thomas. Here is what Newman said about the definite and the limited:

I am what I am, or I am nothing. I cannot think, reflect, or judge about my being, without starting from the very point, which I aim at concluding. My ideas are all assumptions, and I am ever moving in a circle. I cannot avoid being sufficient for myself, for I cannot make myself anything else, and to change me is to destroy me. If I do not use myself, I have no other self to use. My only business is to ascertain what I am, in order to put it to use. It is enough for the proof of the value and authority of any function which I possess, to be able to pronounce that it is natural. What I have to ascertain is the laws under which I live. My first elementary lesson of duty is that of resignation to the laws of nature, whatever they are; my first disobedience is to be impatient at what I am, and to indulge an ambitious aspiration after what I cannot be, to cherish a distrust of my powers, and to desire to change laws which are identical with myself.[2]

I shall not be using the language of metaphysics in this discussion of the finite. I must, however, note here a certain difficulty that arises in choosing a precise, non-technical, and non-philosophical vocabulary in which to deal with these finite, concrete things and images that are at the center of every act of the imagination. (I am, of course, not using "image" here in its specialized literary sense, but rather, as applying to all the situations, large and small, that have bearing on the creative act.) If I were to characterize our

definite images of the world and of man as the "first materials" of the imagination, the very externality of the term
would seem to be an admission that there are materials of
the imagination that have an existence prior to being touched
by the spirit and attitude of man—that are, as it were, free
and unstained by thought or theology. The use of the term
"first materials" would thus commit me to an aesthetic I consider highly dubious, one that assumes we can act in a "free"
area of the imagination, in which all ideas about the finite,
as well as all theology, are relegated to the category of secondary and even extrinsic imaginative acts. If I acceded to
this, I should be well on the way to viewing poetry as "pure
poetry" and to an understanding of theology as purely "celestial."

If I try to use a less innocuous term than "materials," and
call our first images the "first facts" of the imagination, I
am again in trouble, for I am making an autonomizing declaration that a fact is a fact is a fact, just as a rose is a rose
is a rose, without having determined the dimensions of such
facts, or how many levels of being or of human sensibility
are possibly involved in them. The difficulty becomes if anything a little more acute if I use instead the phrase, "first
problem of the imagination," to describe the finite. For the
word "problem" is anything but innocuous: it *is* connotative,
and, as it is often used, would seem to be saying here that
the imagination is a **high** and glorious faculty, born with an
intent desire to produce insight and to bring us to some
kind of absolute, but that between us and these goals lie the
rough, limiting contours of the finite, as a kind of obstacle.[3]
When we speak of problems, we speak of things that are ir-
ritatingly in the way. And this is the way a certain kind of
artist looks theologically at the whole finite world. Thus we
see prefigured, in this difficulty of vocabulary, some of the
questionable attitudes toward the finite with which this chapter, among other things, will concern itself.

ATTITUDES TOWARD THE FINITE

Whatever the self is seeking in its interior life—whether
its goal be simply insight of a human kind, or some transcendent emotional ideal such as peace—it cannot help taking
certain attitudes, forming certain judgments in an immediate,
spontaneous way, toward the images of limitation it experiences.[4] I shall call such attitudes "theological," using the

word deliberately in its broadest sense, to indicate that there is more in ourselves and in our images than meets the eye. These attitudes penetrate the images themselves, and the two are always mutually forming, creating, sometimes distorting each other.

My own attitude toward these images of limitation—which I shall state briefly before I take up the contending points of view—is that the images are in themselves the path to whatever the self is seeking: to insight, or beauty, or, for that matter, to God. This path is both narrow and direct; it leads, I believe, straight through our human realities, through our labor, our disappointments, our friends, our game legs, our harvests, our subjection to time. There are no shortcuts to beauty or to insight. We must go *through* the finite, the limited, the definite, omitting none of it lest we omit some of the potencies of being-in-the-flesh. This does not mean that we should go through it violently, looking for a means to a breakthrough; that would be to try to accomplish everything at one stroke. The finite is not itself a generality, to be encompassed in one fell swoop. Rather, it contains many shapes and byways and cleverness and powers and diversities and persons, and we must not go too fast from the many to the one. We waste our time if we try to go around or above or under the definite; we must literally go through it. And in taking this narrow path directly, we shall be using our remembered experience of things seen and earned in a cumulative way, to create hope in the things that are not yet seen.

But this narrow and direct path through the finite is only one of the possible attitudes toward things, people, and the self that the imagination may adopt. I shall cite here four other attitudes that run markedly counter to this one:

1. Some imaginations try to achieve a tenuous, mystical contact with the finite, touching it just sufficiently, they tell us, to produce mystical vision, but not solidly enough, they add, for their vision to be impaired by the actuality of things. These imaginations I think of as "exploiters of the real." They believe the real can be "used" in the name of beauty or God, and they will exploit persons or things without being particularly interested in either. There would seem to be much of this attitude toward finite things in Proust ("for often I have wished to see a person again without realising that it was simply because that person recalled to me a hedge or hawthorn in blossom").[5] The same attitude can be

seen in certain Catholics who are more interested in baptismal statistics than in people. The latter too are performing an act of the imagination before the finite, and their act in this case has a theological disease rooted in it—a disease that may affect either theology or the imagination or both, and which we may call "magic."

The "magical" view takes the finite as a bag of tricks, or as a set of notes to be played lightly and delicately, in order to send the soul shooting up, one knows not how, into some kind of infinite or absolute; that accomplished, the devil take the finite. I think of the imagination that displays this attitude (or affliction) as going around or under or above the real, or using it as a sort of resilient, rubbery surface off which to rebound as quickly as possible into various parts of the sky.[6]

Such an imagination tries to get as much as possible of heaven out of as little as possible of earth, and even the little of earth it does touch is not taken seriously in a cognitive way, but is regarded as an obstacle and a necessary evil. The effort of this imagination is always to remain as uncommitted to the finite as possible.[7]

2. A second and similar imaginative attitude toward the real world is that of those who desire to touch the finite as lightly as possible in order to rebound, not into a quick eternity of beauty, but back into the self. Their aim is to create states of affectivity, areas of paradise, orders of feeling within the self. Proust again provides an example:

I drink a second mouthful, in which I find nothing more than in the first, a third, which gives me rather less than the second. It is time to stop; the potion is losing its magic. It is plain that the object of my quest, the truth, *lies not in the cup but in myself* [italics mine]. The tea has called it up in me, but does not itself understand, and can only repeat indefinitely, with a gradual loss of strength, the same testimony; which I, too, cannot interpret, though I hope at least to be able to call upon the tea for it again and to find it there presently, intact and at my disposal, for my final enlightenment.[8]

Intensified or ordered subjectivity is the goal of this attitude; again the means are the exploitation, the manipulation, distortion, or reduction of the real. I shall call this attitude "psychologism." Its disdain or impatience with the world is implicit in its images; there is no confrontation of reality.

Psychologism finds its counterpart in speculative theology and in the nineteenth-century movement within the

Catholic Church known as Modernism, in which all dogma was safely removed from application to the real and reduced to a set of symbols for the production of religious affectivity.[9] The poetic manuals of the psychologizing imagination patronizingly declare literature to be non-cognitive, in contrast with science and philosophy, and only serviceable, therefore, to the purposes of the emotional life. One critic, I. A. Richards, speaks of "objectless belief" in describing the liberation from the real that the psychologistic imagination would have its literature enact. "Poetry conclusively shows," he says, "that even the most important of our attitudes can be aroused and maintained without any belief entering it at all." [10]

3. A third attitude of the imagination is well known, and has been given various names. I shall call it the imagination of the "double vacuum"—the two vacuums of heaven and earth. This imagination penetrates, at least to some degree, into our human flesh and environment; then it recoils, with the weight of some emotion (and judgment) such as disgust, boredom, or anger, and flies, in a second movement that is unrelated to the first and constitutes an act of rebellion and escape, into a tenuous world of infinite bliss. It is as though the imagination were divided into two parts, each making a separate movement. On the one hand it plunges down into human reality with the attitude, and perhaps the wish, that such reality may be hell; on the other hand it plunges back up into heaven and ecstasy, though in this case too (as in that of the "magical") by what means, literary or human, we know not.

Lionel Trilling, in his *The Liberal Imagination*, discovers a double motion of this kind in the novels of Theodore Dreiser ("I have said that Dreiser's religious affirmation was offensive; the offense lies in the vulgar ease of its formulation as well as the comfortable untroubled way in which Dreiser moved from nihilism to pietism"), and in a later chapter I shall discuss the plays of Eugene O'Neill as examples of this same type of imagination.[11] Sometimes, as Mr. Trilling suggests of Dreiser, such an imagination merely reproduces the real order passively, according to its flattest dimensions. But in general it seems to me that this imagination cannot be accused of failing entirely to confront or to penetrate reality, though later I shall raise the question of whether it confronts it in its full depth. It often glories, in any case, in the confrontation and the facing of facts, and can be rather patro-

nizing in telling us what the facts are and in setting itself
up as the only realist in the world. Its most ironic feature
is that its plunge back into heaven is accompanied by vague
assertions and undifferentiated thrusts of will; in these it
becomes more "theological" than any of the other attitudes
of the imagination with which I have been dealing.

The closest parallel I can find in speculative theology to
this third imaginative attitude is in the writings of Karl
Barth, whom I name somewhat hesitantly, since I have no
wish to oversimplify important issues for the mere sake of
providing examples. Barth's theology displays, however, certain aspects that are crucial to my central argument regarding the attitude of the imagination toward the finite, and I
shall be dealing with it in some detail later in this chapter.

4. Those who hold a fourth attitude—a very contemporary
one—of the imagination toward the finite might be called the
"facers of facts." They tell us that nothing much can come out
of our reality; that the earth is a kind of Hell Revisited,
and that there are no forms in men or in things to which
we can relate ourselves effectively and cognitively so as to
produce out of them either beauty or salvation.[12] The
beautiful thing, say these facers of facts, is to accept the
absurdity and limitation of reality with nerve, sincerity,
courage and authenticity. They do not admit the validity of
the leap back out of this earthly vacuum into some infinite
realm which the third type of imagination makes. The fact
facers believe themselves to be more honest, logical and
consistent than the double-vacuum imaginers; and I for
one must confess a certain grudging sympathy with their
position—if we are to be forced to accept the premise that
the finite *is* a vacuum. R.W.B. Lewis has summed up the
difference between the two imaginative positions—the third
and the fourth—in a comment on the work of Graham
Greene and Albert Camus:

> Greene induces in us, or seeks to induce, a desperation of the
> senses, whereupon we can, if we are so inclined, make "the leap,"
> and desperately infer the divine perspective out of the ruins of the
> human. . . . Faced with absurdity, says Camus, these men will
> not cry: Absurd! they cry: God! It is the quarrel between Camus
> and Greene, representing as it does a radical division in the
> whole substance of contemporary culture, which lends the shock
> of immediacy to *The Power and the Glory.* . . . Heaven is at
> best a dubious inference from Hell; and only by accepting the
> reality of evil can one have the scantiest hope of heaven.[13]

The existentialist literature of the last generation provides many examples of this fourth, hell-revisited-without-bouncing-back-if-you-are-honest attitude, of which I am giving here only a brief sketch.

THE GENERATIVE FINITE

Having described four possible attitudes of the imagination toward the finite, I now return to my own position, which pictures the imagination as following a narrow, direct path through the finite. With every plunge through, or down into, the real contours of being, the imagination also shoots up into insight, but in such a way that the plunge down *causally generates* the plunge up. This movement might be diagrammed as:

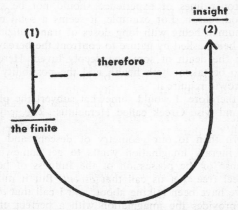

Actually it will take the rest of this book to describe what I mean by these geometric phrases of descent and ascent. But meantime I am using phrases that are meant to do no more than parallel some of our simplest ways of putting things when we are giving advice ("directions") to errant characters who are getting nowhere (have no real insight). People tell them to come down to earth, to get down to business, to come out of their ivory tower, to come down before they go up, to learn the hard way, to make haste slowly, to stop thinking and start doing, to put up or shut up, to put in the details if one wants the whole.

The geometry of the phrases and metaphors may differ

somewhat, but the sense is always the same: the arrival at insight requires a basic entrance into the finite and the limited. The philosophers will put it in their own way: Plato tells us that we should not go too fast from the many to the one. The theologians have their own vocabulary, sometimes with divine sanction: St. Paul seems to attribute the ascension of Christ into Heaven causally to His descent into the earth, and generally we ourselves will be stressing the great fact of Christology, that Christ moved down into all the realities of man to get to His father.

The homely truth is that there are thousands of people who could put this matter better than hundreds of writers, so that nothing nebulous is meant at all. What we are saying can have endless concrete senses and can only be filled in by wisdom, by the accumulated wisdom of the race, in life and in art. Even clinically we are today increasingly aware that the proper lines of experience should not be skipped without good reason. For example, it seems a solid mistake to feed a human being with long doses of tranquillizing pills when he is being asked by nature to confront the bereavement involved in the death of someone deeply loved. Here there is a path to be taken; both health and the possibility of insight and growth require it.

In sum, therefore, I would somewhat subvert the phrasing of an old and wise Greek called Heraclitus: *The way up is the way down.*

We return then to our geometry of descent and ascent. Surely the literary imagination wants to get somewhere, it wants a sense of the possession of the fullness of being, it wants to feel free. Let us call that *ascent.* But it must pay the price we have been talking about, and I call that *descent.* This path provides the imagination with a perfect entrance into things, and yet a perfect separation from them; and the separation is accomplished by the fact of the entrance. This is not a formula originating with me; it has been stated most precisely, so far as I know, by a sixteenth-century Jesuit writing a funeral eulogy of St. Ignatius: *Non coerci maximo, contineri tamen a minimo* [it is a divine thing not to be hemmed in by the largest limitation and yet to be contained in the smallest], I quote here from a commentary on this *Elogium:*

This double and contrary drive of the spirit is the universal soul of the Exercises [i.e., the Spiritual Exercises of St. Ignatius], because

the problem of my free decision—*id quod volo*—is their center, as
it was the central concern of St. Ignatius. In the famous fragment
of his Pensées, entitled *Disproportion de l'homme,* a Pascal will
later use the same method of showing us that "man is himself the
most extraordinary object of nature." St. Ignatius, who is less
speculative, goes beyond Pascal in taking hold of liberty as the
mystery of our being. Whatever the range of its domination, is
not liberty, much more than the intelligence, the faculty of the
possible, a "movement that goes beyond" and a negation of limitations? *Non coerceri maximo.* On the other hand, the more distant and extraordinary is its goal the more must it locate itself in
the most immediate and the most proximate if it is to reach or
move toward this goal. *Contineri a minimo.* Rather than destroying each other these two movements generate each other. . . .[14]

The formula as stated thus answers an objection that may be
raised in the name of liberty, or freedom: that such a penetration into the definite or limited will keep our imaginative
instincts from achieving that free, lofty, or wide vision to
which they aspire, and which gives the taste of liberty despite
all confinements. For the movement described is predi-
cated not only upon total involvement in the finite, but
at the same time upon total freedom—not freedom *from* involvement, but freedom *in* and *through* involvement: *contineri a minimo.* We are being told by the author of the
Elogium that the imagination or the soul must involve itself
if it is to achieve freedom or insight. He was speaking, of
course, about the nature of the spiritual life, and I am
speaking about poetic and literary processes, but there is no
reason why the one should not illuminate and assist the
other, provided the differences between them are respected
but not exaggerated.[15]

Even this description of the imaginative process is not altogether satisfactory, however, and must be regarded as provisional, for it still has somewhat the effect of locating the
things called insight or beauty in the sky—where I wish at
all costs to avoid placing them. What I am attempting to
formulate throughout this book is an ideal attitude for the
imagination in relation to the finite—ideal in the same sense
that it preserves a balance, somehow avoiding the conflict
that threatens the imagination in an act in which it is apparently being drawn in two directions at once: *down* into
the concrete, *up* into the unlimited.

We are all driven by a need for maximum beauty and
insight, and at the same time we wish for a habitation in

the inescapable minima of human life. Yet we cannot tolerate
a permanent dissociation between the two. We wish on the
one hand to grasp "meaning" to the full, so that there is no
pain of questioning left; on the other hand we have an
equal longing for pure, unalloyed, concrete objects, and for
not having to go beyond them to get at meaning, joy, or illumination. This double longing exists in all of us. We
want the unlimited and the dream, and we also want the
earth.

The problem of imagination, confronted by the concrete, is to avoid this dichotomy; the attitude I am proposing
as a model for it is exemplified in Christology, where the
conflict has been resolved once and for all, I believe, in a
continuous, open, and dynamic way. In the words of St.
Paul, "Wherefore he saith: Ascending on high he led captivity
captive; he gave gifts unto men. Now, that he ascendeth,
what is it, but because he also descended first into the lower
parts of the earth? He that descended is the same also that
ascended above all the heavens, that he might fill all
things." [16] God Himself has no need to go further than
his eternal Christic, anointed Word to grasp Himself from
all eternity; and certainly, being no better than God, we too
need go no further than the earthly, concrete, limited
Christ and descend with Him for the grasping of everything. Whether we believe in Him or not, He represents an
ideal point at which the imagination can relax the strain
of its double aspirations; if He is there, then at that point at
least we can keep penetrating more and more deeply into the
detail of Him, who is penetrating the detail of life as a
way to life, and let the other side of the picture—the dream,
the divine, the unlimited, the beauty—take care of itself.

We would be disparaging Christ and disparaging the finite
if we were to assign to Him an improperly transcendent
character and were to assign to the finite, through which
He walked, any negative or deprecatory quality. This is precisely what is done, however, in the attitude I have called
that of the "double vacuum"—which I mentioned earlier
as being displayed in the theology of Karl Barth. In that
theologian's work we find an attitude that is precisely the
opposite of the relaxed and affectionate attention to the
detail of Christ's penetrating life that I have set forth as an
ideal for the imagination to follow in its relation to the concrete.

Karl Barth shook the theological world by the publication of his magnificent commentary on the Epistle to the Romans. I use the word "magnificent" here to denote the powerful, prophetic quality of this work, and I feel the same word can be applied to traditional Protestant theology in general (just as it may be used in connection with many ventures of the contemporary imagination). Much of the public strength of Protestantism lies in its magnificent poetic defense of the unconditioned transcendence of God, and its glowing picture of human nothingness, while Catholicism is often caught, as a result of its own logic, in a state of "nonmagnificence."

Barth would seem, at first glance, to be insisting in his Christology on the definiteness and particularity of Christ as the narrow gate, with all the scandal and religious vulgarity this still represents to the pure intellectual. For he declares that "His [Christ's] life is a history within the framework of history, a concrete event in the midst of other concrete events, an occasion in time and limited by the boundaries of time; it belongs to the texture of human life." [17] No one—not even Kierkegaard—has declared with a more admirable rhetoric that Christ is the isolated, solitary, and unique Moment in the presence of which all other befores and afters have no power. In a sense, therefore, Barth represents Him as the greatest possible Particularity ever to enter the cosmos.

If Barth had in his commentary been satisfied with this Particularity as a focus for the imagination's progress toward insight, or the soul's toward the absolute, he might have ended with a more complicated, and more valid, theology. As it is, however, this Particularity of Christ serves only as a means to the destruction of Christic and *all* Particularity before the face of the living God. Christ, for Barth, becomes merely the historical moment that most closely corresponds to the deepest existential sense of nothingness in man. He it is who smashes the definite before the unconditioned, and thus makes possible the great Protestant cry of "nevertheless" that Barth tells us comes from the unconditioned Will (God loves us despite all). It is impossible to have a "therefore" in this theology. The great historical Christic moment is meant to cancel all history. Drama, which at every step involves a "therefore" or a "consequently," is thus made impossible, for Barth, by Christ. "Men are forgiven by God only when He condemns them." And finally Barth has this to say of the great Particularity:

His [Christ's] greatest achievement is a negative achievement. He is not a genius, endowed with manifest or occult powers; He is not a hero or leader of men; He is neither poet nor thinker;—*My God, my God, why hast thou forsaken me?* Nevertheless, precisely in this negation, He is the fulfillment of every possibility of human progress, as the Prophets and the Law conceive of progress and evolution, because He sacrifices to the incomparably Greater and to the invisibly Other every claim to genius and every human heroic or aesthetic or psychic possibility, because there is no conceivable human possibility of which He did not rid himself . . . Messiah is the end of mankind, and here also God is found faithful. On the day when mankind is dissolved the new era of the righteousness of God will be inaugurated.[18]

I do not wish to minimize the dimensions of the theological problems confronted by this thinker, but I cannot discuss them fully within the confines of this book.[19] I am concerned, rather, with the kind of imagination that is created for us by such a theological prototype.

It is, it seems to me, an imagination that takes, as I indicated in calling it the imagination of the "double vacuum," one existential and non-historical plunge into the complete Otherness of God, and there is, according to Barth's Commentary, the adversative connection of "nevertheless" between the two plunges. Superficially the lines of the movement of this imagination are the same as those of the twofold path I diagrammed earlier, the path defined by the author of the *Elogium* of St. Ignatius, in which the connection is "therefore." But in fact the two imaginative movements are completely different, as can be seen if the two diagrams are put side by side:

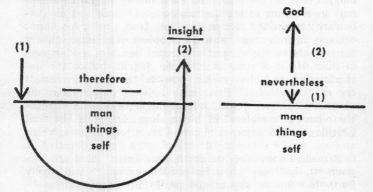

In the one instance there is real causality and creativity in the relation between the passage through the finite and the movement toward insight; in the other there is *no* causal or cognitive relationship between the two, unless the word "recoil" can be said to involve a relationship.

DOSTOEVSKI: THE VISION OF FINITUDE

The question posed by the above discussion of contrasting attitudes of the imagination toward the concrete would seem to be: How can the literal and the transcendent be brought together in anything resembling a harmony? It is not, it seems to me, a question of the one overcoming the other, as some would have us believe. We are told that symbols will "overcome" the element of the literal in our lives; but who wants to overcome the literal? Who, if he were honest, would not be happier if he knew that beauty and understanding were completely contained within the literal, the plain, ordinary, completely self-enclosed fact that meets the eyes and ears?

The ideal solution would be that the world should "signify" without becoming less actual in so doing.[20] Our hope must be to discover such symbols as can make the imagination *rise* indeed, and yet keep all the tang and density of that actuality into which the imagination *descends*. It might be well at this point to look at the work of a great writer who dealt precisely, in literary terms, with this problem of finding the means for relating our highest dreams to the human.

There is no reason to think that Dostoevski ever came in contact with the terms of the present discussion. But if he had troubled to formulate his idea of the function of the literary imagination, he might have been tempted to think of it as an instrument with which to break through to some kind of absolute and unlimited realm that had little, if any, relation to the concrete. Dostoevski was an epileptic, and it is possible that he hoped literature could provide consistently the kind of unearthly illumination that epilepsy seemed to give in occasional flashes. One piece of evidence for this is the remarkable moment of vision described by the epileptic Myshkin in *The Idiot:*

That there was, indeed, beauty and harmony in those abnormal moments, that they really contained the highest synthesis of life, he could not doubt, nor even admit the possibility of doubt. He felt that they were not analogous to the fantastic and unreal dreams due to intoxication by hashish, opium, wine. Of that he could judge, when the attack was over. These instants were characterized—to define it in a word—by an intense quickening of the sense of personality. Since, in the last conscious moment preceding the attack, he could say to himself with full understanding of his words: "I would give my whole life for this one instant," then doubtless to him it really was worth a lifetime. For the rest, he thought the dialectical part of his argument of little worth; he saw only too clearly that the results of these ecstatic moments were stupefaction, mental darkness, idiocy. No argument was possible on that point. His conclusion, his estimate of the "moment," doubtless contained some error, yet the reality of the sensation troubled him. What more unanswerable than a fact? And this fact had occurred. The prince had confessed unreservedly to himself that the feeling of intense beatitude in that crowded moment made the moment worth a lifetime. "I feel then as if I understood those amazing words—'there shall be no more time.' " And he added with a smile: "No doubt the epileptic Mahomet refers to that same moment when he says that he visited all the dwellings of Allah, in less time than was needed to empty his pitcher of water." [21]

Whatever name we give to what impelled Dostoevski, whether it was "the wonderful yearning for the abyss" or something other than that, he did undergo temptation, as he describes the immediate infinites accessible to Myshkin (and to his own imagination) in the supreme moment of the epileptic seizure—and, in his work, we can see him overcoming it. His absolute desires must often have been in terrible conflict with his instincts as a writer, but he did finally, judging from the work, reject the possibility of any real insights emerging from such flashes of illumination.

Let me take as an example of this rejection a few scenes from *The Brothers Karamazov*, dealing with some critical moments in the life of the character Alyosha. The passages I shall quote, from the end of Book VII of *The Brothers,* are quite rhetorical, read out of context, and are not without their own spiritual overstatements and excesses; but the rhetoric and the excess will help at this point, I think, to clarify the issue by showing the antipodes which the imagination manages to reach, for Dostoevski. Here is Alyosha in ecstasy with relation to heaven:

The vault of heaven, full of soft, shining stars, stretched vast and fathomless above him. The Milky Way ran in two vast streams from the zenith to the horizon. The fresh, motionless, still night enfolded the earth. The white towers and golden domes of the cathedral gleamed out against the sapphire sky. The gorgeous autumn flowers, in the beds round the house, were slumbering till morning. The silence of earth seemed to melt into the silence of the heavens. The mystery of earth was one with the mystery of the stars. . . .

and with relation to the earth:

Alyosha stood, gazed, and suddenly threw himself down on the earth. He did not know why he embraced it. He could not have told why he longed so irresistibly to kiss it, to kiss it all. But he kissed it weeping, . . . and vowed passionately to love it, to love it forever and ever. "Water the earth with the tears of your joy and love those tears," echoed in his soul.

What was he weeping over?

Oh! in his rapture he was weeping even over those stars, which were shining to him from the abyss of space, and "he was not ashamed of that ecstasy." There seemed to be threads from all those innumerable worlds of God, linking his soul to them, and it was trembling all over "in contact with other worlds." He longed to forgive everyone and for everything, and to beg forgiveness. Oh, not for himself, but for all men, for all, and for everything . . . never, never, all his life long, could Alyosha forget that minute.[22]

Now the whole question is, how did Alyosha get there? How did he get to the top of the heavens and down to the earth, in such a way as to embrace in fullness the whole of both *(non coerceri maximo)*? If we look carefully through the earlier parts of Book VII, I believe it will become quite clear that he got there through having first of all embraced the definite by a complete and humanly perfect entrance, and found it to be creative and cognitive. He makes a perfect passage through the whole of a situation, and we as readers do it with him. The situation is partial; it is only one step in the adventure of the imagination, and therefore limited. But as it is met and walked through it is not partially human, a half-human act, but totally human and able therefore to produce the reverberations of the totally human in Alyosha and in us *(contineri a minimo)*.

It is just as well to note here, for future discussion, that this question of how the part can contain the whole is possibly the crucial question, not only for the imagination but for the whole of human life; how we answer it determines whether or not partial quantities of any kind—of action, of commitment, or simply of literary form, such as metaphor or synecdoche—make any sense for human or for poetic cognition, or are merely futile. Watching Alyosha now will help us to deal with this question later.

He has arrived at the earth and the heavens and the fullness thereof. But he had first arrived at Zossima, and at Grushenka. Father Zossima is the holy monk whose dead body has putrefied much sooner than the reigning dogma of the Russian Church allowed in the case of the reputedly holy. It is the sudden moment of consternation which this event causes in the monastery, and in Alyosha, that sets the imagination of Dostoevski working so brilliantly in Book VII. In the famous Grand Inquisitor scene, in Book VI, he had allowed himself to picture a battle of pure dialectic between Ivan Karamazov, who attacks God and discredits the earth, and Zossima, who champions God and restores the earth, but by a dubious kind of transcendental thinking and by literary sleight-of-hand. Perhaps, the scene completed, Dostoevski became caught up in the powerful charge made by Ivan and a little ill-at-ease over the defense offered by Zossima. At any rate, with the embattled dialectic of Ivan and Zossima still rolling about the sky in splendid fury, the novelist decided to put the two positions into the lists against each other on the lowlier and more fateful level of the literal and the limited human scene, thus setting himself a task of limited but ultimately real cognition. The deceased elder had said in one of his exhortations, "Men love the downfall and disgrace of the righteous." Dostoevski now proceeds to test this idea against the conscience, not of speculation but of reality itself, against his own Russian reality and not that of the cosmos. Where Ivan and Zossima had wrestled in the sky, he as man and artist now descends into the finite for the truth, for the insight, for the peace.

He had performed such a feat of descent before, in the *The Possessed*. The solitary, incredibly strong revolutionary has become a stock figure in our time, though a dangerous one. It is part of the romantic myth that surrounds this figure that he is the arch-enemy and the great challenger of God, the splendor of occupying such a position being undeniable and quite satisfying. I am not the first to point out that the legend of the revolutionary is but a mask to hide his real intention: behind his challenge of God lies a desperate desire to reduce all mankind to a least common denominator of life, in order to present a united front against every invasion by the spirit. Dostoevski knew this, but also knew that to communicate his insight he had to expose the pretensions of such a figure, lay them open for judgment, within the terms of a human act. The pretensions of Stavrogin, the arch-revolutionary of *The Possessed,* are so exposed in the terrifying final moments of the confessional scene, in which he comes to the monk Tihon, confident, without being aware of it, that he has at last committed the ultimate crime in his seduction of a young child. (This same kind of breakthrough has been tried, elsewhere in the novel, by another character, Kirillov, in the form of suicide.) Dostoevski could have failed, in this scene: celestial admiration can get in the way of insight. But in *The Possessed* the splendid movement of the revolutionary toward confession is matched by terror on the part of the monk, who knows he must respond to the confession with a terrible word—and that word is "ridiculous."

Surely this word, spoken at this moment and in this action, is more shattering than an army with banners in battle array. It is a poetic, an imaginative, a cognitive word in the highest sense of these terms. It cuts like a two-edged sword into the Buddhistic dream of Stavrogin, the revolutionary who stands above all reality, poised like a dancer in infinite space, whose movements, unlike ours, need not be executed upon the floor of the earth, who need not breathe Russian air or face the reality of a Russian child.

Such dissociations from the real very often produce, not the mysticism or the dream or the power or the poetry they seek, but, as in this case, the *ridiculous.* The word is a vision into an inscape, and a choice: it chooses the lines of the real as they are determined by poetic insight; it is judgmental and prophetic, as the imagination of Dante in the *Purgatorio* is always both judgmental and prophetic, seeking this ledge and not that, seeking the truth in the flesh as the narrow and definite way. Any judgmental exposure or routing-out of this revolutionary based on celestial judgments, arrived at by means of the pure concepts in the top of the head, as it were, has been made unnecessary by this one word, "ridiculous." The weapons of art, we may conclude, are terrible and not merely ornamental. They are the cognitive allies of the Holy Ghost and, as Aristotle said, they are indeed more philosophical than history; they are superior to history and superior to pure concepts. The mind that has descended into the real has shot up into insights that would have been inaccessible to pure concepts.

In Book VII of *The Brothers* Dostoevski catches some of the very forms of envy and love in a similar act of limitation, using the same weapons he used in this scene of *The Possessed*. Earlier in *The Brothers,* as I have said, in a great "celestial" debate, God, the Mighty One, had been pulled down from His seat by Ivan, and Zossima, using concepts from the top of his head, had not quite succeeded in putting Him back. Now Dostoevski attempts an act of earthly cognition. Let me see, he says to himself, if the corpse of the monk, stinking beyond expectation, will do better than the top of his head, or at least work with it in a posthumous alliance.

The monk *is* dead and stinking, and this apparent outrage against all sanctity *has* happened. It is a time to try men's hearts, for "men love the downfall and disgrace of the righteous." "It was the most natural and trivial matter," Dostoevski tells us in his adroitly unassuming way. "I should, of course, have omitted all mention of it in my story, if. . . ." But he is about to use the trivial matter as an instrument for the exploration of various individuals' hearts and ideas. I count fourteen such explorations within a few pages, and the importance of the total must not be minimized, for each heart, though different from that of all the other actors on the scene, serves to illuminate every other, and all serve to illuminate the counter-heart of Alyosha. The imagination of the novelist is not entering into one heart of one "finite," but into many, for this is the way the finite is made: first by number and later by time.

We start at the very surface of the soul, with the monk from Obdorsk, who is all ears to the general excitement, listening everywhere and whispering on all sides. All he knows is that something is up, and this is for him the holy and the unholy; it is all accomplished on the level of "something is up."

Then the action shifts to Madame Hohlakov, into a certain kind of feminine finite, onto the level of intense curiosity (yes, men are curious too), where it is necessary to have a report, *à la* TV, on "everything that takes place," delivered quickly, succinctly, every half-hour. This is fun, this failure that has overtaken the righteous, and now we are beginning to have some insight into what kind of fun it can be. Of course, next, "the unbelievers rejoiced," but we miss the point of the fun of some *believers* if we do not see that they are having more fun out of the situation than the unbelievers. Now, further, Father Zossima, like every holy man, had his enemies, and their delight at the smell of decomposition "can hardly be imagined"—and yet it can, through the penetrating help of all these other imaginings. There is an irony here, that the instrument Dostoevski uses to reveal the vindictive state of the souls of Zossima's enemies should be the revelation of the equally vindictive state of the souls of his friends. They take the whole affair personally, with a "you-can't-do-this-to-me" attitude.

We are beginning to see the whole picture now, but only through the light cast by all the different and definite souls depicted. Even when the revelation seems to come from the top of the head or through certain rationalizations drawn from theology, it is still the heart and the soul speaking: "It shows God's judgment is not as man's," or "It must be a sign from heaven," begin to be quoted learnedly all over the place. This marks the entrance of a type of theologian on the scene. And then, the strict old monks begin to use their righteous piety as an instrument with which to pull down the mighty from their seats. The mad hyper-ascetic, Father Ferapont, speaks for them in a passage whose effect is astonishing, for we are now far below the first surfaces of the finite:

"Casting out I cast out!" and, turning in all directions, he began at once making the sign of the cross at each of the four walls and four corners of the cell in succession. . . . "Satan, go hence! Satan, go hence!" . . . He was wearing his coarse gown girt with a rope. His bare chest, covered with gray hair, could be seen under his hempen shirt. His feet were bare. As soon as he began waving his arms, the cruel irons he wore under his gown could be heard clanking. . . . "The dead man, your saint," he turned to the crowd, pointing with his finger to the coffin, "did not believe in devils. He gave medicine to keep off the devils. And so they have become as common as spiders in the corners. And now he has begun to stink himself. In that we see a great sign from God." . . . "He did not keep the fasts according to the rules and therefore the sign has come." . . . "He was seduced by sweetmeats, ladies brought them to him in their pockets, he sipped tea, he worshiped his belly, filling it with sweet things and his mind with haughty thoughts." . . . "You learned men! You are so clever you look down upon my humbleness." . . . "Tomorrow they will sing over him 'Our Helper and Defender'—a splendid anthem—and over me when I die all they'll sing will be 'What earthly joy,' a little canticle." . . . "My God has conquered! Christ has conquered the setting sun!" he shouted frantically, stretching up his hands like a little child, shaken by his tears and spreading out his arms on the ground. Then all rushed up to him; there were exclamations and sympathetic sobs . . . a kind of frenzy seemed to take possession of them all.[23]

The dialectic of the previous Books V and VI, much of it in the name of a righteous and victimized humanity, had come close to pulling God from His throne, exposing Him as the villainous one, while man, poor man, is victimized by his innocent pain. But in Book VII the tables are turned; now the search turns for one or two just souls who would not gladly pull anyone down from his earthly seat. For the moment the young Alyosha and Grushenka, the woman of ill repute, will serve. Each had intended to destroy the other's cause, and Rakitin would have destroyed the cause of both. But Alyosha is saved (as Grushenka in another way) by his grief for the monk, in the midst of the stench ("the sting of it all was that the man he loved above everything on earth should be put to shame and humiliated"). We are confronted here by the simplest situation in the world: the straight and unbending entrance, despite the floods of distortion by which it is surrounded, of a human imagination into the real. The eye, as it sees, enters into the thing as it is seen. "He whom I loved is dead." It is as simple as that, and everything else around Alyosha is a lie of non-being. His is an absolute and unswerving commitment to the exact articulations of reality, the commitment of grief. This is the beginning of insight and of the grasping of heaven and earth and of salvation ("The great grief in his heart swallowed up every sensation that might have been aroused, and if only he could have thought clearly at that moment, he would have realized that he had now the strongest armor to protect him from every lust and temptation"). All the other actors are twisting reality, in the name of some private dream or infinite; they refuse to enter by the narrow gate. It is by this gate, narrow but full of cognition, the part containing the whole, that Alyosha arrives at the fullness of heaven and earth.

It is clear that as this total imaginative act of Dostoevski took place within his own mind, so all these characters represent the history of that one mind as it ploughs, in a short span of time, through the images of non-being and into that narrow gate that leads the imagination to freedom and to truth. In this same way, God's imagination has in His own creative act cut through all the lies of impossibility, penetrated into the last bit of mud at the hidden bottom of the sea, to illuminate the lines of possibility and reality. *Infulsit* is His word. He hath "shone through" to bring into view the articulations of reality, as the imagination of every great artist shines through the darkness. The few simple words which Newman, that great analyst of the concrete, chose for his epitaph might be used to sum up the whole vocation of the human imagination: *Ex umbris et imaginibus in veritatem*. Out of shadow and phantasy into truth.

But within our present earthly context the truth is narrower than the lies. It is indeed a narrow gate, the gate of the finite, the limited, and the definite. It is very small (*contineri a minimo*) but it is full of power (*non coerceri maximo*). It is narrow but complicated, and the imagination must seek it by all the ways that are proper to it. The first of these ways of finding the gate is that of time.

NOTES

1. *Principium igitur cujuslibet nostrae cognitionis est in sensu.* (*In Boetium de Trin.* q. 6, a. 2, c.)
   Impossibile est intellectum nostrum secundum praesentis vitae statum quo possibili corpori conjungitur, aliquid intelligere in actu, nisi convertendo se ad phantasmata. (1 a, 2.84, a.7, c). ad 2. For a discussion of the total Thomistic implications of these sentences, see Joseph Donceel, S.J., "A Thomistic Misapprehension," *Thought,* 32 (Summer 1957), pp. 189-198.

2. John Henry Newman, Cardinal, *A Grammar of Assent* (New York: Doubleday, Image, 1955), pp. 272-273.

3. This attitude is something like what Allen Tate calls the poet's "illusory pursuit of essence." For various strong statements by Tate against every angelic form of the imagination that seeks its food elsewhere than in the human fact, see his essays "The Symbolic Imagination," "The Angelic Imagination," and "Our Cousin, Mr. Poe," collected in his *The Man of Letters in the Modern World* (New York: Charles Scribner's Sons, 1955: Meridian Books edition), pp. 93-145.

4. As a corollary to the preceding discussion of vocabulary, I may note here that I prefer to stick to human words such as "insight," "awareness," "illumination," "realization," for the goals of the

imagination. If I thus avoid showing the traditional concern for the relation of the concrete to "universal" forms of knowledge, it is because I feel it is extremely dubious that the imagination— or metaphysics, properly understood—has as its goal the reaching of "universals" in any of the ordinary philosophical senses of that word.

5. Marcel Proust, *Swann's Way* (New York: Modern Library, 1928), p. 239.

6. For a literal example of this taking off into space, cf. the analysis of the imagination that informs contemporary science fiction done by Robert Plank in the article "Lighter Than Air, But Heavy as Hate," *Partisan Review,* 24 (Winter 1957), pp. 106-116.

7. In this chapter I am not using the word "commitment" in any narrow social or political sense, though the latter is not necessarily excluded. Cf. the general discussion of the position of contemporary international literature *re* commitment and non-commitment in the special number of *The Times Literary Supplement* entitled "A Sense of Direction, being an examination of the efforts of writers to keep or regain contact with the everyday realities of life in terms of modern literature." (August 16, 1957.)

8. Proust, *op. cit.,* p. 55.

9. I am indicating possible relationships between certain forms of speculative theology and literary images of the world only as a method of illustrating the various attitudes the imagination may adopt toward the finite. To establish such relationships conclusively would require formal historical studies (some of which have been made), which are outside the range of this discussion.

10. In his essay "Poetry and Belief" (in R. W. Stallman, ed., *Critiques and Essays in Criticism,* New York: Ronald 1949, pp. 330-333), Richards justifies the "pseudo-statements" of poetry by saying: "A pseudo-statement is a form of words which is justified entirely by its effect in releasing or organizing our impulses and attitudes (due regard being had for the better or worse organizations of these *inter se*)." And his remedy for the collapse of belief is "to cut our pseudo-statements free from belief, and yet retain them, in this released state, as the main instruments by which we order our attitudes to one another and to the world."

11. Lionel Trilling, *The Liberal Imagination* (New York: Viking Press, 1950), p. 30.

12. For some excellent studies of this problem of the frequent contemporary conviction that no positive and really cognitive insight can come out of the structures of human nature, see

L'Humanisme et la grâce, "Semaine des Intellectuals Catholiques," édit. de Flore (Paris: 1950), especially the chapter "Y a-t-il une nature humaine?" by Jean Guitton, pp. 125-149.

13. Richard W.B. Lewis, "The Fiction of Graham Greene: Between the Horror and the Glory," *The Kenyon Review,* 19 (Winter 1957), pp. 70-72.

14. Gaston Fessard, S.J., *La Dialectique des exercices spirituels de Saint Ignace de Loyola, Théologie,* 35 (Paris: Aubier, 1956), p. 173.

15. In the Prayer-and-Poetry tradition of Henri Bremond and others there is a tendency to confuse the poetic process with the concerns of the spiritual life; but there is an equal tendency in others to exaggerate the differences between the two.

16. Used by the Church in the epistle of the Mass for the eve of the feast of the Ascension. Cf. Epistle to the Ephesians, 4, 8-10.

17. Karl Barth, *The Epistle to the Romans,* trans. by Edwyn C. Hoskyns (New York: Oxford University Press, 1950), p. 103.

18. *Ibid.,* p. 97.

19. It is with hesitation that I refrain, in these pages, from substituting the word "Barthians" for the name of Karl Barth; I am aware that the latter is probably not happy to be ranked among the Barthians. I leave it to the professional theologians to determine how far Barth has moved away from the troublesome dichotomies of his original position. A review article (by Xavier Tilliette, *Etudes,* January 1958, pp. 112-115) of Father Henri Bouillard's three-volume study in French, *Karl Barth* (Paris: Aubier, 1957), indicates that the great reform theologian is "moving toward a re-evaluation of the Incarnation and of the 'humanity of God.'" Father Bouillard's work, the fruit of ten years of research and based on a defense of Barth delivered at the Sorbonne in his presence, is praised in *Etudes,* as magisterial and sympathetic; the review of it closes with a quotation from Lacordaire, as descriptive of the spirit of Bouillard's study: *"Je ne cherche pas à convaincre d'erreur mon adversaire, mais à m'unir à lui dans une verité plus haute."*

20. There is an analogy in Biblical exegesis for this notion of the world's "signifying." Nicolas of Cusa cites three different possibilities: What is a figure or sign can be a thing only, *ut res tantum;* or a sign only, *ut signum tantum;* or a thing and a sign together, *ut res et signum.* This would seem to be the kind of double operation within one thing that I have been describing. (Cf. P.C., Spicq, *Esquisse d'une historie de l'éxègese latine au moyen age,* Paris: J. Vrin, 1944, p. 341.)

21. Feodor Dostoevski, *The Idiot* (New York: Dutton, 1953), pp. 214-215.

22. Feodor Dostoevski, *The Brothers Karamazov* (New York: Modern Library, 1950), pp. 436-437.

23. *Ibid.*, pp. 402-405.

2 Time

Our first exploration into the structure and dimensions of the finite images of literature is into the basic and all-pervasive phenomenon of time. This is what might be called the horizontal dimension of the definite, both in literature and in life, for neither life nor the literary organism is given in a single stroke. Both are basically actions, achieving themselves in the growth, the moving structure, the flowing pattern. The literary imagination often exhausts itself looking for absolute or infinite points of time; very frequently it rebels, in the name of a specious eternity, against the whole image of the definite as temporal, and conceives that the function of the imagination is not to explore the time pattern as fruitful source of insight but to destroy it as obstacle to vision. Theologically this kind of imagination is more transcendental than theology itself. Problematic materials are suggested from Poe, Baudelaire, Proust, Eliot and others. A positive analysis is drawn from the Spiritual Exercises *of Saint Ignatius.*

THE QUESTION of time has always been a disturbing one for the human spirit and imagination, for in the question of time are focused all the human feelings of puzzlement about the relation of the finite or definite to the infinite. Of all the finite, limited things with which the imagination is confronted, time is perhaps the most limited. It is a succession of pure instants, each incredibly small and incredibly brief, each of which can itself be broken down into even briefer parts. In each of these instants nothing survives of the past; no mo-

ment of the present can be made to stay, and there are no
resources in either the present or the past that can totally
dictate the character of a single instant in the future. Such is
the inexorable flow of temporality.

There is an instinct in all of us which rebels against time.
We come upon a moment of goodness or of peace—a moment such as Keats was contemplating when he wrote his
ode on the Grecian urn—and we try desperately to hold
onto it, or else we strive to make all the moments run together
into one fine moment, a single, static thing which will, from
the very fact that it has ceased to flow, resemble some kind of
eternity. Man feels himself, in his most inward being, alien to
the whole sweeping movement of time, thinks of himself
as a creature able to derive virtue or peace out of immobility
alone, but who has fallen by some mischance into a cursed
thing outside himself, into a rushing, uncontrollable stream
called time. But our rebellion against this flow of moments is
precisely a rebellion against the finite and the limited, as
these are caught in the mode of temporality; and it is not
perhaps too much to say that on the attitude we take toward
time, as the most intense form of the limited, on our decision either to strain against it or to accept it, depends all
our peace.

Later in this chapter I shall discuss time in relation to
theology. But here I am posing the question of the human
attitude toward time, not as a technical or philosophical
question, but as one to be confronted on all the levels of
life that exist "below" the formally theological, hoping thus
to approach the theological with a felt form of understanding—with insights that will more nearly penetrate the nature, impact, and meaning of the subject. The insights I
shall aim at in this case will be based chiefly on materials
produced by the literary imagination.

TIME AND THE MODERN MIND

There are basically two contrary and hostile positions
now held by the contemporary imagination regarding time.
According to one, time is a thing that must be escaped from,
since it leads neither to insight, beauty, God, peace, nor to
anything else. It must either be destroyed or immobilized,
or must be *used* in such a manner as clearly indicates that it
is external to ourselves. In this view, it is assumed that the
intelligence can somehow stand outside the flow of time and

be thereby more clear-sighted, gain greater intellectual understanding of things by remaining apart from their rough contours. Such an intelligence, even though human, is thus seen as "pure" or angelic, having a quality of eternity and immobility about it because it need not enter into the confusing pattern of concrete time.

According to the other position, time—at least human time—is nothing but *ourselves,* as we move without pause through all the phases and stages of our lives, and therefore in a certain sense all talk about whether we accept or reject temporality is so much idle patter. Those who hold this view, moreover, believe that though time is always in motion, it is a motion that has a structure and therefore a meaning, and that only by staying within this structure of temporality and moving with it can one gain access to real insight. For this more realistic intelligence, true understanding is gained only through entering into the contours of reality, for such understanding is an illumination that comes out of a passage through *experience,* this illumination leading to another experience, and this to further illumination, and so on, even unto death.

There are many other points of cleavage between the two intellectual positions, in practically all of which the man who despises the definite, limited thing and insists that infinites of some kind are the true metal of human destiny seems to carry off a quick victory. The man of the infinite bears the marks of romantic enthusiasm, apparent greatness of soul, imagination, and ambition, while he who chooses and respects the finite, the limited and concrete actual as a way to glory and beauty—he who, in other words, respects the power of real being—comes to be regarded as an unimaginative plodder and an intellectual primitive. I shall try to show whether or not these distinctions are deserved, in the context of the debate over temporality, for there is no point at which the differences between the two positions emerge with greater clarity than that at which men begin to tackle the joys and agonies of the fascinating thing called time.

For many writers of the last few literary generations, time is not only an enemy, but *the* enemy. The feeling may be expressed as a purely natural aversion, or it may take a religious form, as in the remark of Simone Weil: "We must get rid of our superstition of chronology in order to find eternity." But whatever the form, it is clear that we are living in the midst of a fairly widespread cultural assault on the limited nature of the moment, and unrealistic but highly imaginative intellectual efforts are made to stop the coursing of time, or to transform the brief, sad instant into an infinite.

Of course this tendency is not a new one. I shall not deal here with the historic statements of the position, however, but will remain for the most part with modern texts, for in our time the attempt to transform the instant into an infinite has become increasingly passionate and scientific, as well as forceful and refined.*

A principal mode of attack on the movement of time and the finiteness of human reality can be described under the heading of "simultaneity." The term covers the impulse to pack the past and the future, indeed the whole of scattered being, into the present moment—thus to possess all things in a single instant and to demolish the narrow gates of both space and time.

Let me take as an example of this some images from the work of Marcel Proust, whose great novel, *Remembrance of Things Past*, I cited in the previous chapter. That novel is a brilliant study, in fictional form, of the problem and place of time in human life. For Proust, the great enemy of the human race and of human happiness is time, which must be overcome by the genius who can, by using all his resources, discover or create within this inimical element some kind of eternity. Thus the novelist uses all his skill, whether it be a form of art or, in some cases, hysteria, to overcome the necessity mankind has always been under of regarding the things of space and human life from one point of view after another. The passenger on the train is confronted with a beautiful scene, and he darts desperately from one window to another, trying to assemble in one totality, one simultaneous impression, the beauty of it all. Or, in another place in the novel, a character stands upon a steeple, which represents the surmounting of temporal existence, and "encompasses at once things he can habitually see only one by one." [2]

The same technical passion is involved in Picasso's famous painting of a violin as in Proust's work—the passion to reproduce not what the body must see or live, but rather

* Many useful examples of this modern attempt have been collected by Georges Poulet in his recently translated *Studies in Human Time*, to which I acknowledge a considerable debt for what follows.[1]

what the mind, standing at some allegedly supra-temporal point, can see. Thus the Cubist painting contains all the angles, all the impressions, all the possible views of a violin, brought to life at a single instant on the canvas.

One recalls the stormy protest of the surrealists against what they might have called the *rhetoric* of life and time, the clear and limited outlines of the forms they were creating. The spokesman for the movement, André Breton, rebelling against what I propose to be the very essence of the human spirit, that is, drama and dramatic growth in time, finally cried out for non-dramatic simultaneity in the secret souls of geniuses:

Everything suggests the belief that there is a certain point of the mind where life and death, the real and the imaginary, the past and the future, the communicable and the incommunicable, the high and the low are no longer contradictions.[3]

Baudelaire had said: "One must always be drunk. That says it all. There is no other point. In order not to feel the horrible burden of time that bruises your shoulders and bends you to the ground, you must get drunk incessantly." [4] Drinking halts time and provides the gift, in the instant, of an artificial eternity. Baudelaire knows the trick, too, of doing in a refined way what our present-day civilization does in a cruder way, that is, of extending the moment by the sheer multiplicity of sensation:

This imagination lasts an eternity. An interval of lucidity with a great effort permits you to watch the clock. The eternity has lasted one minute. . . . The proportion of time and of being are disturbed by the innumerable multitude and intensity of sensations and ideas. One lives several lives in the space of an hour.[5]

And similarly with Poe (another example of the disease of supra-temporality for which I am in Poulet's debt) whose instrument for the conquest of time and the creation of simultaneity is the dream, or "nocturnal time" as opposed to ordinary daytime. ". . . Possessing neither past nor future, existing within itself, unattached to any antecedent or subsequent life, dream has its own time," says Poulet of this notion of Poe's. "It is a perpetual present . . . if the nocturnal time is long it is because the hours that compose it are not differentiated one from another like the hours of solar time

. . . actually they do not pass. They remain." [6] The return of Poe from the dream to the actual moment, to insertion into daylight time, is accompanied by fright.

It would be facile to dismiss this idea of Poe's by saying that since Poe was a romantic, and an esoteric dreamer, his texts, while suitable objects for the literary critic, have nothing to do with our souls' salvation or with any reality of contemporary culture. I wish we could so pleasantly isolate the literary problems and diseases of time from what goes on in the depths of our spiritual and our social life. But there are many today—and hard-headed sociologists among them—who are convinced that this distinction made by Poe between the eternal and infinite life of the night and the frightening actuality of the daytime may be used to describe symbolically the cleavage within our present technological civilization. Due to the growing encroachments of automation and the terribly repetitive, unfeeling nature of much of our daytime work, we have been led to create a night-time culture, and a kind of time within it that has no relation to the day or to the work we do during the day. This night-time culture is largely an attempt to provide a sensational and sentimental dream life in which real time is arrested or forgotten, and the coming of the next morning indefinitely put off. As Allen Tate has said so well, we all have a little bit of Edgar Allan Poe in us; he is cousin to us all. [7]

Perhaps the most ambitious, most brilliant, and most sophisticated vendetta launched against time was that of Descartes, who first put forward the notion of a pure intelligence within us which is not subject to time, and which can make brilliantly simultaneous the whole of existence, past, present, and future. We cannot question the legitimacy of the mathematical mind's ambition to relate things, and to reduce as much of the world as possible to a single, unified, simultaneous concept expressed by a formula or an equation. But when that ambition takes the form of a desire to wipe out the succession and the partial quantities of time, and to *live* in an isolated area of the personality where the temporal has no meaning or power, then a grave folly has been committed.

Perhaps it is the gravest folly of all to believe that by sheer thought the whole dramatic quality of life can be ignored or wiped out. And this is what seems to have happened in the Dream of Descartes, when he discovered that by standing still, by doing nothing, by becoming completely non-dramatic, and by thinking of one thing and after that of another, he could perceive in one great simultaneity the unity of all the sciences.

Since Descartes an increasing number of men are dedicated to what we call the "clear idea," to what I shall later call the univocal idea, which attempts to stand in its moment of glory free of the muddiness and vicissitudes of time. An example is André Malraux, who in his *The Voices of Silence* discusses the fight of man against fate or destiny. He defines the latter as "the mortal element in all that is doomed to die,"[8] by which I take it he means the flow of time and all that goes with it. In the "victory" of any masterpiece of art, says Malraux, time-ridden man somehow rises into grandeur and timelessness. What this large aesthetic statement amounts to concretely is that art and all its forms are so many conquests over time, chaos, and fate. Art, for Malraux, is at once the conqueror and the destroyer of time.

When the man dedicated to such an idea descends actively into the temporal order of human affairs, in which he does not really believe, and is given power, he becomes a rigid planner with no capacity for adaptation to the temporal mutability of the things around him; he is ruthless against any form of reality, human or material, that gets in the way of his idea. This man, with whose qualities I shall deal in detail in a later chapter on the univocal, is literally saying: To hell with time, because like God my pure intelligence stands outside it. But he is also saying: If I step into time I shall, unlike God, not save it but destroy it. There is danger in this notion of a pure intelligence, with its pretensions to living an eternal life outside time, with its perfect, immovable plans, its desire to think apart from and without the aid of being, its geometrical aims at destroying all our pasts and all our pluralisms in the name of angelic simplicity, its wish (as simple-minded as that of a child) to control the future perfectly so that it really need not be lived at all.

THE GENERATIVE MOMENT

For the pure intelligence, with its aspirations toward brilliant, univocal clarity, inflexibility, totality of vision and simultaneity, any proposal that a descent into the finite and a movement through time are the necessary modes of the major and crucial forms of human knowledge is a proposal that it submit to a kind of dying. The finite intelligence—my

term for the intelligence that is devoted to the finite and
the concrete—*does* accept as a basic premise of its own
functioning the idea of death. The words "death" and "dying"
must, however, be subjected to a closer scrutiny than the men
of the infinite are generally willing to give them.

"Death" is a wide word. It can mean dying to many
things. In connection with temporality it literally means dying
every moment to the past and the present. Human life is a
moving structure of phases (birth, childhood, adolescence,
prime, middle age, old age, death) so put together as by its
very movement to produce insight and illumination—such
experimental insights and illuminations as are totally beyond
the ken and function of all static, logical forms of thought.
The temporal flow of human life is therefore a *formed*
thing, a significant form. It is a progressive and planned
movement into and within the infinite, slowly uncovering
and penetrating those secrets of the latter which are barred to
all the forms of so-called "pure," non-temporal thought. Seen
geometrically, the movement has a truly dramatic simplicity:

The horizontal line represents the passage through time and
the barbs the points of illumination, each one necessary to
and creative of the next.

Human time, when lived according to its basic flow, is a
highly subtle, complicated, and sophisticated intellectual process. Yet many an intellectual, devoted to the pure intelligence, rejects this process as though it were a sickness. We
have learned from modern psychology how deep is the
temptation of the human being to escape into his mind, so
to speak, and to think out his reality in that safe spot, untouched by the processes of living through experience. This is,
of course, a lordly and magnificent way; it is also an easier
way. But the psychologists are now aware—as the saints
always were—that this way of knowledge is really a defense
against knowledge, a clever though covert attempt on the
part of the self to avoid insight; and that out of such an
attempt finally comes not knowledge, and not health, but ill-
ness. The withdrawal from the flow of time is such an escape from experience; the attempt to reject or to ignore any

part of the temporal movement, to hold on too tightly to any part of it, produces not freedom and not inviolability but a kind of slavery. We pay a terrible price if we try to remain children in the literal temporal sense; in fact, we grow old before our time, because of all the stresses and strains of the fight against time.

The "man in the street" often understands what the intellectual does not: that true reality is contained within the dramatic temporal life of the body. The peasant knows that if he is sick he will be healed not only by doctors but by time. He knows very well that time simply will not coalesce, and that it is really a child's game to wish that it may do so. He knows, when he goes to the movies and begins to be entertained by all the tricks of a new simultaneity that can stretch out the present into an infinity, that can restore the past and bring the future into the immediate present, that what he is witnessing is also a game. If his instincts remain uncorrupted he understands that he himself must continue to live his life moment by moment; that time is not an enemy lying in wait outside himself to trap him, but is nothing but the phases of his own life, as much a part of him as his own skin, out of which he cannot leap.

In his introduction to Cervantes' *Don Quixote*,[9] Samuel Putnam suggests the essential theme of that book to be the final return of the infinite-directed, the romantic mind to the few basic, narrow realities which in the flesh confront each living soul—a return and a yielding which may, however, make an agony of experiences and decisions. The death of Don Quixote the dreamer is very like that of Socrates. As Quixote dies, he insists that in his will careful provision be made for a new dress to be bought, for twenty ducats, for his housekeeper. Readers of the *Phaedo* will recall how in his last moments Socrates says in a businesslike way to his friends: "I owe a cock to Asclepius; see that it is paid." The Christian generally believes that time is a passageway to the infinite, and that the latter goal cannot be reached by any other means. He believes that the infinite is not a reward for having lived through so dreadful a thing as temporality, but rather that, in a very powerful sense, such an infinite— whether it be beauty, or God, or peace—proceeds out of time by a kind of extraordinary structural logic. The process is, for the Christian, a weaker but nonetheless true analogue of the manner in which Christ Himself passed through the stages of human life, back into the bosom of His heavenly

Father. I shall be dealing with the Christological parallel at a later point; here I am simply concerned to establish that, even in the natural order, human time is a divine construction, narrow indeed but powerful as all real being is (as dreaming is not), all of its phases important for natural and sacred knowledge, none of its phases to be omitted without paying a price.

Some of the noblest works of art created by the human mind have had as their aim the portrayal of such a steady march of the soul through irrevocable events. Each of the events in such a work is an action or a decision which, once it has happened or been made to happen, causes the future, causes another event, and makes altogether impossible the facile and childlike desire to recall or regain the past as though nothing had happened since. Sometimes the decisions that cause the future are not entirely on the level of consciousness, but art at its highest is never a dream world in which the protagonist seeks to escape from the meaning and consequences of time. Rather it is a highly conscious submission to and movement through the forms of time, even unto death (as with Christ) and a relentless search for insight into what happens to a human soul as it courses through event after event.

I could illustrate this passage of a soul through time by that of the mother of Hector in the *Iliad*, or that of the mother of six sons in Synge's *Riders to the Sea*, but a more modest and perhaps more effective example is that of the traveling circus man in the movie *La Strada*.

This man's passage through time leads him along all the roads of Italy, and brings him at last to a deserted beach, where he sits, a broken man, in the presence of his first thought: the thought that he had incredibly abused the love of the dim-witted girl-child he lived with along those roads. He has murdered her one friend, and taken away the one thing in her life that made her believe the cosmos had need of her, has betrayed and abandoned her and has given her over to the death of utter metaphysical loneliness. We watch the illumination pour into the face of the man on the beach, see his reaching arms, and the effect is overwhelming. It is indeed his first thought—and yet, as with all of us, it is not. For no organization of experience is wholly spontaneous. Each has its genesis in many different seeds spread along the roads we have traveled. It is possible that the action of "paying the price" is central to all creation, and to all real knowledge. Thus the circus man, before that moment of first thought, has traveled many roads and made an odyssey through many cities, he has raged at innocence, and has shielded his mind from all possible perception and his heart from feeling by a thousand savageries and insensitivities; but who is to say finally that that broken conscience on the beach is not experiencing love—for love, like being, has many forms, is never without a body all its own. And our insight into the reality of this one soul's situation comes out of our knowledge of the events through which the soul has passed.

THE FLIGHT FROM TIME

I am not saying that all those who do not agree with the view I have described of the reality of time and the necessity of a passage of the soul through it are anti-religious. The longing for eternity, for a habitation outside temporality, is a theologically valid feeling. We do want God, or something like Him, and are impatient about securing Him or it. But the theological or religious impulse is much more than a simple, inner, affective reaching out for the divinity. It is an extremely complicated aspiration and so, therefore, must be the thoughts and feelings that come under it.[10] The theological picture is not complete unless the ultimate and finally desirable goal of religion is reached by a passage through time. Thus the concept of the worthlessness of time, and the profound rebellion against it, can only be in part a religious protestation; another part of it is non-religious and non-theological.

Let me again use Proust as an example of the non-religious aspect of this rebellion against time. André Maurois, in his *Proust: Portrait of a Genius,* says not only that "Proust was obsessed by the flight of the passing moment, by the perpetual state of flux of everything that makes up our environment, by the changes wrought by time in our bodies and our minds," but that:

There is an antimony between his anguished sense that all vanishes, men no less than things, including himself, and the deep conviction that there is in his nature something permanent and even eternal. Proust knew this conviction in certain brief moments *when suddenly an instant of the past became real to him,** and he discovered that sights and feelings which he had thought of as

* Italics mine.

gone forever must, obviously, have been preserved somewhere in him, since, otherwise, how could they reappear.

The role Proust was destined to fill, says Maurois, was "the role of the artist who, by fixing such moments and all that they contain, *can stop the flux of Time.** Life as it passes is but Time lost; but all can be transfigured, found again, presented 'under the aspect of eternity, which is that of art.'" "It is at this moment," Maurois continues (in a long passage which I quote here in its entirety, for it makes my point very clearly),

> that salvation comes to the artist, and to all human beings. From the medley of relative worlds, an absolute world emerges. In man's long struggle with Time, it is man, thanks to the talismans and charms of art, who remains the victor. Thus we see that the subject of *A la Recherche du temps perdu* is the drama of a marvelously intelligent and agonizingly sensitive being who, from the very threshold of childhood, sets forth to find happiness in the absolute. He tries to reach it in all of its forms, though refusing, with an implacable lucidity, to deceive himself as most people deceive themselves. For human beings, as a rule, accept glory and love and the triumphs of the world at their face value. Proust, declining to do so, is led on to seek an absolute that lies outside this world and outside Time itself. It is the absolute that religious mystics find in God. Proust, for his part, looks for it in art, thereby practicing a form of mysticism that is closer to the other than might be supposed, because all art in its origins was religious, and because religion has often found in art the means of communicating to the human consciousness truths which the intelligence can discover only with difficulty.[11]

Note the disarming deception behind this quotation. Maurois is claiming that there is a connection between the spirit and method of Proust and the spirit and attitude of Christianity and the saints toward temporality, whereas they are in considerable conflict. It is an identification of opposites that is facile, to say the least, for such an artist in reality sets himself up in complete opposition to the Christian saint and the Christian theology of time.

Proust, as Maurois himself shows, has no hesitation in declaring that time is an enemy, and that the whole function of human life and art is to enter into a kind of contest with time, whereby time can be brought to immobility. His

* Italics mine.

great work is devoted to an attempt to overcome the actual movement of time, to bring the past back into existence at some point at which it possessed the taste of beauty, of peace or joy. In making such an attempt, far from seeking "the absolute that religious mystics find in God," Proust is committing an act that is non-religious and non-mystical. Instead of accepting the structure of time, which is essentially the structure of a thing perpetually in motion; instead of trying to see, with all the resources of genius, that such a movement might be leading somewhere; instead of exploring what will happen psychologically and spiritually once the movement is entered into fully—instead, this kind of artist rejects the possibility of beauty emerging from such insight.

I say *this kind of artist* advisedly. For it is simply not true to say that the function of all art is to immobilize time, to freeze into permanence some instant of peace or illumination so that we may have it forever, and thus share in that quality of eternity that does not move but simply *is*. There may be artists, and forms of art, that are afflicted with such a desire—but it is, to my mind, precisely that: an affliction. The impulse itself represents a disease of the feelings and a collapse of the true metaphysical mind; it is a fraudulent aping of religion and Christianity, and of that final religious idea of eternity as the one eternal now, without sequel, and without insecurity, or the loss of any good thing.

In order to clarify this position in further terms of the literary imagination let me turn for a moment to the *Oedipus Rex* of Sophocles.[12] There is no need here to summarize the action of the play. Suffice it to say that it advances relentlessly through event after event, each event carved out with clarity and with a note of the irrevocable. This is the poetry of action. Even at the moments where the action of the play is interrupted to indulge what we may think of as pure poetry [13] (that is, by the choral odes), there is no relaxing by Sophocles into an escape through magic or dreams; the choral odes are, rather, the focal points of the drama, which give us in high lyric form the illuminated meaning of the event that has just taken place, the decision that has been made, or which give us—as life itself does at such points— some insight into, some anticipation of what will follow inevitably from what has occurred.

Nowhere is time forsaken. The *Oedipus* is a story of a

soul moving through time, from greatness into the dust;
everything inside and outside of this masterpiece is
meant, down to the last iambic rhythm, to help us see more
deeply into time and to flow more deeply with it. I use the
word "outside" deliberately, for there seems to be little doubt
of the meaning, to the Greeks, of the general Dionysiac
myth upon which their theater was based: the splendid birth
and youth and final dismemberment of the god Dionysus
were accepted by them as reflecting, in the order of feeling
and sensibility, the same profound temporal order they saw
in nature and in their own lives. Thus the viewing of a
play like the *Oedipus*, which is the story of the initial glory
and the final dismemberment of a king, did not by its master-
liness provide them with a distraction from the time process
that is the play's central theme, but rather drove them even
more deeply into their own consciousness of time—drove
them to a level of it that is overwhelming in its grandeur
and actuality. For there are two levels of time: one that is
hustle and bustle, and the other the feeling for that deeper
movement of human life that leads into something great. The
rhythm of the *Oedipus* helps to re-create and intensify the
awareness of this kind of temporality, and the play makes no
pretensions, at any point, to destroy temporality.

But—and here I follow the analysis of Francis Fergusson [14]
—there is another way of writing a play. In it, unlike
Sophocles' procedure in the *Oedipus*—a purely rational
"idea" is isolated at the outset, and the elements of human
character and of action (the elements of time) used merely to
demonstrate this idea; or else a single passion or emotion is
isolated in the same way, and the elements of time used similarly to demonstrate it. Illustrating this procedure, Fergusson
says of Racine: "He is interested in individual characters as
illustrations of his abstract idea, insofar as they are required
for the concrete situation he uses"; and of Nietzsche's comment, in *The Birth of Tragedy*, on Wagner's *Tristan*:
". . . Nietzsche says nothing about the intelligible elements
in the opera. The characters, the story, the events themselves,
are regarded merely as expressions of the underlying passion. Even the myth of Tristan, on this basis, would be
regarded as superficial, a necessary concession to our mortal
darkness, but essentially illusory." [15] And, as Fergusson
makes clear, the same attitude toward the concrete, the
same view of the universe as a "worldless world," was
true of Wagner himself.

TIME, ART AND THEOLOGY

It is evident that modern man, and particularly modern man in America, wishes to escape from the rigors of time. But another element of his personality makes him pride himself on his apparent total immersion in the rough processes of temporality, and makes him despise, either openly or secretly, anything that sets him apart in a "feminine" way from his own achievements, his own daring, his own apparent immersion in the temporal. The American may go to church on Sunday, and subscribe formally to membership in the Christian religion, but does he not often secretly conceive of this church-going and this membership as a kind of escape from the temporal? We are a partially changed people because of the inroads of recent history, but the image the American had of himself in the nineteenth and early twentieth centuries—described by Henry Steel Commager, in his *The American Mind,* as that of an amazingly resolute "new man" who plunges into the future, into the uncharted wilderness, into experience and experiment, into daring and time —still holds true. A part of this man, however, is exhausted by the effort, by all this daring, and feels he is entitled to some form of escape. And for some, it is clear, Christianity is no more than such an escape. Church-going is on a level, for these people, with going to a romantic movie in the evening after having worked hard all day; having soaked themselves in time and experience, they feel they are now entitled to something altogether different.

I believe the seeds of such an attitude lie dormant in all of us. We at all times like to hide within the hope that Christianity may, please God, have nothing to do with the temporal, and that at least within its confines we may be safe and may rest from the temporal process.

It is in answer to this yearning, common to us all, that many of the most intelligent men of our day have attempted to reduce the idea of Christianity to a set of non-temporal "doctrines"—to purely intellectual statements, in the Cartesian sense, that appeal only to the superficial parts of the intelligence and are to be adhered to by this intelligence only, and that have, they maintain, no relation to modern experience and the human condition.

The effort to fix the human intelligence in a realm apart,

to make of it something pure and perfect and quite able to manage by itself without reference to the contingent and the temporal, is nothing new. Such philosophers as Leibniz, Spinoza, and Kant, among others, have held that temporal things do not lead to a deep, possessive awareness on the part of the mind, but rather that they are in themselves no more than weak imitations of that mind, which is already quite full of truth or quite well able to become so without being bothered by complications raised by the human personality or by the business of living through time.

This notion of the intelligence as absolutely divorced from human reality is all very well for philosophy. But when it is transposed, as is being done today, onto the level of theology, when Christian doctrines are conceived of as a set of pure statements to be accepted by the pure mind as unrelated to anything as low as plain living, the situation is much more serious. The philosophy of the transcendental and lordly mind is at least respected as being sophisticated. But when religious belief becomes a pleasant unrelated-to-anything haven for the minds of the naïve and for those seeking to escape reality, it is *not* respected.

Those who attempt to convert Christianity into a set of static, celestial statements, with no relation to actuality, usually profess to represent, in their own persons, the modern, experimental soul to which religion is no longer related. They are, I believe, falling into the error of historicism. They are subtly saying to themselves: we are what we are in the order of feeling and experience, we are not what another age was, and we can do nothing about it. This is partially true, but it also is a form of self-protection. Those who, in the name of the imagination or of science, declare that they represent an historically defined state of soul and that anyone who takes up Christianity is not being faithful to authentic modern experience have, at least in my view, no right to defend themselves against Christianity in such terms. It was precisely against such historicist attitudes that St. Paul aligned himself, when he preached Christ to the two orders of sensibility that were either violently or scientifically opposed to the idea of Him: he preached to the Jews a Christ who came to liberate them from their racial law, and to the Athenian intellectuals a Christ who by His particularity and concreteness demanded the beginnings of a new intelligence, as against their ideal universalism. The historicist argument deserves no more consideration, it seems to me, in our own time.*

Christians imprudently try to defend themselves against this argument by calling it an attack of time against eternity; whereas actually Christians are the men of time, under attack by many spurious but highly intelligent and imaginative forms of eternity. The simple fact is that time is indeed an experience, and the modern sensibility has explored it very fully, usually without even a natural faith in it. And Christianity is a *doctrine* that defends eternity, and is in apparent opposition to the autonomous right which the contemporary imagination claims for itself to explore the full extent of the human condition. But a curious twisting of vocabularies has taken place, much abetted by the failure of some Christians to realize what total Christianity is. Both poetry and science not only claim the right, understandably, to penetrate the human situation, but they claim it as opponents of (rescuers from!) a supposititious Christianity which is "doctrinal" in a perverse sense of that word, which is purely con-

---

* At the moment of writing there is a recurring quarrel going on in the literary journals that on the surface is a quarrel between men of the eternal and the historicists, between fixity and relativism. Both sides to the conflict are zealous in two ways: in launching a criticism and in admitting that the two things, principle and fact, truth and history, must be brought and kept together. Roy Harvey Pearce initiated the latest debate with an article in *The Kenyon Review* (Vol. XX, No. 4, Autumn 1958, pp. 544-591) entitled "Historicism Once More," in which he boldly asked that the new critics make an intrinsic incorporation of time, history and passing language marks into the "eternal" achievements of art. René Wellek ("Literary Theory, Criticism, and History," *Sewanee Review,* Vol. LXVIII, No. 1, Winter 1960, pp. 1-19) attacked with considerable concern and a warning against the "relativists," even against his colleague Erich Auerbach. A third recent document of interest would be Francis Fergusson's final chapter, "Two Perspectives in European Literature," in his *The Human Image in Dramatic Literature,* in which he joins himself to the concern about relativism and historicism but adds something like my own fundamental question: "It is time we raised once more the ancient question of art's truth to reality." I must confess that, while I share Mr. Wellek's concerns about historicism, it will be clear that I am firmly on the side of Mr. Pearce's sincere attempt to incorporate the passing historical moment into the work of the artist. He is basically right. For if history and our new and unpredictable tomorrows are not most tightly fitted into our final and best visions, then what is the use of creating or living? But I also think that the whole discussion would be more profitable if the word "historicism" were omitted from the vocabulary of all concerned in this *present* debate. There is no historicist in the current discussion.

ceptual, non-temporal, angelic, and hostile to the entire intention of literature and scientific investigation.

Now if this were the final character of Christian belief—if it were no more than a way of escaping into a world of false peace where the mind may rest untouched by its own humanity, or by any movement of human time—and if Christ Himself were no more than an "idea," safely perched outside temporality and beyond the reach of testing by experience and sensibility, then there might indeed be reason for suspecting or condemning Christianity and for rejecting Christ. But the truth is, of course, that Christian belief is in its essence belief in a person who, having "created" time, could not possibly be hostile to it; who had directed it from the beginning by way of His providence and His having substantially and inwardly shaped it (so that He is the master of both history and psychiatry), who finally entered it and grew into it with such subtlety and power that He is not the enemy of but the model for the imagination and the intelligence. He is the enemy only of the romantic imagination and the pure intelligence as ways of life.

Even when the human soul is in the highest of contemplative states—that is to say, when it is locked most securely in the embrace of the timeless divinity—it cannot forego its grip on the humanity and temporality of Christ. The men of the infinite would have us believe that at least in prayer, at least at the moment of union with God, time is transcended and some kind of motionlessness, some kind of quasi-eternity, is reached. But time, even on the natural level, *is* a kind of ontological prayer. There is no other form of union with God. Ultimately the most solid form of prayer for the Christian, no matter what spiritual state he may be in (including that of high contemplation), is not rest but motion: a coursing, with all the powers of the mind and will and body, through the mysteries—that is, the stages—of the life of Christ. It is no idle phrase that the Church repeats when she says again and again: *per ipsum et cum ipso et in ipso,* through Him and with Him and in Him.

I have used the word "subtlety" to describe the Christic passage through time, in the sense in which either Dante or St. Ignatius would have used it. For indeed it requires subtlety to know, for worse or better, the roles of temporality at each moment. Dante, about to make the great journey of human life in his poem and knowing the way was narrow but not infinite, says at the beginning of the *Purgatorio:*

> O you, who are there in your little boat,
>   longing to listen, following in my way
>   behind my timbers singing as they go,
> turn you back to find your own coasts again;
>   do not trust to the open sea; for perhaps,
>   once losing me, you would be left astray.[16]

And St. Ignatius, knowing the perplexities of each moment of time and the infinite forces of darkness which lay around every real moment and true decision, composed an intricate set of rules called "the discernment of spirits," to help the soul judge its own confusing sensibilities in the midst of each new instant. But these are only instances of masters copying the supreme mastery of Christ as He handles and moves through every detail and phase of human life.

I have also used the word "power" to describe the progress of Christ through temporality. It is fashionable to question the miracles in the life of Christ and to say that they are in accord with the modern temper. I do not wish to discuss that question here, but wish merely to point out that there is an amazing refusal on the part of modern "sensibility and experience" to discuss, much less take as an example, the non-miraculous quality in Christ's resolute living and penetration into human time. He assumes a body, which has been the scandal of every docetist (the heretic who holds that Christ did not have a real body), from Marcion to our own day. He gives up His childhood decisively, telling His parents that He must be about His Father's business. In the desert He refuses the devil's temptation of cheap, immediate glory. He weeps over Jerusalem instead of leading it as a great military messiah. When He is taken prisoner, He tells His captors that, if He so wishes, His Father would send Him legions of angels—but that He would not ask for them. On the cross He is offered a kind of medication but refuses it. There is no other who could say as authentically, of human time, as He: "It is consummated." It is not accurate to say that Christ redeemed time. For time has never needed redeeming; it only needed someone to explore its inner resources fully, and add even further resources to it, as He did. And so powerful and new is the exploration, in His case, that it is crowned not only with insight but with the Resurrection.[17]

I have gone this deeply here into the Christological position because it gives me a forceful means of expressing the concern I feel when people talk about the splendid autonomous right of the imagination and the intelligence, over against religion, to explore, experience, and objectify "the human condition." I suspect that such talk is only, in its own apparently more realistic fashion, a restatement of Keats's plea that the imagination be allowed to be a chameleon, taking on the shape of anything and everything it meets, but never in the order of temporality and decision, becoming anything. "The freedom of modern art," says Francis Fergusson, "is precisely the freedom to respond, directly, and without premeditation, to any and every human experience." [18]

More often than not the imagination refuses the prophetic role, declines to determine, as Dante did, the true and narrow temporal shape and direction of the human situation; for this would be to abdicate its right to react freely to all the infinities that surround the moral and dramatic reality of man. The human imagination is afraid of the narrow and non-simultaneous character of time. And it is doubly afraid of the narrowness of Christic time, not being able to abide the idea that the already narrow path to insight or salvation through time has been further straitened and thinned down to the measure of the time structure, the event structure, the mysteries, of the life of a Nazarene carpenter.

This hesitation on the part of the imagination, confronted with temporality, is perfectly understandable and can be very honest. It is, after all, only the most exacerbated form of the quarrel between the men of the finite and the men of the infinite. The important thing to recognize, however, is that the true division in the world is not between the men devoted to the definite and the dramatic and those who are ranged, with all the weight of human sensibility, on the side of "the human situation." The division is rather between the universal chameleons, the men who wish to take on, without commitment, the form of all things plus the simultaneity of all time, and those who are willing to begin with a narrow, specific, highly concrete focus in the imagination and to move along a narrow line of time, accepting *that* as the only true mode—a dramatic mode—for the acquisition of insight into the thing called "the human condition."

Aeschylus was possibly the first to teach us that this insight into the human condition comes only through a descent into the deeper temporality that is the very moving life of the soul, rather than to the superficial levels of time found in mechanical motion, successive sensations, and the ticking of clocks. No one would pretend that this descent onto the deepest level is smooth, that it is without its unique and painful zigzaggings. If it were, it would not have been so decisively rejected by the romantic imagination or by a certain variety of scientific intelligence. But certainly it is the moving line of earned insights and a cognitive life that is full of sensibility, of real assents, and of statements about existence which are come by legitimately through the developing dramatic rhythms of life, and not through the illegitimate and unrooted leaps of what Cardinal Newman might have called the purely notional mind.[19]

THE SPIRITUAL EXERCISES

There will come a place in these explorations when we will want to look into the formal question of whether there is a theological level at the innermost core of the literary image. But even at this early stage we can perhaps afford a few anticipations of that question, especially if they be the kind that are thoroughly concrete and fundamentally "poetic" in the best meaning of that word. I should like to propose the *Spiritual Exercises* of St. Ignatius as a source of poetic as well as spiritual insight at this point, where we are concluding our first investigations into the image of the definite and the image of time, for he has much to say about both.*

Certainly he wished to lead the soul to God, and if people wish to call that escape they are at times entitled to the use of their own words. But his method was not the method of escape or magic. Magical or instantaneous methods of getting at God are marked by a hatred and fear of human time and of the full, long human process. Basically they wish to

---

* To those who will be bothered, whether personally or impersonally, by my emphasis on the eminence of time for life and art I can only say that it is hardly something new but is only an attempt at the further concretization of a few simple facts. According to St. Thomas all knowledge of and movement in being is always both total and partial, partial according to the limits of our human situation, total in that we are always in touch, no matter what the limitations, with the whole of being. The element of time does not weaken the direct approach to God in prayer, according to all the uses of the idea of *direct approach* in traditional piety. But time taken as an enemy can be such a preventative. What seems most important to me is to restore time to its proper context, as located in being and, in a very important sense, in eternity—and thus to eliminate the destructively absolute dichotomy between the two.

do two things—and I want to lay strong emphasis on this because both contrast strongly with the Ignatian method of coming to God; because of this hatred of time they wish to use but a single, special moment of it, one that by some strange, inexplicable "trick" will lead them to full glory, and they wish to deprive even that single moment of as much of its highly questionable actuality and concreteness as possible, thinking that these are blocks to the cognition of glory and beauty. Ignatius, thoroughly representative of Catholic theology, works entirely in the contrary direction. An analysis of his method will show in detail after detail that, as a seeker of God, he is completely devoted to the time process and completely devoted to its definite actuality, no matter what it is at each particular moment. Therefore his method of prayer or, shall we say, his directive for leading the soul to God, has two main structural points behind it:

1. He leads the exercitant, the man making the exercises, *proportionally* through the life of Christ. Therefore, he leads him through it step by step, forbidding him again and again to take the way of magic impatience or hatred and commanding him to stay within the pure time process as such. It is hoped that the texts which are used later will make perfectly clear what is meant by this.

2. He is remarkably definite in his demands on the soul that the latter be altogether concrete in its consideration of that moment of time. This is that point of his technique and, we should also say, of his *theology* which is called the "composition of place." In it he insists that the one praying should submit his mind and will completely to perfect and complete *detail*, the detail of that moment which is being separately and patiently considered. Once again I hope that the naked texts will reveal precisely what he meant, and in their complete simplicity. For nothing could be simpler and barer in their style, save a mathematical treatise, than the *Spiritual Exercises*. It is only the impassioned and actual quality of the theology behind them which reveals the high and thoughtful life behind these few bare pages.

But we must remember that it is exactly through such proportional and definite methods that he wishes to lead the soul to God and beauty, and that that is his only and ever-recurrent theme. In his method he is completely human, time-possessed and definite. But in his ultimate aim he is what some people would choose to call altogether single-minded and "fanatical." The sentences in which he reveals this aim are there to the point of abundance. For example, and most significant for his identification of the passage through the time process and the reaching of the infinite, he calls the second week of the Exercises, that in which the coursing through time is most insistent, "the illuminative way" (cf. Annotation X). There are other phrases, repeated again and again, which, in the midst of the total detail of human life used by him, reveal his total single-mindedness: "For the sake of the honor and glory of God, . . . solely the service, honor and glory of His Divine Majesty" (Annotation XVI); "to approach and unite itself to its Creator and Lord" (Annotation XX); "only the service of God Our Lord" . . . "the service and praise of His Divine Goodness" (meditation on the Three Classes); "the greater service and praise of His Divine Majesty" (consideration on the Three Degrees of Humility) and so on according to the same note through the entire little book. Finally, one has but to read the last page of the Exercises, the Contemplation for Obtaining Love, to see that the only Ignatian objective is contemplative love, such a one, too, as soars far beyond all the loves and ecstatic, timeless leaps of the new escape-theology.

Thus, then, we have an extraordinary and at times disconcerting document which combines, in unified and sharp strokes, time, detail, definiteness, actuality, and glory.

But Ignatius is not coursing through man and the human self, with all the reality that goes with it, as a purely secular fact. Rather in his prayer he is coursing through the *mysteries of the life of Christ* as the latter advances through the full human scheme. For him, then, there is no separation between our advance through Christ and our advance through man and time, even unto death, even unto the death of the cross. Therefore, it is impossible to find in his thinking any form of "pure theology," that is, pure angelism, or pure secularism. His Christology and his humanism are one and the same thing. He was remarkably strong in his sense of fact, history and the present moment, but he took these strong perceptions from the study of theology and the life of Christ. We now come to some of the texts of this double but unified method.

1. First of all let us notice the Ignatian devotion to the time scheme and his great patience in marching through it, part by part.

The Exercises are divided into different weeks of prayer, according to the different subjects of each; it is to be especially emphasized that the second, third and fourth weeks have as their simple subjects different parts of the life of Christ.

As early as the Eleventh Annotation, the saint has this to say about method: "It is of advantage to him who is receiving the exercises of the first week, that he should know nothing of what he has to do in the second week, but that he so toil in the first in order to arrive at what he is seeking, as if he did not hope to obtain anything in the second."

Methodologically the exercitant is always restricted, in a way that is almost severe, to the subject matter of each moment; in the directions for the first week we read: "The petition ought to be according to the subject matter, i.e., if the contemplation is on the Resurrection, the petition ought to be to ask for joy with Christ rejoicing; if it be on the Passion, to ask for grief, tears and pain with Christ in torment . . ."

In the "Additions" for the first week we read: "In the point in which I shall find what I desire, there I will rest, without being anxious to proceed to another, until I have satisfied myself."

In the "Notes" given as directives for the second week the point is made even more clearly: "It is to be noted that during the whole of this week, and the following weeks, I ought only to read the mysteries of the contemplation which I am immediately to make; so that, for the time being, I do not read any mystery which I have not to make on that day or at that hour, in order that the consideration of one mystery may not disturb the consideration of another."

For the third week, which is given over to a study of the Passion, the directive is simple: ". . . consider what Christ Our Lord suffers, according to the portion of His Passion which is being contemplated." And further on we are advised "not to endeavor to admit joyful thoughts, even though good and holy, as on the Resurrection, and of Paradise . . ."

But all these are only formal and explicit directions to guide the soul through the structure of the Exercises, and it is the structure itself which gives us an even more solid picture of the method of Ignatius. This structure at its heart is given over to the *events* of the life of Christ, and it is important to emphasize this word. They are separate and consecutive actions that are marched through by the mind seeking the way of illumination. Thus different subject matters are assigned "on the events from Herod to Pilate"; "on the events from the Sepulchre, inclusively, to our Lady's arrival at the house, to which she went after the burial of her son"; "take the events at the house of Pilate." And he adds the advice for one making the exercises in a shorter time: "take each day five distinct exercises, and in each exercise a distinct mystery concerning Christ Our Lord."

One may be tempted, looking at these directives and at this *event structure,* to say that the whole of it is only a special and Ignatian form of prayer, with its own limited validity, and why therefore conceive that it has a mountain of relevancy for our day, for our problems? Well, it is true that Ignatius has a special genius in formulating the Exercises. But there must be a special reason why he has been selected by the Church as the patron for all prayer in retreat form. I believe that the partial reason for this election of the saint on the part of the Church is that with a unique genius he has hit off the Catholic idea of the march of the self to God through event, through Christological and human event.

We must understand that in the long debate which is going on, especially between Christian and non-Christian writers, a debate in which this book pretends to be a tiny part, we are at loggerheads about the use of words. We are accusing each other of the use of magic and escapism in our separate theologies. We have said something of their vices in this direction but what of one of their fundamental attitudes toward ourselves on the same subject? I think that that attitude could be reduced to this: that fundamentally all *dogma,* all religious belief, is an abstraction, a separate formula, an invention to help us escape from the reality in which they, more than ourselves, are immersed. Moreover, we cannot expect that they will understand in a flash what our idea of doctrine, when accurately put, really is. But what essentially is that idea? If the reader will pardon my own brevity in an enormous subject for my own limited purposes, I think that Catholic doctrine is the very reverse of this magical idea; rather it is a divine command of the mind and the will to enter, on the divine and the human planes, into an historical, actual and *eventful* set of facts which penetrate reality to the hilt. And for this kind of summary there are two major pieces of evidence with which every reader is certainly somewhat familiar. The first is the liturgy of the Church which in its changing year reviews

the events in the life of Christ. The second which comes
to mind is the Apostles' Creed itself, that central statement of
belief which has no magic whatsoever in it. It is a sort of
summary of the *actions* of God in three forms, in the form
of His eternal majesty, in the form of Christ, and in the form
of that Church which claims no warrant with men unless it
be itself Christ as His larger and growing Body. The Creed
begins with God and ends with eternal life for men, but in
between is time, that time through which Christ passed and
that time through which doctrine implicitly commands us to
pass. Ignatian theology is, therefore, only a scientific structuralizing, for the sake of prayer, of the fundamental shape
of Catholic doctrine. The saint would have completely sym-
pathized with Erich Auerbach's sentence: "The stern hand of
God is ever upon the Old Testament figures; he has not only
made them once and for all and chosen them, but he continues to work upon them, bends and kneads them, and, without
destroying them in essence, produces from them forms which
their youth gave no grounds for anticipating." And he would
have completely rejected that phrase of Proust which sums up
so much of the real magic of modern times: *"le plus grand
intérêt de la vie non pas placé dans les aspirations actives
vers l'avenir et nouveau, mais dans le réassurement du passé
et dans l'inaction."* Time, Ignatius knew, was only a fruitful
passage through all the stages of the self, but he placed all
this firmly on a Christological and theological level. Moreover, there is not a single "leap" in the whole book.

2. We turn now to the way in which the Exercises
handle each moment of time, a way which is referred to
technically as the "composition of place." Of it we have said
that, as Ignatius allows himself to be absorbed by every
distinct moment of Christological time, so it is that by the
composition of place he will have the exercitant enter as
fully as possible into the entire concreteness of each of
these moments. Thus, in the directives for the first week the
saint says: "The first prelude is a composition of place, seeing the spot. Here it is to be observed that in contemplation
or meditation on visible matters, such as the contemplation
of Christ our Lord, Who is visible, the composition will be
to see with the eyes of the imagination the corporeal place
where the thing I wish to contemplate is found. I say
the corporeal place, such as the Temple or the mountain
where Jesus Christ or our Lady is found. . . ."

In the meditation on the Kingdom of Christ, the directive

is: "The first prelude is a composition of place, seeing the spot. It will be here to see with the eyes of the imagination the synagogues, towns, and villages, through which Christ our Lord used to preach."

For the first contemplation of the second week he directs: "The second prelude will be a composition of place, seeing the spot: here it will be to see the whole space and circuit of the terrestrial globe, in which so many divers races dwell: then likewise to behold in particular the house and chamber of our Lady in the town of Nazareth in the province of Galilee." And the first point for the actual contemplation reads thus in part: "the first point is to see the persons on either side: first, those on the face of the earth so varied in dress and carriage; some white and others black; some in peace and others in war; some weeping, others laughing; some in health, others sick; some being born, others dying. . . ." The second point continues in the same fashion: "hear what people are saying on the face of the earth; how they converse together, how they blaspheme . . . likewise what the Three Divine Persons are saying . . . and then what the Angel and our Lady are saying; and afterwards to reflect thereupon. . . ." And so with the third point which has to do with what the people of the world, God and our Lady are doing at the moment.

A perfect example of Ignatian concreteness is given in the composition of place for the following contemplation: "it will be here to see with the eyes of the imagination the road from Nazareth to Bethlehem; considering its length, breadth, and whether the way be level or through valleys and over hills; and likewise seeing the spot or cave of the Nativity, how large or small, how low or high, and how it is prepared."

Even more interesting in this regard and not quite falling under the domination of a composition of place is that form of Ignatian meditation within the Exercises which is called an "application of the senses." Thus, he states: "The first point is to see the persons with the eyes of the imagination, meditating and contemplating in particular their circumstances and deriving some fruit from the sight. The second is to hear what they are saying, or might say. . . . The third is to smell and taste the infinite sweetness and delight of the Divinity, of the soul, and of its virtues. . . . The fourth is to feel with the touch; as, for example, to kiss and embrace the spots where such persons tread and sit, always endeavoring to draw some fruit from this."

It should be unnecessary to go any further with this analysis of the Ignatian plea that we direct our search for God through time, reality and the self. Perhaps it is evidence enough for us to call him the full secularist and the full theologian in the one breath and moment. I leave to others the point of the full relevancy of this evidence for our times. But surely we can say, at a minimum, that there are many more souls today than Simone Weil who are crying out implicitly and explicitly, in a kind of despair over the dichotomy in which they are caught: "We must get rid of our superstition of chronology to find eternity."

An adequate discussion of time is one that will take the shapes of direction and indirection. By "direction" I mean formal theological debates on the issues raised in these chapters. By "indirection" I mean again all the analogical and more completely human or social levels on which these issues occur. Thus we have just been discussing the place of time and the "dramatic" in the Christian theological view of things. The word "dramatic" has of course been a little unusual if not mildly shocking in this superior context. But I should like, in the following two chapters, to attempt an analysis of the actual state of the drama and the dramatic among us. In very brief we will ask some such questions as the following about both tragedy and comedy. 1. How, possibly, can this discussion about the roles of the finite and the infinite in human life affect the status of our tragedy and comedy for good or for bad? 2. Is it possible that even in so homely and non-theological a situation as our theater the same twisting and corruptions of vocabulary have been going on to the detriment of the substance of the modern stage? We could have looked at other fields through the microscope of our present problem, but let us hope that some light will come from these we have chosen.

NOTES

1. Georges Poulet, *Studies in Human Time*, trans. by Elliott Coleman (Baltimore: Johns Hopkins Press, 1956).

2. Marcel Proust, cited by Poulet, p. 320.

3. André Breton, "Second Manifeste," *Les Manifestes du Surréalisme* (Paris: Éditions du Sagittaire, 1946), p. 92.

4. Charles Baudelaire, *The Essence of Laughter*, Peter Quennell,

ed. (New York: Meridian Books, 1956), p. 149.

5. *Ibid.*, p. 85.

6. Poulet, *op. cit.*, p. 330.

7. Allen Tate, "Our Cousin, Mr. Poe," p. 134.

8. André Malraux, *The Voices of Silence*, trans. by Stuart Gilbert (New York: Doubleday, 1953), p. 630.

9. Miguel de Cervantes, *The Ingenious Gentleman Don Quixote de la Mancha*, trans. by Samuel Putnam (New York: Viking Press, 1949), pp. viii-ix.

10. According to some critics, the whole religious picture should be left surpassingly and beautifully simple. They like to think that, while human life may be all twists and turns and facets, religion by some strange good fortune involves no twistings, turnings, efforts, struggles, on the part of the mind, the heart, or the imagination. But is there not a kind of softness in the type of simplicity these critics wish to introduce into some of the great human images that recur at the center of art and of the religious life? I should like to suggest that, on the contrary, there is a high virility in the way doctrine, action, and feeling have "complicated" both art and theology.

11. André Maurois, *Proust: Portrait of a Genius*, trans. by Gerard Hopkins (New York: Harper, 1950). The citations here are all from Chapter VI, pp. 156-192.

12. It is only by accident that I am drawing examples here from classical literature. However, I should like to note some further instances of the same way of regarding time, from W. F. Jackson Knight's *Roman Vergil* (London: Faber & Faber, 1944), p. 133. Of Aeschylus, Knight says: "(In him) each problem is solved not algebraically but by living. It turns as you watch into a new problem . . . not timeless, but in time. . . ." And of Vergil himself he says (p. 133):

    From Aeschylus he [Vergil] took creative conflict of loyalties, and indeed the Pythagorean formula of antagonisms everywhere, each destined to have a solution of its own, leading to new antagonisms and new salvations. And from Aeschylus, too, he took the long reach of time, and a solution, by living, in the far future, when even God can learn from man. But from this he left something aside. God is for him more Homeric than that, timeless and unchanging. He also added something. He defined and shewed in actual, practical forms the solutions that time could bring. This too might be missed; how intensely the main fabric of Vergil's poetic thought, with its solution by conflict in the mysterious power of time, is Aeschylean.

13. The reader will note a recurrent mention of the concept of "pure poetry." It seems to me that Francis Fergusson in his *The Idea of a Theatre* (Princeton: Princeton University Press,

1949), and *Dante's Drama of the Mind* (Princeton: Princeton University Press, 1953), has done as much as any one to help us escape from that limited notion of the literary imagination. But, like the rest of us, he sometimes wavers (cf. *Dante's Drama of the Mind*, pp. 151-160) between the narrower and the larger, or Dantean, understanding of poetry. Fergusson is trying courageously, it seems to me, to reconcile many concepts of poetry: the Aristotelian idea of imitation; the Scholastic theory of poetry; the enormous Dantean view of it as an endless poetizing of the human spirit according to all its modes and according to the inner drive of the widening sea of love; Jacques Maritain's partial view of a poem as a quasi-secondary *executive* act of the poet; the modern, pure poetic conquest which is described by Maritain as poetry's perfect *pris de conscience* of itself. This reconciling is, to put it mildly, a vast undertaking, and it remains to be seen whether all these strands can be put together successfully in the interests of the literary imagination. It would take an entire essay to comment satisfactorily on Mr. Fergusson's work in this direction.

14. Francis Fergusson, *The Idea of a Theatre.*

15. *Ibid.*, p. 74.

16. *Purgatorio,* trans. by Francis Fergusson, *Dante's Drama of the Mind,* p. 5.

17. I have been delighted to find my view of the absolute centrality of time in the Christian scheme in agreement with that of this great Protestant theologian, Oscar Cullman, as set forth in his *Christ and Time.* Catholic writers cannot help but affirm Cullman's recognition that the "folly" and "scandal" of Christianity, as it strikes the pure intelligence, is not restricted to the messy particularity of the crucifixion; this scandal, he says, extends to the whole idea of redemption occurring in and through time, and through a narrow line of time within universal time. Cullman objects, as well he might, to every attempt to eternalize and de-historicize the temporal structure of the life of Christ, every attempt to reduce it to some kernel of ideas that can get along without its historical frame. He knows that there is no such thing as a moment of pure intuition that grasps eternity and saves the soul. Rather, there is a dramatic line of action which must be followed by the soul. It must live with Christ, die with Him, be buried with Him, and rise with Him. Everything—insight, beauty, salvation—depends on our giving ourselves over to this dramatic movement. Oscar Cullman, *Christ and Time,* trans. by Floyd V. Filson (Philadelphia: Westminster, 1951, pp. 27-33.)

18. Francis Fergusson, *Idea of a Theatre,* p. 223.

19. So true is this that I consider the insistence on the temporal dramatic process of cognition to be the primary contribution of much of modern literary criticism; namely, that there are no statements in poetry that are not dramatically lived into by

true sensibility. **One of the first rules of this criticism seems to me to be: Let there be no non-temporal short cuts to the truth.** No matter what their aberrations, the basic intention of many of the new critics seems to me to be a reuniting of the orders of pure thought and temporal sensibility—orders that had been torn asunder, made into two separately operating parts of the human being, by the combined movements of Cartesianism and Romanticism.

3 Tragedy

The next dimension in the finite and definite image of the literary imagination that we confront is that of tragedy. In a sense it is the first time that we confront the finite, not horizontally though powerfully as in the case of time, but vertically and in depth. These geometrical images are not altogether accurate but they will serve their rough purposes.

The tragic image moves down into the most finite moments of the finite; it discovers its most limited points. These are final moments and points of weakness, collapses of energy, failures of the human will to raise itself, of itself, into an equation with the fundamental situations of living and being. The evidence of life and of the Greek and Elizabethan literary images are at one in saying that there is such a dimension.

Nevertheless, our recurring theme is again true. The finite, even at its weakest and most limited, is creative and generative of beauty. Tragic beauty is the most beautiful of all our literary images. The modern tragic playwright is a romantic; he avoids the final confrontation with this dimension and leaps off into unfounded infinites; thus he actually fails to capture the tragic creativity of the finite. Examples are taken from Odets, Miller, Anderson, Sherwood, Sartre and others. A particular analysis of the plays of Eugene O'Neill is made.

THIS CHAPTER is intended as an analysis of some of the basic problems lying behind the questionable status of tragedy in the modern theatre. It is in no sense a tangential chapter, for

I would suggest that the root cause of our constant failure to achieve the truly tragic level in our theatre—and I take it that almost everyone admits the failure—is our hidden abandonment of the finite and our refusal to admit the possibility that the beauty always pre-eminently associated with tragic art can only be achieved through a direct imaginative confrontation with and extrance into human finitude.

In the previous chapter we discussed time, and suggested that, evanescent though it be and unstoppable as each of its instants is, time is nevertheless an ordered, subtle and highly powerful structure which, when caught at its proper depth, does not stand outside of real being or eternity or infinity, but is moving into them by an intensive construction of its own. Nor is this statement to be equated with some easy theory of progress, because human temporality can be discerned, both by the honest literary imagination and by the theological or Christological intelligence, to be moving through many forms of death. It seems to take death as its weapon and, by some sort of extraordinary process, is always rising through it to insight in the natural order and resurrection in the supernatural order.

THE TRAGIC VISION

I have used the phrase "the honest literary imagination"; it is my deep conviction that the literary imagination, as it has been used in the theory and making of modern tragedy, has been "dishonest." It knows quite well, as we all do, that tragedy, when it is really achieved, produces an extraordinary impact of beauty and exaltation in the spectator. My own conclusion is that this achievement of tragedy has always occurred when the dramatic text has allowed itself to move through human time to the very last point of human finitude and helplessness. Here we have once again a form of the remarkable human law we have discussed, that a kind of infinite is reached by marching through a finite. It might be put this way, somewhat paradoxically but truly, according to the feeling and the actuality of the great tragic texts: in tragedy the spectator is brought to the experience of a deep beauty and exaltation, *but not by way of beauty and exaltation.* This is indeed what we have called a natural mystery, understandable to the deep, experiential intelligence but not to the purely rational intelligence.

But the terms of this situation (and the textual facts) have been completely switched around by very many of the theorists and playwrights of our day. Apparently quite incapable of believing that anything good (much less beauty and exaltation) can come out of so enslaving a thing as the limited finite, the narrow gate of final human helplessness, they have insisted, both as critics and writers, that exaltation must come out of exaltation, that infinites must come out of infinites. They therefore do a very "dishonest" thing and a very incorrect thing: 1) a dishonest thing, because they proclaim, against all the evidence, that the achievement of great tragedy has always been rooted in mystical conquests of the human spirit over pain, in the emergence of godlike strength and qualities in man in the very midst of tragic defeat. The tragic figure is really an exalted conqueror. But any straight and fresh reading of the Greek and Elizabethan texts, uninfluenced by later Romantic theories of beauty, would find that this is simply not so; 2) they do a very incorrect thing, because they base their own playwriting practice on this theory, and thus, without quite knowing it, they help to make the writing of tragedy even more difficult than it is usually granted to be in our times. We might put the matter in this way:

1. In the case of whatever we have been accustomed to call great and successful tragedy, the text takes the experienced dramatic line of movement from great *energy* in its first acts to a final absolute and experientially valid point in its last acts where all energy is dead and gone. The will has not been able to measure up to the issue. There is no equation, if I may so put it, between human energy and existence. In the end the decision of every one of the great tragedies is that, left to itself, the human will at the very height of its straining stands broken and defeated. If, for example, we should picture the fact of defeat in terms of the metrical pattern of a production of the Oedipus, it should be in terms of the confident, forward iambics of a machine of perfect dignity which bit by bit begins to disintegrate, in the end loses all sense of a formed beat in the pattering, stuttering rows of consecutive short-syllabled feet of a blinded man, and in the very end does not even have the energy to complete the final iamb. It hangs in the air and there is nothing left. The limited finite of the thing called man has been explored to its depths by the imagination. I do not say that our helplessness has been explored

with relish and gloating and rhythmic exaltation after the manner of a Marquis de Sade or a Swinburne—who gave us a theology of pleasure in pain—but rather that our final helplessness has been a final dramatic discovery, moved into by the sub-conceptual power of the logic of the movement of the soul and the situation. There has been no direct assault on beauty. Beauty has been left to take care of itself—and it has very well taken care of itself.

In the *Antigone,* the *Medea* or the *Seven Against Thebes,* the evidence is the same. In the great *Oresteia* trilogy finitude is faced unblinkingly everywhere by the artist: if there is any dramatic relenting away from it in the last play, *The Eumenides,* it is only by a widening of the theological picture: the iron, inevitable, mathematical quality of the universe that is summarized in the trilogy by the Furies and that has driven man to sin upon sin and defeat after defeat has been tempered by a discovery in the depths of the godhead of the principle of mercy and understanding; but the solution has not come by discarding the finitude of man, nor by discovering violent, interior Romantic energies in man at the end of the drama.

I have restricted myself here to the case of the Greeks because they are sufficiently distant in history from the complications introduced by Christian revelation for good and Romantic aesthetics for bad to be able to state the natural tragic spirit in all its purity. But the same kind of evidence can be culled from Elizabethan tragedy. It would, in fact, seem to make much sense to calculate that Shakespeare is *appraising* the "energy" of the Elizabethan period rather than joining in some kind of unqualified exaltation of it. (And do we not today know that we have roughly the same problem on our hands, the problem of an incredible burst of energy and achievement that needs appraisal and criticism, not so much the criticism of the satirist—for we have plenty of that—but rather the undeviating criticism of the tragic artist who reminds us of *all* the rhythms of man and of the seasons?) Thus Macbeth is catching one rhythm of life when he cries out:

Bring me no more reports. Let them fly all!
Till Birnam Wood remove to Dunsinane,
I cannot taint with fear. What's the boy Malcolm?
Was he not born of woman? The spirits that know
All mortal consequences have pronounc'd me thus:

'Fear not Macbeth. No man that's born of woman
Shall e'er have power upon thee!' Then fly, false thanes,
And mingle with the English epicures.
The mind I sway by and the heart I bear
Shall never sag with doubt nor shake with fear.

But a little later he is surely talking of another rhythm:

Tomorrow, and tomorrow, and tomorrow
Creeps in this petty pace from day to day
To the last syllable of recorded time;
And all our yesterdays have lighted fools
The way to dusty death. Out, out, brief candle!
Life's but a walking shadow, a poor player,
That struts and frets his hour upon the stage
And then is heard no more.

And so is Brutus, a little before the end:

Night hangs upon my eyes; my bones would rest,
That have but labour'd to attain this hour.

And many others with him, including Richard II:

For God's sake, let's sit upon the ground
And tell sad stories of the deaths of kings.

At any rate both sets of texts would be more than enough
to make nonsense of the fairly usual statement that life was
lived on the crest of greatness in the Athens of Pericles and
in Elizabethan England, and that the tragic "hero" emerged
with the same kind of greatness in those periods.

2. But the older and more accurate idea of tragic movement has been completely reversed both in the theory and
practice of the modern theatre. This theatre has always posed
as realistic with a vengeance, "sincere," authentic, bravely
willing to face the facts of the human situation. But surely
the ironic thing to be noted is that until our time the pride,
dignity and strength of man had been the subject material of first acts: whereas the "tragic figures" of the
modern stage are usually doing very nicely indeed in our
last acts in point of strength, energy and exaltation. Up to
the very last act the new theatre was able to look at the
truth like an eagle. But in the last act, it became incurably
romantic, abandoned the finite, and grasped desperately a

any kind of infinite. There was simply no downing of its characters.

The important point is that this energy, these exalted endings were not come by through that legitimate logic of experience which belongs to the art of true dramatic motion. They were tacked on: the men who were the severest critics of theology were the very ones who were guilty of adding on to their plays these vague theological appendages about the immortal greatness and strength of man—a strength and greatness which could be vindicated by neither history nor personal experience. They were non-evidential statements, attitudes which were blind assertions and thrusts of the will. There were earlier playwrights who had taught them the trick. There was Ibsen, for example, with his rhetorical ending in *Enemy of the People* when Dr. Stockman is able to cry out in the midst of his pain, as Oedipus never could, "The strongest man in the world is he who stands most alone." [1] And there is the same type of line in *When We Dead Awaken*, where Ibsen solves all by an "Up to the peak of promise." [2] As tragedy these things are nonsense, but the tragedians have been making similar gestures ever since.

Let us cite some of our tragic theorists. The following almost identical statements could have been picked up at random from books of the immediate past. They all indicate an abandonment of the finite as a way to beauty:

No man can conceive it [tragedy] unless he is capable of believing in the greatness and importance of man. Its action is usually, if not always, calamitous, because it is only in calamity that the human spirit has the opportunity to reveal itself triumphant over the outward universe which fails to conquer; what distinguishes real tragedy from those distressful modern works sometimes called by its name is the fact that it is in the former alone that the artist has found himself capable of considering and of making us consider that his people and his actions have that amplitude and importance which make them noble. Tragedy arises then when, as in Periclean Greece or Elizabethan England, a people fully aware of the calamities of life is nevertheless serenely confident of the greatness of man . . . [3]

The sturdy soul of the tragic author seizes upon suffering and uses it only as a means by which joy may be wrung out of existence, but it is not to be forgotten that he is enabled to do so only because of his belief in the greatness of human nature and because, though he has lost the child's faith in life, he has not lost his far more important faith in human nature. A tragic writer does not have to believe in God, but he must believe in man.[4]

Why is the death of the ordinary man a wretched, chilling thing which we turn from, while the death of the hero, always tragic, warms us with a sense of quickened life? Answer this question and the enigma of tragic pleasure is solved. So the end of a tragedy challenges us. The great soul in pain and in death transforms pain and death. Through it we catch a glimpse of the Stoic Emperor's Dear City of God, of a deeper and more ultimate reality than that in which our lives are lived.[5]

Tragedy is not concerned with the pain or the suffering, but with the dignity with which they are endured. There are no retreats for the tragic protagonist. Neither in madness nor in the self-absolution of confusion may he retreat. No single tremor is to be lost even in the "forgetfullness of sleepe." The truly tragic hero "will weep no more," he "will endure." The ecstasy is not to be shunned. At this height he is alone, unique and sufficient. This is tragic dignity.[6]

So much for a new theory, in which there is very little recourse to the definite and the limited, but an abundance of vague theological terms and vague, unrooted dreams. Let us now look at the new theatre in its actual, tragic practice (especially in its closing acts), a practice that follows the new theory and sings exactly the same tune:

In Clifford Odets' *Till the Day I Die,* the very factual line "Let him die" is cancelled out by the next and mystical line "Let him live." The play with the significant title, *Awake and Sing,* by the same playwright, contains such lines as:

RALPH: Right here in the house! My days won't be for nothing. Let Mom have the dough. I'm twenty-two and kickin'! I'll get along. Did Jake die for us to fight about nickels? No! The night he died I saw it like a thunderbolt! I saw he was dead and I was born! I swear to God, I'm one week old! I want the whole city to hear it–fresh blood, arms. We got 'em. We're glad we're living.
MOE: So long.
(They go and RALPH stands full and strong in the doorway seeing them off as the curtain slowly falls.) [7]

The same exalted creature is seen in Paul Green's *The Field God,* where a very real approach to high tragedy is colored over by the new theology's final: "We are God— Man is God. That's the light, that's the truth. It will set them free. And love shall abide among us to the end." [8]

In the case of *Death of a Salesman* by Arthur Miller, it is not altogether easy to make a judgment, because it is not easy to decide what final direction the judgment of Mr. Miller is itself taking. It is surely not a great play, and derives much of its power from that unilinear kind of strength which belongs to a case from a psychiatric textbook. The play is the story of the slow and sickening collapse of a man's own ideal image of himself, and perhaps of a civilization that imposes this type of image. But in his preface to the play, Miller inevitably hits off the standard line of "infinite theory"; indeed, he repeats the line verbatim when he tells us that:

... if it is true that in essence the tragic hero is intent on claiming his whole due as a personality, and if this struggle must be total and without reservation, then it automatically demonstrates the indestructible will of man to achieve his humanity ... It is curious, although edifying, that the plays we revere, century after century, are the tragedies. In them, and in them alone, lies the belief—optimistic if you will, in the perfectibility of man.[9]

Then there is the new tragedy of defiance, of endless defiant energy, which is another form of the use of the infinite image. Here it is as we find it in Maxwell Anderson's *Winterset* (notice particularly the use of the phrase "emperor of the endless dark"):

> And Mio-Mio, my son, know this where you be,
> This is the glory of earth-born men and women.
> Not to cringe, never to yield, but standing
> Take defeat implacable and defiant
> Die unsubmitting. I wish that I'd died so,
> Long ago: before you're old you'll wish
> That you had died as they have. On this star,
> In this hard-star adventure, knowing not
> What the fires mean to right and left, nor whether
> A meaning was intended or presumed,
> Men can stand up and look out blind, and say:
> In all these turning lights I find no clue,
> Only a masterless night, and in my blood
> No certain answer, yet is my mind my own,
> Yet is my heart a cry toward something dim
> In distance, which is higher than I am
> And makes me emperor of the endless dark
> Even in seeking! What odds and ends of life
> Men may seek otherwise, let them live, and then
> Go out, as I shall go, and you.[10]

Then again we may briefly remember all those tragedies of
the "new dawn," which, having succeeded with great competence in reducing the human actor to the rock-bottom of
defeat, promised to resurrect him or dress him with that
power for raising a new seed to humanity once ascribed to
the blood of martyrs. With the dawnists the inevitability of
growth for human society as a whole or of victory for some
part of it constituted the salvation of the individual and
was for him the solution of the tragic fact. He undergoes
a mystical personal rejuvenation through the victory that
shall be.

Such a solution was of course very fashionable. One might
have expected a spate of such writing in the inevitable war
plays with their inevitable mystical jingoism, and no one was
surprised. But the theme had been in the air for generations
and it needed no war nor triumph of arms to give it
courage to express itself. Nor was it limited to the leftist
theatre, though certainly it could be anticipated that here
the theme would be played loudest.

As an illustration of the dawn technique (which may, with
some want of charity, be called the technique of the exclamation point—witness the greater part of the following citation)
we may cite the source of salvation for Odets' beaten ones
in *Paradise Lost.*

> No! There is more to life than this! Everything he said is true,
> but there is a future. Now we know. We dare to understand. Truly,
> truly, the past was a dream. But this is real! . . . Everywhere now
> men are rising from their sleep. Men, men are understanding the
> bitter black total of their lives. Their whispers are growing to
> shouts! They become an ocean of understanding! *No man fights
> alone.* Oh, if you could only see with me the greatness of men. I
> tremble like a bride to see the time when they'll use it. My darling,
> we must have only one regret—that life is so short! . . . Yes, I want
> to see that new world. I want to kiss all those future men and
> women . . . Oh, yes, I tell you the whole world is for men to possess.
> Heartbreak and terror are not the heritage of mankind! The world
> is beautiful . . . Ohhh, darling, the world is in its morning. . . .[11]

Much more of the same, some better, some worse, some
left, some right, can readily be found in George Bernard Shaw,
in O'Casey, in Sherwood, in Anderson, in Lawson, in Irwin
Shaw. Chekhov had been tempted toward the same finality,
and almost begins to say the same things, but he cannot quite
bring himself to it. All he can finally promise is rest and

peace, and not salvation in a future society. At least he is right in rejecting the mechanism of the future. For the honest tragedian must deal with the person as he finds him, the continuous and not the continued person. No one else can solve the problem of this kind of person and it must be solved in him and for him. To introduce a Cartesian concept of personality is only a subterfuge. For a true person is cribbed, cabined and confined within himself and his own generation. He cannot become anything but what and who he is, not, at any rate, by any human way. And for the true artist there is nothing else but the unbreakable continuum of personality to deal with: to convert it, by a trick, into a future society becomes a complete avoidance of the problem and of true, experientially developed drama as we have previously defined it.

We must, in brief, stick to the facts. At least we must begin with the facts and the final road we take under our own power must not be into the shadows. True tragedy has always been a sober calculation of the relation of human energy to existence. Such calculating has always required profound honesty and a rejection of the cheaper forms of mysticism. St. Paul himself had weighed the matter well and found it impossible to work out the equation. And he therefore cried out: "Who shall deliver me from the body of this death?" We need not cite his famous answer. It has also been suggested that the truth will set us free if we follow it with docility, to the best of our ability at any stage. This is precisely what tragedy in our time has often failed to do.

To summarize: the kind of physical gesture before the cosmos that has become quite common in our theatre is worlds apart from the gesture of true tragedy. But as it is more than possible to retort that this is a purely academic question—for in a sense everyone can hold on to his notion of what true tragedy is—I shall attempt to go further. The contemporary gesture of defiance and exaltation is completely foreign to the basic ritual gestures of the simple man. The contemporary theatre has been largely a place created by and for "intellectuals," a place of rarefied concepts producing unauthentic art that does not attract the ritualistic man, the common man. And one reason for this is that the innate ritual in him is more honest and profound: it is a movement of final helplessness and appeal.

How this movement leads to the peace and tranquillity of

pure tragedy, and to a paradoxical exaltation, but not by
way of exaltation, is another question—which we might
again leave to the contemplatives. At any rate, it is a question which was not meant to come within the purview of
this discussion. What we have been elaborating is the
necessity, borne out by textual fact, of sticking to the
finite image and to human finitude if we are to reach that
quasi-infinite which has always been the strange but real
mark of true tragic beauty.

TRAGEDY AND LEVELS OF LIFE

I have suggested that the tragic finite is a movement
through and within the infinite which takes the ordered and
significant form of a march through different phases, culmi-
nating in the final *instrument* of death and helplessness. This
infinite is a vast reality, and we will let the matter go as
simply as that until the next paragraph. This finite of
human temporality is a very narrow reality, and yet it is
only by its mediation that we can achieve any goal at
all. The simplest metaphor to express this necessity is that
of a fish: it must breathe its air (the infinite) through the
water (the finite); if it should pursue its goal more directly,
the process of abandoning the water to get the air would end
in agony and death.

As we have seen, this fundamental relationship between
finite and infinite has been reversed in most modern attempts
at tragedy. Let us translate "the infinite" into a theatrical
analogy and consider it as the whole world of being and
situations in which we human actors live, the issues in
which we are involved, the total world through which we
move. Let "the finite" be the will and personality of the human actor. Against this background we can note an incredible thing about the incredible "theology" of the new tragedy:
to the Christian, it represents the rebirth, in new forms, of
the old heresies of Manichaeanism and Pelagianism.

1. This school of tragedy has attached a very dubious
quality of worthlessness, threat, evil, absurdity, to the whole
world of situation and existence. Its attitude is Manichaean.
Its actors operate within a structure of non-importance.

This "new tragedy" traces its beginnings to the great
creators, in the second half of the last century, of that
realistic and naturalistic drama which we are accustomed to
call "social tragedy." These dramatists had come, validly

enough, to view the social environment as the great enemy, corrupted and corrupting, thoughtless, small, machine-like, contemptible, and in every case the origin of the tragic fact. This kind of theatre could have been produced only by a social structure of such meanness as deserved the reaction it received from Ibsen, in part at least, Strindberg, Hauptmann, Björnson, Zola, Becque, Antoine and many others.

Their tragedy often operated on a level no deeper than the social and, had they belonged to an intellectually secure and balanced age, they might have fought and won their social crusades without affecting the whole climate of tragedy for generations after. But so many men in those generations had become what Hamlet was thought to be, not knowing what or whither, and the vocabulary and mood which the realists formulated became the vocabulary and mood of the attempts at tragedy on deeper levels. Not society but life itself now came to be seen as a nightmare: the world had gone mad. How often in our generation have we seen the tragic protagonist who is cursed by the necessity of walking, victim and innocent, through an insane world. We need only recall such plays as Sherwood's *Idiot's Delight,* Paul Green's *Johnny Johnston,* or Anderson's *Key Largo* and *Winterset,* while Sartre gave a definitive formulation, in theory and on the stage, to the principle of the absurd.

One of the quarrels between the thinkers revolved around the question whether we should meet this problem of the new smallness and futility by illusion or disillusion. O'Neill, in the disappointing *The Iceman Cometh,* held out for illusion, though in this he only copied the theme from similar pleas by Ibsen in *The Wild Duck* and Barry in *Here Come the Clowns.* These all placed their curse on the men who force us to look at the truth and the whole truth, no matter what the price—for the truth, such as it is, cannot set us free.

But by far the majority were those who, disillusioned by lies and disillusioned of the hope that existence has greatness, called for "facing the facts."

Men had become suspicious of any form of greatness and any form of belief and even an Eliot, though his poetry be charged with belief, apparently could no longer approach with directness the Christian sensibility about existence; he began to use the flat and ineffective myth of *The Family Reunion.*

2. So much for the "new Manichaeanism." What of the new Pelagianism? Pelagianism was a heresy which, accord-

ing to an analogy we have been constantly using, tried to translate the energy of the human will into an infinite. It proclaimed that man could achieve salvation by his own inward competence and energy, without the aid or need of grace. In the first part of this chapter I have tried to show that successful tragedy has always fought its way to beauty through the story of the insufficiency of the human will; it is not necessary to repeat our evidence that the modern attempts at tragedy have abandoned this finite image for a new Pelagian tactic, for a new type of third act, the third act of power and the exclamation point. It has thus corrupted the idea of being on every plane; it has corrupted the idea of the infinite, making it crazy, guilty and absurd; it has destroyed the idea of the finite. It may claim that at least it has faced the facts with sincerity and authenticity. It has not.*

There are three different levels on which life can be lived. First, there is the level of surfaces and superficiality, above pain and problem, on which it is perhaps true that we have, at times, as a technological nation, tried to live. Secondly, there is a level much deeper than this (where pain is indeed confronted, and chaos, too), which to my mind is the level to be equated with what is today so often grimly called "the human situation." Is it going too far to say that there is in this region of things a certain dark attraction for the modern intelligence and sensibility, an attraction toward and almost a love of the chaotic, the absurd, the resentful struggle of it all? Thirdly, there is a still deeper level of human existence, a place where the human spirit "dies" in frequent real helplessness; and this we may call the really tragic level of existence.

This is the region of the soul into which Christianity descends in order to operate its unique effects. For example, the theologian says that it is the place of faith. By this he means that there is a point to which the mind must come where it realizes it is no match for the full mystery of existence, where, therefore, it suffers a death; it is only at this point that it will consent to put on the mind of God—as that mind is given us through the revelation of the Christian mys-

---

* The writer confesses to an abiding irritation at what often seem to him arrogant claims to courage, sincerity and the facing of facts (over against religionists who are often accused of a "failure of nerve" in the face of the same facts). It strikes me that this kind of language does make irritation altogether permissible.

teries—and thus rise to a higher knowledge and insight. Here the points of death and life coincide in the one act. In this sense Christian faith has the tragic at its very core and is never a simple or easy intellectual act. It is always an extremely complicated mixture of dying and living; at no stage in the whole life of faith can death be screened out.

The theologian also says that this third level of which we speak is the place of hope. He means by this no simple state of the will when it is in the state of theological hope; for, like faith, hope contains at every moment of itself a death and a resurrection. The principal message of the theologian about hope is that it is the meeting ground of the tragic awareness of helplessness in the human will and its taking up (in that same moment) the strength of God. Again there is no division of moments here. The discovered weakness (how clear and finite it is) becomes a gate to the infinite. But the weakness is permanent, and hence a permanent gate, not to be discarded in the name of some fraudulent and cheap leaping out of the skin of our helplessness into the arms of God.

It may seem that I have argued myself into an awkward situation. I had confessed irritation at those who, looking deeply into the chaos and pain of the second level of the human situation, had proclaimed that they at least had the nerve to face its facts. Am I not guilty of the same pretentiousness, indeed worse, in suggesting that the religionist is willing to face an abyss of yet deeper facts? In all courtesy I beg leave to say no.[12] For I am not saying that the Christian claims to descend into a region of deeper pain, or that he has more courage than his brothers of the second level. What I wish to suggest is almost the reverse of this: perhaps less pain, perhaps less courage. For at the point of complete helplessness, what happens, if only the soul so decide to open itself, is that it should seek help and ask for it. This is the mysterious point where it transcends the straining, painful situation of the Romantic hero who has shut himself off in solitude from man and God in order that he may stand brilliantly on his own.* To shut oneself off in

* The necessity of being on our own and of approximating the condition of the romantic hero seems to be a special American problem. To be on one's own two feet and to be active is certainly the mark of the masculine, but it is hardly the whole of a man. Yet our cultural requirements, for the moment, tend to compel us toward total activity and the fear of passivity. The questions is, has

solitude may very well be the ultimate in pain. But it is not the ultimate of the finite; it is not that place where the soul at last lets go its mad attempt at privacy. This final opening of the self to man and God, opening in weakness and opening in strength, may be part of the explanation of that remarkable kind of tranquillity which is given off to us as we sit in the theatre watching the thing—unique in beauty—called successful tragedy. And it may darkly explain, in part, why the latter is so deep an instrument for the meeting, the wedding, of the finite and the infinite. It may also be the place where the soul, opening itself to man and God, finds the place of theological love, and this would complete our perspective on the tragic but powerful point of the three great theological virtues.

But what happens to the attempt at tragedy when the writer remains, I do not say deliberately, on the second level of experience? Two things may happen. 1. So far as the human finite is concerned, he will live and write in a region which he will certainly need courage to face, but it will also very likely produce disgust, resentment and other gestures of the soul which are not effective tragic gestures. 2. So far as the forging or discovery of any kind of infinite is concerned, he is likely to formulate a tenuous, unreal dream that has no roots in the earth. He will have been forced to jump out of his own skin to solve the problem, and his theology will be the kind of escapist fabrication which traditional Christian theology is often accused of being.

We have already examined textual fragments for this kind of inevitable consequence in the modern theatre. Let

---

this anything to do with our inability to handle the tragic in art? Still this is only a single though a quite fundamental part of the issue. The issue has, in fact, many profound reverberations on the final level of the metaphysical and the theological. The best and the most striking treatment of the problem by a philosopher that I have been able to find is that by Frederick E. Crowe, "Complacency and Concern in the Thought of St. Thomas." (*Theological Studies,* March 1959, pp. 1-39; June, pp. 198-230; Sept., pp. 343-395.) It is a Thomistic analysis of the will as basically though not totally a receptive and quiescent faculty. It suggests that surely, in the midst of our anxiety and restlessness and striving, we have not given sufficient attention to this factor as an enormous part of the structure of man. The theological implications would also seem to be quite important, for this basic factor in the human and the finite illuminates the relation of man to the idea of revelation as well as the great dictum of St. Paul *fides ex auditu,* faith is from hearing.

us now concentrate more fully on the work of a single playwright whom we have good reason to view as an accurate reflector of much of the contemporary dramatic temper: Eugene O'Neill.

O'NEILL AND THE FINITE

O'Neill was an American who had been deeply affected by the American scene and had clearly recognized in it depths which will not abide living on the surface. Even in the theatre his sensitive reaction to pure surfaces must have occurred early in life as he toured with his father in the highly profitable *The Count of Monte Cristo*. As Joseph Wood Krutch remarks, *Monte Cristo* was "a typical and outrageous example of the kind of play wholly divorced from life, and the violence of O'Neill's reaction against everything which was conventional in the theatre may have been in part the result of his intimate association with drama at its most absurd." [13]

Even a melodramatic play such as *The Emperor Jones* is a clear and powerful indication of one of the central problems the writer has set for himself, to indicate, not theologically but biologically, that there are untouched depths in the souls of the men around him. The Negro character of Brutus Jones, ex-Pullman porter, has of course been picked without malice aforethought; we all instinctively remember that the Negro had a parentage in a deep jungle life of depth, complication, power and mystery. It is impossible to reduce this life with finality to an easily manageable surface. But this Brutus Jones has tried to do and has for the time being succeeded in doing. He has risen to an easy greatness on the surface of the jungle and has gained mastery over the simple natives, by every superficial trick which he had learned from the white man. And the surfaces which he has come to confide in do seem to possess a power of their own for the moment; therefore he is depicted as follows:

Jones . . . is a tall, powerfully built, full-blooded Negro of middle age . . . an underlying strength of will. A hardy, self-reliant confidence in himself that inspires respect. His eyes are alive with a keen, cunning intelligence. In manner he is shrewd, suspicious, evasive. He wears a light blue uniform coat, sprayed with brass buttons, heavy gold chevrons on his shoulders, gold braid on the collar, cuffs, etc. His pants are bright red with a light blue stripe down the side. Patent leather laced boots with brass spurs, etc., etc. [14]

I take it that this play has been written on the symbolic
level and that here is the symbol of a soul which has tried to
delude itself into thinking that brass and gold are enough.
But there are other symbols in the play, which belong to the
jungle proper and which begin to tear off the brass and
gold, compelling the modern man to face what is beneath.
So far he has not learned to handle these depths, so that
the instruments for the encounter are only fear, hatred and
flight. Jones begins to be pursued by the vengeful natives,
by ghosts, by darkness, by all the forces which he has neglected or despised. This jungle could be a home, a comfortable,
friendly place. For some people it is, for his forebears it was,
but for Jones it is not:

> His pants have been so torn away that what is left of them is no
> better than a breech cloth. He flings himself full length, face down-
> ward on the ground, panting with exhaustion . . . two rows of seated
> figures can be seen behind Jones. They are seated in crumbled,
> despairing attitudes, hunched facing one another with their backs
> touching the forest walls as if they were shackled to them. All are
> Negroes, naked save for loin cloths. At first they are silent and mo-
> tionless. Then they begin to sway slowly forward toward each other
> and back again in unison, as if they were letting themselves laxly
> follow the long roll of a ship at sea. At the same time, a long melan-
> choly murmur rises among them, increasing gradually by rhyth-
> mic degrees which seem to be directed and controlled by the throb
> of the tom-tom in the distance, to a long tremulous wail of despair
> that reaches a certain pitch, unbearably acute, then falls by slow
> gradations of tone into silence and is taken up again. Jones . . .
> throws himself down again to shut out the sight. A shudder of ter-
> ror shakes his body . . . His voice reaches the highest pitch of sor-
> row, of desolation . . . His face hidden, his shoulders heaving with
> sobs of hysterical fright.[15]

There is man, caught by the jungle, but the play can go no
further than an intuition of terror.

In *The Hairy Ape* the terms of expression are somewhat
the same, only now the symbol for the rough depths is the
stokehold of an ocean liner; suffice it to say that it is as
frightening as the jungle. The reaction of the immaculate
passenger Mildred is enough to indicate what it is like
down there for the dramatist ("paralyzed with horror, terror,
her whole personality crushed, beaten in, collapsed, by the
terrific impact of this unknown, abysmal brutality").

Finally we come, in *Mourning Becomes Electra,* to a picture and a sense of the self beyond which even the unhappy imagination of O'Neill could not go. The play, as we all know, is a version, in modern psychological terms, of the great trilogy of Aeschylus. But one can hardly calculate the different terms and conclusions of the two pieces. There are indeed in the Greek house of the Atreides sin and suffering and evil which continue on and on and on, and with them continues the search of Aeschylus into the self. His conclusion finally hangs upon what we might call an evenly suspended doubt about the goodness or badness of man, but it is a healthy doubt. The jury trying Orestes, the last of the family of Atreus, is evenly split, five for and five against, and it takes the deciding intervention of a merciful goddess to save him.

But with O'Neill the issue is not left in doubt. Now the symbol is neither jungle nor stokehold but a mansion, a home that is seen as worse than either. The play falls back on a typically sick solution, that the self, as represented by this house, is evil and must atone for being evil. This solution, so like and yet so unlike that of the saints, is that the self must be lacerated by the self. Indeed the self has been found and we must not run away from it; we must be locked up within it for the crime of having been born.

LAVINIA (grimly). Don't be afraid. I'm not going the way Mother and Orin went. That's escaping punishment. And there's no one left to punish me. I'm the last Mannon. I've got to punish myself: Living alone here with the dead is a worse act of justice than death or prison! I'll never go out to see anyone! I'll have the shutters nailed close so no sunlight can get in. I'll live alone with the dead and keep their secrets, and let them hound me, until the curse is paid out and the last Mannon is let die . . . I know they will see to it I live for a long time! It takes the Mannons to punish themselves for being born.[16]

So much then for O'Neill's sense of the self. No God is intervening here and certainly no God can intervene internally to make His habitation in such a place. Any true theology of the self which would make the self the scene for the action of God is in our day somewhat suspect, regarded as a fragile tradition incapable of sincerity or of "facing the facts." Nevertheless, this view of traditional theology does not prevent those who hold it from theologizing in their own special way. In this connection let us turn our attention to O'Neill the theologian, for in this respect he will be representative, though always clumsily, of a current trend among us.

THE INFINITE OF O'NEILL

For O'Neill, as for so many of his contemporaries, God, in whatever form, is a reality completely external to man. Man must leap to God by unfounded faith, by sudden, unrooted ecstasy, or even by hysterics, in order to escape from the self. His plays in general turn from despair to hope and faith with brilliant, melodramatic ease. The search for man and the search for God remain totally disconnected.

This is a kind of theology, a kind of faith, a kind of leaping, which leaves the human situation untouched and in terms of which God is only being used as an escape. But all such escape is purely mythical. We cannot jump out of our skins, and if God cannot enter into the inmost part of us and our human reality, then all theology is a farce, a bit of magic which will never work or solve anything. All leaping is futile because leaping out of the human concrete is impossible. But in O'Neill's theological search, there is nothing but leaping.

For example, there is *Lazarus Laughed*, that notable attempt on the part of the dramatist to say something positive about the final nature of human life. In sum, the play is filled with laughter and the demand that men indulge in laughter, yes, happy laughter, as the key and the end of things. But the laughter is utterly mysterious, the result of a vision by Lazarus who is risen from the dead; the play does not grow toward this happiness; the whole process is a miracle that does not relate itself to human life in any way whatsoever. Indeed, one of the characters, "an aged Jew," speaks more truly than O'Neill when he bursts forth with a protest against this new, separated and hysterical theology:

How can we compete with labor for laughter! We will have no harvest. There will be no food! Our children will starve! Our race will perish! And he will laugh.[17]

But Lazarus and his new disciples laugh and do not heed this apparently worldly protest. He keeps crying out Yes, Yes, Yes, and he continues to laugh, laugh, laugh. These lines go on endlessly and anyone who has ever seen a production of this piece knows that, despite all its apparently brilliant

and happy affirmations, it is a tremendously monotonous and
unfounded play:

> Lazarus laughs!
> Our hearts grow happy!
> Laughter like music!
> The Wind laughs!
> The sea laughs!
> Spring laughs from the earth!
> Summer laughs in the air!
> Lazarus laughs! . . .
>
> Laugh! Laugh!
> Laugh with Lazarus!
> Fear is no more!
> There is no death! . . .
> There is only laughter! [18]

Moreover, there is no true object for this love or this
laughter, so that the whole business finally bears no relationship to the story that is its New Testament counterpart.
Magdalene, the former evil one, could at last be joyful that
her joy had an object and a theological foundation; she
could cry out *Rabboni, Master,* and thus enter into some
fully concrete love. But with this new Lazarus there are
only nameless assertions and cheap, easy generalizations.
Thus Lazarus speaks to Caligula:

You are proud of being evil! What if there is no evil? What if
there are only health and sickness. Believe in the healthy God
called Man in you! Laugh at Caligula, the funny clown who beats
the backside of his shadow with a bladder and thinks thereby he is
Evil, the enemy of God! . . . Believe! What if you are a man and
men are despicable. Men are also unimportant! Men pass! Like rain
into the sea! The sea remains! Man remains! Man slowly arises from
the past of the race of men that was his tomb of death! For Man
death is not! Man, Son of God's laughter *is!* . . . *Is,* Caligula!
Believe in the laughing God within you! [19]

I must repeat at this juncture that, despite this very critical
analysis, we must have nothing but the highest respect and
sympathy for this theological impulse of the dramatist,
as we must have a similar awareness of and sympathy for
the unsophisticated theological impulse increasingly observ-
able among every class of people today. Certainly it is there,
precious and valuable, demanding from us not only sym-

pathy and awareness but a new, energetic attempt which, starting from its own terms and genesis, will make it more hard-headed, more articulated, more related, as the "aged Jew" had required, to our labor, our harvests, our food, our children and our race.

Yet for O'Neill, as for many of us today, man seems caught between the two poles of the spirit, man and God, and feels that he can really belong to neither. For man is terrible and God is distant. Therefore "the hairy ape" can say:

I ain't on earth and I ain't in heaven, get me? I'm in the middle tryin' to separate 'em, takin' all de woist punches from bot' of 'em. Maybe dat's what dey call hell, huh? [20]

And what solutions are there for this truly difficult situation so long as one continues to conceive that the ancient theology was a purely intellectual invention which never "faced the facts," when truly it was a tremendous effort to put man and God together? Certainly it would never have tolerated such fragile, magical solutions as that of Brant in some of the worst moments of *Mourning Becomes Electra:*

Aye—the Blessed Isles—maybe we can still find happiness and forget! . . . I can see them now—so close—and a million miles away. The warm earth in the moonlight, the trade winds rustling the coco palms, the surf on the barrier reef singing a croon in your ear like a lullaby! Aye! there's peace, and forgetfulness for us there—if ever we can find those islands now! [21]

It would not be right, in this brief discussion of O'Neill's plays and of his representative separations of life and death, to omit some mention of *Days Without End,* for many, among them many Christians, would say that at least here, in a final moment of retraction, the dramatist has returned to the old objectivity of theology and its ancient unity with the search for the soul. In the last act of that piece Christ is there, and the cross, and the acceptance of both in over-abundance, and there is the exultant cry from John Loving that at last, in these terms, he can forgive himself. But once again, I must in all simplicity say that I am not satisfied. There is too much of violence and suddenness and leaping exaltation, too little relationship to the previous human story, in Loving's mystical bouncing into a saving faith. And it is clear, from the closing lines, that O'Neill still has all the vague, mystical moods of *Lazarus Laughed* in mind as he talks of Christ the concrete man. For thus he has his character conclude:

". . . Love lives forever! Dead is dead! Ssshh! Listen! Do you hear?"
"Hear what, Jack?"
"Life laughs with God's love again! Life laughs with love!" [22]

We might conclude here our examination of the writings of O'Neill, whom we have taken as a symbol of the new tragedy. In his "human" plays there is no theology and the entrance of God is impossible. In his "theological" plays there is nothing left but a vague, distant vision; suffering is gone, death is no more, the gathering of harvests and the doings of men do not enter in. Lavinia shutting herself in on herself in solitude and Lazarus leaping out of himself— these can be taken as substantially all that O'Neill has to say of what is separately true about man and God. All these feelings are based on the principle that the finite is a solitude, the fond place of the romantic hero, echoing in the darkness with nothing but calls for pain and courage. It seems wrong to say this hero has gone too far. He has not gone far enough. If there is a Christian imagination, it can only operate in perfection, in the perfection of Faith and Hope and Charity, at the last of all levels. And it does.

NOTES

1. *The Collected Words of Henrik Ibsen,* VII (New York: Charles Scribner's Sons, 1923), p. 216.

2. *Ibid.,* XI, p. 487.

3. Joseph Wood Krutch, *The Modern Temper* (New York: Harcourt, Brace, 1956), p. 122.

4. *Ibid.,* pp. 126-127.

5. Edith Hamilton, *The Greek Way* (New York: W. W. Norton, 1930), pp. 149-150.

6. William Van O'Connor, *Climates of Tragedy* (Louisiana: Louisiana State University Press, 1943), p. 45.

7. Clifford Odets, *Six Plays* (New York: Random House, 1939), pp. 100-101.

8. Paul Green, *The Field God* (New York: Robert McBride & Co., 1927), p. 301.

9. Arthur Miller, "Tragedy and the Common Man," Drama Section, *New York Times*, February 27, 1949.

10. Maxwell Anderson, "Winterset," *Eleven Verse Plays* (New York: Harcourt, Brace, 1939), pp. 133-134.

11. Clifford Odets, *op. cit.*, pp. 229-230.
    This is one way in which the continued, not the continuous nature of human time is put—by Descartes: "It does not follow that I must still exist afterwards, if, so to speak, I am not created anew each moment by some cause" (cited by Poulet, *op. cit.*, p. 58).

12. It is possible that Mary McCarthy is right in accusing some Catholics, Graham Greene among them, of a certain pretentiousness when they claim, over against rationalism, to have discovered the problem of evil ("That there were brave men among those old rationalists does not occur to Mr. Greene, all bravery being reserved for the present generation, and in particular for Catholics, who have dared to acknowledge God and His corollary, the devil"). See her article-review of Greene's play *The Potting Shed*, "Sheep in Wolves' Clothing," *The Partisan Review*, 24 (Spring 1957), pp. 270-274.

13. *Nine Plays by Eugene O'Neill*, Introd. by Joseph Wood Krutch (New York: Modern Library, 1932), p. xii.

14. Eugene O'Neill, *The Emperor Jones, Anna Christie, The Hairy Ape*, Introd. by Lionel Trilling (New York: Modern Library, 1937), p. 9.

15. *Ibid.*, p. 48.

16. Eugene O'Neill, *Mourning Becomes Electra* (New York: Horace Liveright, 1931), p. 256.

17. Eugene O'Neill, *Lazarus Laughed* (New York: Boni and Liveright, 1927), p. 34.

18. *Ibid.*, pp. 22-23.

19. *Ibid.*, pp. 158-159.

20. *The Emperor Jones, Anna Christie, The Hairy Ape*, p. 258.

21. *Mourning Becomes Electra*, p. 165.

22. Eugene O'Neill, *Days Without End* (New York: Random House, 1934), p. 157.

4 Comedy

The differences between the dimensions at which tragedy and comedy operate are not easy to locate or describe. But one thing is certain. They both live and imagine at a level far below the first and superficial surfaces of man.

The greatest tribute that can be paid to comedy is that its images are as deep but not as painful as those of tragedy (and altogether different from what we today call entertainment). It gets below all the categories within which the most of life is spent and destroys the most of these categories (the rich, the proud, the mighty, the beautiful, the style, the Joneses) in its descent. In this descent it discovers a kind of rock-bottom reality in man, the terrain of Falstaff and Sancho Panza, which is profoundly and funnily unbreakable, which has no needs above itself. It seems to be the most inherently confident rung of the finite. It is ugly and strong.

Our way of ferreting out the true comic image will be to identify all the false images of comedy: the clown, the fastidious man, the too-much-humor that makes a fool of man, the laughter of hatred. What, then, is really funny? Things are really funny—because wonderful realities can come of their lowermost depths.

THERE IS ONE fundamental theme which I have wished to emphasize throughout these studies: the centrality of the *finite concrete* as the only healthy and effective path to whatever has always traditionally been regarded as the goal of the human imagination or, for that matter, of the total human personality. It does not matter whether we call that the infinite or peace or insight or maturity.

The centrality of the thick and limited finite fact or image. That is one way of putting the matter. A neurotic civilization has lost faith and confidence in the ability of these facts and images to lead to the desired goal. Literally, it does not believe in the power of the actual—and therefore tends, on the levels of the culture of both the intellectuals and the people, to construct magical, unreal or phony mansions for the soul to dwell in. Eliot has called it "distracted from distraction by distraction."

Another way of describing our situation is to say that the imagination, to get anywhere, must course through the actual phases or stages or "mysteries" of the life of man. Man is a highly specific and concrete donnée, a "given," a time pattern, a structured and significant movement within and into being, a movement that is meant ontologically to get somewhere in terms of insight and union with God. A bourgeois civilization will use the term "maturity" or "authenticity"; a sacral civilization might use the phrase, "union with God." At any rate, each phase of this movement is highly limited and precise, taking its value not only from itself but from its place in the total rhythm of human life. Earlier chapters tried to analyze what has happened to the image of time in the modern imagination, but suffice it to say again that there has been a collapse of confidence; we have no faith in the dense reality of time. The search for all the forms of intensity in our civilization is a sign of the rebellion against the finite moment of time and time's relentless movement into another such paltry moment.

It is quite customary criticism to say that we have progressively lost contact with being and are an anti-metaphysical generation. This is all very fine, but what in reality does it mean? These pages on comedy and the comic wish to propose, through the exceedingly pointed language of comedy, that we have lost contact, not with a mysterious scholastic entity called being, but with the potent being of that finite actuality which is the whole language and preoccupation of the comic.

THE COMIC COMMITMENT

Dare we commit ourselves to any form of the limited, with a complete and absolute commitment? "Can any good come out of Nazareth?" is the question we ask as we look at what to us is the dreadful face of the limited. As we saw in the previous chapter, tragedy in the contemporary theatre cannot so commit itself. But true tragedy has always thrust itself and the human imagination, without stint or dishonest illusion about the greatness of man, all the way up to the hilt of helplessness, all the way into the abyss of non-being that lies underneath the masks of finitude. It is only in rare moments that we get the taste and depth of this abyss; for the most part we cling to the surfaces and the forms of things, away from their true being which is also an incredible non-being. Distracted from distraction by distraction, by the distraction of the surfaces.

The essential difference between the tragic and the comic is that between the two finites into which each enters. In tragedy the finite is looked at through the narrow and normal end of the telescope; therefore the limited in the human situation is regarded as an enormous abyss of non-being, which indeed it is. For our purposes there would be no better way to describe the size of the nothingness seen through *this* telescopic view than that contained in the actual language of Henry II ("Of comfort no man speak") or of Lear ("Why should a dog, a horse, a rat, have life, and thou no breath at all . . . Pray you undo this button") or of Oedipus ("I dread to speak, O God . . . And I to hear"). In tragedy life is a dreadful sea incarnadine ("O the mind, mind has mountains"), and there is no worst. These are dreadful visions, leading by the inward power of their very depth (no Manichaeanism here) to exaltation and to God.

Nevertheless, especially for us who have lost the taste of being, the way of comedy taxes the imagination and the whole soul more than does tragedy, and requires even more courage as a way into God. It is a more terrible way, requiring a greater *ascesis,* requiring more faith in the finite, the pure finite, as an entrance thereinto. In tragedy there is always a little danger that the very size of the abyss will hide its finitude, the very heroicity of the depth will conceal its littleness. Sometimes the tragic action, with its deep taste of actuality, is assuaged by turning the pain into the beginnings of the romantic dream. Occasionally even Shakespeare nods, as may be seen at the end of *Hamlet*: "Absent thee from felicity a while to tell my story." The rhythms steal in upon the active imagination and induce a kind of sleep that prevents full cognition. Hamlet becomes directly beautiful, the first beginnings of this tendency in modern man. But comedy makes fun even of rhythms. In the face of the finite it is completely, unblinkingly cognitive, entering into it without deception, facing the actual with a great form of courage, the courage of the comic.

In order that we may not be trapped into a kind of theorizing about comedy that avoids the taste of the comic, let us begin by seeing how, in its own unique language about man, comedy turns the telescope around so that the eye looks through the greater end, and everything has become, not sea incarnadine, but a disconcertingly small puddle. There is a theory about art and literature which maintains that these two things create a "psychic distance" between themselves and actuality. In a sense the whole burden of this book is to question the ordinary understanding of this theory and to ask that it be viewed with suspicion, along with all other theories of art which make of it an esoteric thing and a means of distancing ourselves from the real. We are saying that surface actuality may be a block to vision but that the movement into all the true dimensions of reality is an instrument of vision. If, therefore, "psychic distance" is taken to mean a distance between art and that surface actuality which is really a distraction from reality itself, then this theory makes sense. If it means that art itself is a distraction from *reality* itself, then it is arrant nonsense.

At any rate there is no such distraction in comedy. By being turned around, the telescope reveals the actual contours, the interstices, the smells, of the beastie man. Let us listen to the authentic voice of comedy:

Prince Hal, pretending to be the king and speaking of Falstaff, who is, for us, situated in the present discussion, man:

There is a devil haunts thee in the likeness of an old fat man; a tun of man is thy companion. Why dost thou converse with that trunk of humours, that bolting hutch of beastliness. that swoll'n parcel of dropsies, that huge bombard of sack, that stuff'd cloak-bag of guts, that roasted Manningtree ox with the pudding in his belly, that reverend vice, that grey iniquity, that father ruffian, that vanity in years. . . .

This living in the contours and the smells, this native reaction against *pure* greatness, one is tempted to think, must have been a part of the art of the most primitive artist who first rebelled against developing sophistications. Euripides says to Aeschylus (in *The Frogs* of Aristophanes): ". . . is virtue a sound? Can any mysterious virtue be found in bombastical, huge, hyperbolical phrase?" But the sophistic and pure intelligence of Euripides is just as much the butt of the wit of an Aristophanes. And so it goes through the rest of the history of the comic. The angelic in man is always the victim; there is always a new fall of man into man. The new fool is the incomparable man—like Alceste in *The Misanthrope* ("My love is inconceivable, and never, Madam, did any man love as I do")—who will not face into so small a thing.

It would be unfair to tragedy to think that it is only to the tragic that comedy is addressing itself as semantic challenger, vocabulary against vocabulary. As love against love, the comic challenges the whole notion of the romantic love that survives by trying to wipe out the actual. There is a kind of love which is fresh, original, brilliant, sensitive, and blind, adventurously childish, vague, seeking the safety of the womb, until it is trapped by comedy back into the contours of the mud; Racine accurately describes these lovers:

Never does their passion see anything to be blamed in it, and every thing to them becomes amiable in the object beloved; they reckon blemishes as perfections, and know how to give favorably names to 'em. The pale vies with the jessamy in fairness; the black, even to a frightful degree, is an adorable brunette; the lean has shape and easiness; the fat has a portliness full of majesty . . . 'tis thus that a lover loves. . . .

To continue to compare the two techniques of the romantic and the comic, we need only to recall the invasion of the angelic imagination into the world of the courtesan. This woman is to be overcome by the imagination; perhaps it is woman herself that is to be overcome; perhaps she is a symbol of the reality that we seem to wish to overcome and destroy. The imagination of Proust's Swann knows how to do it,[1] and is equipped with all the tricks and potions which can aerize the courtesan into angelicism. Like the hatred behind the love of Alceste, perhaps the hatred behind this romantic love is incomparable. Certainly it cannot endure the very thought of winter woolens as conceived by the comic art of Joyce Cary (*The Horse's Mouth*):

But I got her to the bus stop at last and while her bus was driving up, she came to her senses for a minute, as Sara always could, in the

most exciting situations, and she took me by the coat and turned
up her eyes and said, "I shouldn't have come, Gulley, should I. Just
upsetting us both. But we were happy, weren't we, and I'll bring
those socks and shirts, and there's an old overcoat too, or if I don't
dare to come out so far again, I'll post them to you. Only don't
come to the house or write. It's not safe, truly it isn't. And look after
your chest. You ought to have more woolies for winter, you know
you ought . . . we were the happiest couple. Even if you did spoil
my nose. Oh, I thank God for that time. . . ." [2]

To our inquiry as to what comedy is, therefore, we get
our first if superficial sense of an answer from its vocabulary.
Its image of the finite is the most concrete, the most dense, of
all the images created by the art of man. In terms, then, of
its peculiar images, it is the most cognitive and least magical
of the arts. If, as I believe, it proposes these images as a
road into the infinite, it hides nothing, and reveals most, of
the finite as such a path. Indeed, its whole function is to be
a perpetual and funny, if disconcerting, reminder that it is
the limited concrete which is the path to insight and salvation. Its whole art is to be an art of anamnesis, or memory, of
the bloody human (in the sense in which the English use
that adjective) as a path to God, or to any form of the great.

In *Hobson's Choice,* the cinematic art of comedy revolves
around its center in the form of a brass ring which has
originally tied the fortunes of Maggie and Willie together in
the days of their hardships. In the days of the beginning of
glory Willie wishes to supplant the brass with gold, but Maggie, with her comic memory, will have none of it and clings
to the brass. Comedy is perpetually reminding the uprooted
great man that in some important sense he was once, and
still is, a bit of a monkey. Thus, in the Scotch film, *High and
Dry,* the American great man cries out that "nobody's going
to get away with trying to make a monkey out of me."
But the Scotch peasants *do* make a monkey out of him, and do
reduce the new, "god-like" American rhythms to the subjection of their own incredibly permanent rhythms. The same
thing happens to Jacques Tati in *The Big Day.* As village
postman, he too aspires one day to the dream rhythms and
power of the American postman ("neither wind nor rain . . .").
But the fabulously old lady reminds him in the end that this
is a brilliant task for little Victor the child, and there are
other and more basic musical modes for the soul of a man.
In the movie *Tight Little Island* there are two comic visions
which emerge for the metaphysics of the comic: 1. The bril-

liant power of the finite, the age-old power of the people, i.e., of man, comes forth in the endless resourcefulness of the islanders for the hiding of their whiskey from the "god-like" man of this particular situation; 2. the complete and funny reminding of the collapsibility of the divine man is demonstrated to the echo of the laughter of a whole people. This time the great refrain to be attacked had been: "Anybody who knows me knows that when I start a thing I push it all the way through."

The one offense, therefore, which comedy cannot endure is that a man should forget he is man, or should substitute a phony faith for faith in the power of the vulgar and limited finite. The key sentence which describes its art in terms of its opposite is the sentence of Prince Hal, in forgetful glory, to Falstaff: "I know thee not, old man." The comic hates all the forms of the man who cannot stand the sight of himself, and it would have understood the words of Christ to Judas who could not stand this sight, as Peter could after a sin as great. But this case of Judas is, of course, only the sinful and most serious form of the non-comic. Below it are a thousand other forms of the refusal to remember, ranging all the way from the forgetfulness of Falstaff's friend Justice Shallow ("I will devise matter enough out of this Shallow to keep Prince Harry in continual laughter . . . O, you shall see him laugh till his face be like a wet cloak ill laid up . . . this Shallow, now in glory, was for all the world like a forked radish, with a head fantastically carved upon it with a knife") to the classical example of the dignified man who is disturbed because he slips on a banana. We are not Judas but we are all guilty, in a little way, of the fear of being man.

There are different levels of comic remembrance and, even though we need not equate them, at least they are all somehow one in some kind of love of the human and some kind of refusal to be ashamed of human parentage. Sometimes the deliberate image of the ugly human actuality is only the image of wit, anything not to miss a point (cf. Falstaff's "I will turn diseases to commodity"). Again it may be only the sudden insertion, into the perfect, perfect Morris-dance movement, of a crazy irregularity which simply cannot tolerate the perfect, univocal form. Or it may be the brass ring of Maggie. At the top of the heap of memory is the intense remembrance of the souls in glory in the *Paradiso* who long for the day when again they shall possess those bodies that had budded forth such glory and shall someday add to it.

These present lines on comedy are written on the eve of
Christmas, so that, finally, this writer cannot help but think
of the liturgy's anamnesis, its recalling of the power of the
earth in which the maggots and the Sybil work to bud forth a
Saviour (*aperiatur terra et germinet Salvatorem*). These memories are profoundly one and profoundly different, one
enough to make our point, different enough to save our
reverence.

THE PSEUDO-COMIC

Unfortunately, there are many kinds of remembrance. One
presumes, even from the purely biological feeling in the
stomach which springs out of the comic memory, that it involves funniness and a kind of joy; but not every recalling
does this. Perhaps it is better, before analyzing the anamnesis
which is proper to comedy, to eliminate all the forms of
remembrance which are not at all comic.

1. Let us start with the "comedy" of the clown. I place the
word in quotes because he may be entertaining, but I do not
believe that he is really funny. He is basically sad, and perhaps the word *frightening* is not too strong a word for him.
Indeed, he remembers the human condition, but is it not
clear to all at times that he feels he is *trapped* in that
situation, and really feels he is crucified? Charlie Chaplin is
certainly an artist who sums up many comic strains; when
he becomes rich and in the midst of it is driven by the comic
instinct to pick up the precious cigarette butt from the gut-
ter, the vision of the comic is there. But it is not altogether
surprising, perhaps it is rooted in the deepest corners of the
self-pitying spirituality of the clown, that Chaplin himself
should have hated the role of Charlie ("I've finally gotten rid
of the little bastard"). And it is hard for some of us to
accept the final vision, no matter what our trap today, behind
the clown art of Rouault. This may be an art that does not
leave room, with its clown Christ, for the slightest sense of
the Christus Victor (even on the Cross) who has been so
indigenous to certain periods of Christian art. We shall have
something to say later about this triumphant note in comedy
itself, and we give only an example of it now, again from
The Horse's Mouth. Gulley Jimson discourses as follows
about this remarkable strength of the truly comic figure:

I'm not a wild ass of the desert, I'm an old hoss. I know something. I've been ridden by the nobility and gentry. Millionaires have cut an important figure on my back. Hickson kept me in the stable for years and trotted me out for his visitors. His Gulley Jimson, his pride and his joy. My stomach has had two kicks a day for sixty years, one to put the saddle on and one to take it off. It can take anything. And eat its own hay. And organize its own kicks. And save up a bite that will take the bloody pants off the seat of government. If it likes.[3]

This is surely a kind of theme song of what we conceive to be the truest and the most accurate form of comedy and laughter: this song of indestructibility, the song of the indestructibility of the people. In preliminary theorizing on this subject I had long been tempted to think that the following was one of the basic lines of division between tragedy and comedy: in the first, we are in full unhidden contact with the real world and we suffer its consequences, whatever the consequences of being; in comedy it seemed that the suppositions were different. We were to hypothesize that the man does not really get hurt as he flies out the window or is hit by a pie. The assumption was the assumption of unreality, psychic distance with a vengeance. I now prefer to think that the comic chant is altogether different. It chants the fundamental indestructibility, the strength, of the human thing, of the finite with the vulgar interstices and smells, which lies below all categories. The chant is there. It is there, if you remember, in the five cars that come banging violently together to the sound of hé-hi-hé-hi-hó in *The Lavender Hill Mob*. Nobody gets hurt in this world because this is a region below all temporal status or manners or category where it is impossible that anybody be hurt. Rock-bottom being cannot be hurt. It is not the world of the clown. There is no sadness or self-pity in it. Our only sad lot is that we have lost contact with it; we live in a world of categories where we are always threatened.

It is only on the level of truly popular being [4] that we can find indestructibility, equality before any man, and freedom; but today it is a level not much in fashion. It is regarded with a squint and thought to be a pitiful thing which requires many defenses. Not so, though, with Sancho Panza. He has just been patronizingly asked to the table of Don Quixote, "that you may be even as I who am your master and natural lord, and eat from my plate and drink from where I drink; for of knight-erranting one may say

the same as of love: that it makes all things equal"; to which
Sancho replies:

Many thanks . . . but if it is all the same to your grace, provided there is enough to go around, I can eat just as well, or better,
standing up and alone as I can seated beside an emperor. And if the
truth must be told, I enjoy much more that which I eat in my own
corner without any bowings and scrapings, even though it be only
bread and onions, than I do a meal of roast turkey where I have to
chew slowly, drink little, be always wiping my mouth, and can
neither sneeze nor cough if I feel like it, nor do any of those things
that you can when you are free and alone.[5]

Again there is no clownish sadness here, nor feeling of
being trapped in the desperate predicament of being human.
Rather there is a kind of native confidence, not in power,
but in the power of rock-bottom being. And it is just this
confidence and vitality which this chapter proposes as a
substantial clue to the mystery of comedy.

2. We turn next to the meticulous man. If ever there was a
non-comic man, it is he. For he recalls whence he was born,
but with a refined if not a violent distaste. He is a fastidious,
prim and ritualistic man, not with a ritual that is the crown
of religious passion and a true revelation, but with one that
has a nice geometric movement safely separated from both.
Here is the way *he* remembers the human (it is a pity to
take these lines from a comedian of the stature of George
Bernard Shaw, but he was indiscreet enough to have written
them and thus for a moment to have revealed as much of his
contempt for his trade as did Chaplin):

In Italy, for instance, churches are used in such a way that price-
less pictures become smeared with filthy tallow-soot, and have
sometimes to be rescued by the temporal power and placed in na-
tional galleries. But worse than this are the innumerable daily serv-
ices which disturb the truly religious visitor. If these were decently
and intelligently conducted by genuine mystics to whom the mass
was no mere rite or miracle, but a real communion, the celebrants
might reasonably claim a place in the church as their share of the
common human right to its use. But the average Italian priest, personally uncleanly, and with chronic catarrh of the nose and throat,
produced and maintained by sleeping and living in frowsy, ill-
ventilated rooms, punctuating his gabbled Latin only by expec-
torative hawking, and making the decent guest sicken and shiver
every time the horrible splash of spitten mucus echoes along the
vaulting from the marble steps of the altar: this unseemly wretch

should be seized and put out, bell, book, candle, and all, until he learns to behave himself.[6]

It would be hard to find another paragraph which images forth so perfectly the meticulosity of the new religious man. And this writer cannot but feel that there is a marked, if somewhat elliptic, parity between this Shavian distaste and the distaste with which the sophisticated instincts of every form of pure intellectualism, and every form of "pure" and invisible religion, confront the historicity of Christ and Christianity. The sins of Rabelais and the guilty conscience of Chaucer are much less remote from the truth. If it were only a problem of belief, of an inability on the top of the head to believe in the actual, then the problem would be relatively light. But this non-comic sense, the lack of confidence in rock-bottom being, has invaded every level of the human personality. Even with the people, it begins to lead to a tenuous and seductive culture which must lure them away from that true comedy which was the proud invention of their fathers' fathers.

Is not this, indeed, our greatest cultural crime, that we unpeople the people and steal from them their comic sense of their own inward worth, which needs no cheap potions or irrelevant magics? But much of our present situation is the work of meticulous men who hardly dare to remember their parentage and who have accomplished the stunningly clever trick of telling us *ad nauseam* that this is what the people want, that those who wish rememberingly to defend the people are eggheads. In this whole matter of eggheads, we must alas realize there are two kinds: one who roosts among the intellectuals of the far Left and has scant regard for the tradition of the people—and another, a far more baleful threat, who is artificially concocting in his Hollywood and TV factories a new tradition of a cheap angelism for all the people, and is, unfortunately, totally accepted by them for the moment—as his alienated, nonconformist brother of the Left is not. Let us only hope that what Chesterton said of England ("The poeple of England have not spoken yet") is also true of this country. And hasten, O Lord, the day of speech.

3. We could at this stage spend a great deal of time on the genesis and the history of the idea of disgust. Jean-Paul Sartre and some of his colleagues have made a profession of the idea, but theirs is only a sleight-of-hand, a brilliantly dia-

lectical summary of the wave of nausea that has plagued the poets since the latter part of the nineteenth century. However, to trace history here is deceptive; what seems truer is to recognize that disgust is an indigenous, ever-cropping strain of the human spirit, very close to comedy but with a devil of a difference. Indeed, that is why it is essential to treat the subject here, in order to sort out the laughter of the disgusted man from the comic. There is such a thing as a love of disgust, a professional love of the monstrous, which is as far away from Falstaffian man as night is from day. One of the great technical (and theological!) questions, therefore, is: How far can you go in inventing interstices and smells for man before you are lodged in the disgusting, the monstrous, and (this is the point) the non-human? This is the critical problem of the difference between laughter at the human and the non-human.

There is a little section in the play within a play in *Midsummer-Night's Dream* which may be taken as a miniature essay on this problem of disgust. Its simple, total point is that in penetrating to the concrete human which is the subject of comedy one cannot pass beyond the point where the memory of the human has been transgressed or annihilated. Despite its length, I include it; only recollect how the playlet, in its wildest fantasy, is only dealing with Bottom the weaver and Snug the joiner.

BOTTOM: There are things in this comedy of Pyramus and Thisby that will never please. First, Pyramus must draw a sword to kill himself, which the ladies cannot abide. How answer you that?
SNOUT: By'r laking, a parlous fear.
STARVELING: I believe we must leave the killing out, when all is done.
BOTTOM: Not a whit: I have a device to make all well. Write me a prologue; and let the prologue seem to say, we will do no harm with our swords, and that Pyramus is not killed indeed; and, for the more better assurance, tell them that I Pyramus, am not Pyramus, but Bottom the weaver, this will put them out of fear.
SNOUT: Will not the ladies be afeared of the lion?
STARVELING: I fear it, I promise you.
BOTTOM: Masters, you ought to consider with yourselves: to bring in, God shield us!—a lion among ladies, is a most dreadful thing; for there is not a more fearful wildfowl than your lion living, and we ought to look to it.
SNOUT: Therefore, another prologue must tell he is not a lion.

BOTTOM: Nay, you must name his name, and half his face must be seen through the lion's neck; and he himself must speak through, saying thus, or to the same defect, 'Ladies,' or 'Fair Ladies,' 'I would wish you,' or, 'I would request you,' or, 'I would entreat you, not to fear, not to tremble: my life for yours. If you think I come hither as a lion, it were pity of my life: no, I am no such thing: I am a man as other men are:' and there indeed let him name his name, and tell them plainly he is Snug the joiner.

Enter Puck. You may love him but he seems a dubious comic spirit: he is intent on transforming the human. Why are we frightened at his work?—because we are frightened at that which comes into our world as the strange, the totally non-human, the Other, the invader, man as *really* an ass. In the following scene, Bottom is no longer recognizable as Bottom.

QUINCE: O monstrous! O strange! we are haunted. Pray, masters! fly masters. Help!
PUCK: I'll follow you, I'll lead you about a round,
  Through bog, through bush, through brake, through brier:
Sometime a horse I'll be, sometime a hound,
  A hog, a headless bear, sometimes a fire:
And neigh, and bark, and grunt, and roar, and burn.
Like horse, hound, hog, bear, fire, at every turn.
BOTTOM: Why do they run away? this is a knavery of them to make me afeard.
SNOUT: O Bottom, thou art changed! what do I see on thee?
BOTTOM: What do you see? You see an ass-head of your own, do you?
QUINCE: Bless thee, Bottom! bless thee! thou art translated.
BOTTOM: I see their knavery: this is to make an ass of me; to fright me, if they could.

The variety of levels of Pucks in human history have been endless. They are never comic. In most cases they are harmless; in others their essentially non-human point becomes startlingly clear. In some periods there is an intellectual finesse about the abandonment of the human as a way into being (witness the story of the decadents in the nineteenth century); in others the professional interest in the monstrous is open, flagrant and public; you are protected from the fright because other fools are laughing with you; it is a public act of laughter. Let us go further:

Lampridius tells us that Alexander Severus could make no use of all the male and female dwarfs, fools, worthless chattering fellows, actors and pantomimes collected by his predecessor, Heliogabalus, so he gave them away to the people. Plutarch describes how in the market in Rome many purchasers would pay no attention to the most beautiful slave girls and boys who were exposed for sale and would seek out horrible freaks and monstrosities. Longinus tells us that children were deliberately stunted, and Quintilian observes that the greater the deformity the higher was the purchase price of these unfortunates. Imbecility, like deformity, had evidently a real pecuniary value: "He has been described as an idiot," says Martial indignantly, "I bought him for twenty thousand sesterces. Give me back my money, Gargilianus, he has his wits." [7]

This is indeed degenerate curiosity and the love of disgust, witless laughter at the witless. But we need not be too quick to judge. There is in our own air many a Puck and many a Heliogabalus trying to turn us humans into asses and witless people, who will think as they do that their comedy, their songs, their rhythms, are funny.

4. We come at last to the laughter of hatred. The fundamental rationale behind this form of non-comic humor is that it hates the human and, desiring to wipe out the memory of it, desires to destroy the thing itself. In Adrian Leverkuhn, the hero of Thomas Mann's *Doctor Faustus,* we have the pure intellectual, the kind of brilliant student who lives off the very topmost part of his head, unmothered by the earth. It is always so hard to tell whether the laughter he moves toward is that of a child or a devil. Leverkuhn begins with un-interest:

Oddly enough, it was best at the grammar school, there I was pretty much in the right place, because in the upper forms they dealt out the greatest variety of things, one after the other, changing the subject from one five-and-forty minutes to the next—in other words there was still no progression. But even those five-and-forty minutes were too long, they bored one—and boredom is the coldest thing in the world.[8]

The genesis of diabolical laughter continues ("I am embarrassed at the insipidness which is the supporting structure of even the work of genius"). Nothing is serious, everything is a parody of itself, about to laugh at itself. It has to laugh, it was born laughing, it suddenly sees that the most divine beauty carved by man has a trick of matter or man behind it, stupid, produced, and grown out of mud or an onion.

("And I, abandoned wretch, I have to laugh, particularly at
the grunting supporting notes of the bombardone, Bum, bum,
bum, bang!") Can you imagine, O Beauty, O Angel, being
born of a double bassoon? Can any good come out of Nazareth? "I have always had to laugh, most damnably, at the
most mysterious and impressive phenomena. I fled from
this exaggerated sense of the comic into theology, in the
hope that it would give relief to the tickling—only to find
there too a perfect legion of ludicrous absurdities." [9]

There is the problem of the comic and theology in a
nutshell. The scandal of the double bassoon and the earth and
Christ and the hatred of the pure intelligence for all three.
The permanent debate of our time is really between
two forms of intellectualism, the forms which I will take
the liberty of calling the analogical and the univocal intelli-
gences. Much may be learned about the comic by observing
how it aligns itself in this debate. We will deal with the
univocal and the analogical imaginations in later separate
chapters, but let us briefly treat them in the present context.

COMEDY AND THE UNIVOCAL

The comic is par excellence the great enemy of the univocal
mind. I call univocal that kind of mind which, having won
through to all the legitimate unities and orderings of the
logical and rational intelligence, insists, thereafter, on descending through the diversities, densities and maelstroms of
reality in such a way as to give absolute shape to it through
these unities and orderings. This mentality wishes to reduce
and flatten everything to the terms of its own sameness,
since it cannot abide the intractable differences, zigzags and
surprises of the actual. It is, therefore, impatient, rigid, inflexible, intolerant, and even ruthless.

Here the rigid thinker and the classical dreamer are at
one. Alceste in *The Misanthrope* has simply made up his
mind that his lawsuit is just, and therefore will not make
a single contact with the realities of his legal situation ("I am
in the wrong, or I am in the right"). There are moralists like
that: Pascal thought the Jesuits impious because they polluted themselves with the realities of moral cases. And
what shall we say of the incredible purity from reality of
Don Quixote; he rescues a young lad from a cruel switching
by a country tyrant, and then tells the lad to go home

with his master who will no more switch him ever ("It is sufficient for me to command, and he out of respect will obey"). Notice the hankering for divine power, free of the mud of detail or precaution. And notice how the human comic, aware of the absurd in reality, inverts the phrase ("I have but to say a word, and my dog does what he pleases").

On the surface, comedy, with its antipathy to the order of things, seems anarchic (and, indeed, it does have a propensity for thieves, villains, drunkards, fools, idiots, lawbreakers and other people like the reader and the writer). But it is not at all anarchic; it is only a defender of another and more human order (more muddy, more actual, more free). Metaphysically it is a defender of being against the pure concept or category. We have seen how in the perfect Morris dance it must introduce the note of irregularity for very sanity's sake. In *Tight Little Island* it is inveighing against a pharisaical order, upon all those who from the chair of Moses impose too great a burden upon the people. In the medieval Feast of Fools, it annually gave itself a bit of a foolish fling because of its little fear of the non-human in the sacred order. And it is significant that this comic intrusion into the liturgy began with the singing of the Magnificat at vespers, with the words "He hath put down the mighty from their seat and hath exalted the humble and meek."

Eliot has said that "human kind cannot bear very much reality." I am not so sure of that. The bigger truth is that they cannot stand very much unreality. At any rate, he might also have said, were he writing a comedy, that men cannot stand too much order. Observe the characters who are so classically non-comic: the heretic, who sees all reality as simple and reduces a multitudinous creed to a single, exacerbating, crusading formula; the scrupulous man who reduces the overflowing life of being and the mind to a worrisome pin point; the great conquerors, the men who have the universe under perfect control and have it forever fixed in an icy stare.

COMEDY AND ANALOGY

We must, then, look for a form of order that orders indeed, but leaves reality, every iota of yours and mine, intact —multitudinous, different and free, but together at last. This is what we call analogical order, and it is the home of the comic. What is it?

The medieval idea of the analogy of being is a fascinating doctrine. On the surface all it says is that being is the same and one everywhere, but everywhere profoundly different. Every difference this tremendous drive in the world creates is being and is one. Thus this unity cannot proceed one generative step without creating difference (the many) and without creating itself (the one). Therefore, it need not move out of itself to be enormously creative, open and free. But this is the most fundamental statement of comic remembrance: that a thing need not step out of the human to be all things, and to achieve the liberty of the children of God. The mud in man, the lowermost point in the subway, is nothing to be ashamed of. It can produce (St. Thomas would call it *potentia oboedientialis*) the face of God. *Aperiatur terra et germinet Salvatorem.*

What is funny? Things are funny, precisely because they can recall the relation between God and themselves. In tragedy the fact of the comic is concealed precisely because the inner logic of the action (a man moves from unawareness to awareness) is so extraordinarily logical, tied together and complete (as in the case of Oedipus). Nothing is omitted; step calls for step, emotion for emotion, word for word. Until we forget, for the logic, that "my end is my beginning." To recall this, to recall this incredible relation between mud and God, is, in its own distant, adumbrating way, the function of comedy.

This anamnesis is accomplished in either of two comic ways. By foreshortening the steps between the beginning and the end, or by multiplying them—far beyond the perfect logic of tragic action.

1. By foreshortening: the comic is sudden, and full of surprises and skippings of intervening steps; the man of dignity (he could be the saint) slips on the banana peel. The lion is Bottom. The Pope is dust. Let us not talk of incongruity as the secret clue to comedy, but of congruity, of the tie between the earth and Christ, with all the logic omitted. Why should we laugh or magnify the Lord? Because this is the way things are.

2. Or by multiplying the intervening steps. So that the bewildering vitality of the finite, within the analogical form, goes beyond the logic of tragedy and everything is seen as lively and extraordinarily bouncing. This is the method of

Rube Goldberg. That this should lead to this! The buffoon exploits his own weaknesses. Falstaff says: "I shall turn diseases into commodity." Gulley Jimson says: "See what my mother became in the years of misery; a great human; a person in the grand style. Yes, by God, you need technique to make a good job out of life. All you can get. You need to take necessity and make her do what you want; get your feet on her old bones and build your mansions out of her rock." And St. Paul said: "I glory in my infirmities."

It is ridiculous, in a Catholic world, to be afraid of the irreverent in so many secret places. Therefore, the thoughts of the writer, as he thinks of the glory of the comic, turn to the Mother of God. In the office of the Feast of the Circumcision there are these words which think of her: *cum essem parvula, placui Altissimo, et de meis visceribus genui Deum et hominem. Beatam me dicent omnes generationes, quia ancillam humilem respexit Deus.*

Cum essem parvula. Though I was small, and very small, I was pleasing to the Most High. Does this not seem, we say it with reverence, to be the final clue to a theory of the comic which, if pitched below the theological level, would make stupid sense indeed? The sins of comedy are many but not incarnadine. They are vulgar, but being blessedly vulgar— and completely literary in the most decent sense of the word—they pass far beyond that world where in the morning Walter Pater put in a comma and in the evening took it out. The sins of comedy have been many indeed; but they have never been in the direction of the fastidious or the aesthetic or the magical. Therefore, much will be forgiven it. Comedy, on its own modest level, has stood in the adumbrated presence of that Lady who was herself surprised that this could lead to that.

The abyss of the finite, tragedy stands, as it were, in the presence of God (abyss calls to abyss). Therefore it does not laugh. But comedy stands, with full, cognitive confrontation and remembrance, in the presence of man, down to the last inch of the little beastie. And seeing what can come of it, seeing how safe and strong a way it is, seeing, through its own ruses and techniques, what St. Thomas meant by being and *potentia oboedientialis*, it laughs indeed. For things *are* funny and a final theory of comedy must be as simple as that.

NOTES

1. My betters in literary work could sketch the modern history of this romantic non-comic image, and here I only briefly indicate the materials suggested to me. Chateaubriand's *Sylphides* in the "Memoires d'Outre-Tombe" are the first of a whole century of imaginary idols, of which Proust's Odette is the last. Théophile Gautier's Mlle. de Maupin is one of the major ones, and is a conscious symbol of the "ideal" in art. The hero tries to visualize the perfect woman; she must be wealthy (no material needs); she must be young (twenty-six was the correct age) and strong and free (no family ties). A widow would be perfect. Here, in this insistence on the predefining of reality before ever one encounters a single inch of it, one cannot help but think of the univocal mind we will in later pages discuss, and of the kinship between rationalism and the romantic mind . . . Romantic novels, for example Balzac's, are full of these independent, rich women whose lovers idolize them. Those like Anna Karenina who could not be the Sylphide are damned to imperfect love. In this whole idea of perfect love—that is, no love at all, for what else can one love but the actual—one has to hoist a strong warning sign in our day. And who better for the hoisting than comedy?

2. Joyce Cary, *The Horse's Mouth* (London: Michael Joseph, 1953), p. 85.

3. *Ibid.*, p. 114.

4. Throughout this chapter the image of "the people" recurs a good many times. There is a little danger that if this image is read on a completely literal level our whole discussion of comedy will be reduced to a mere sociological point: the so-called quarrel these days between the intellectuals and the people. I wish to dissociate my point from such a discussion. There is as much phoniness, as much unreality, among many of "the people" as among the intellectuals. By the word "people" in this chapter, therefore, let us understand that real and rock-bottom reality, under categories, which can finally be reached in anybody, however clever or stupid. This is not, then, an essay on contemporary class differences.

5. Miguel de Cervantes, *op. cit.*, p. 80.

6. Bernard Shaw, *An Essay on Going to Church* (Boston: John W. Luce & Co., 1905), pp. 50-51.

7. Enid Welsfird, *The Fool, His Social and Literary History* (London: Faber & Faber, 1935), pp. 58-59.

8. Thomas Mann, *Doctor Faustus* (New York: Alfred A. Knopf, 1948), p. 130.

9. *Ibid.*, p. 134.

5 The Univocal and Equivocal

Here we begin our study of the manner in which, well or badly, "ideas" enter into the formal structures of different literary images. What we call "ideas" have been variously denominated as themes, structures, patterns, meanings, unities, extensions, connotations. The problem is always fundamentally the same: how does "meaning" get into the image? Thus we might say that we are now exploring the metaphysical dimension of the literary image.

The basic drive behind the univocal mind is the tendency to reduce everything, every difference and particularity in images, to the unity of a sameness which destroys or eliminates the variety and detail of existence. In its descent into existence, therefore, the univocal idea is superficial or destructive. This pattern is exemplified in Parmenides. The univocal imagination shares the same weakness. Illustrations are taken from Camus, Greene, and the "aesthetic man" of Kierkegaard.

The greatest weakness of every univocal pattern in literature is that it stays outside of the image and is not at all, therefore, strictly speaking, a real dimension of the literary imagination. This is the imagination that is really guilty of all the charges that are brought against the "theological" imagination. It does not respect reality; it exploits and uses it.

For the "equivocal" imagination, on the other hand, there is neither spontaneous movement toward nor exploration into the related dimensions of any image or situation. If there is both sameness and difference everywhere in our lives and in our literary images, the equivocal opts always for difference alone. Every experience must be an isolated ex-

perience, unpolluted by the taste of any other. Thus with the imagination of Gide, and thus with the man of Eliot's Waste-land who can connect nothing with nothing. The "equivo-cal man" makes spurious claims to both experience and freedom.

THE FINAL preoccupation of this section will be the nature of analogical thought. But we shall defer that subject until we have looked at the two forms of thought and imagination which fall short of it, forms which we shall call the univocal and equivocal. We shall first deal with the character of univo-cal thought, and I shall propose that in its most general operations, in all these areas where it makes its presence felt in the actual life of our culture, it is usually a vice, a disease. This univocal mentality is not a disease until it invades the order of the actual—where it has no place. But as soon as it does so invade our real world, it is responsi-ble for forms of pain and sickness that strike into the most intimate parts of the human heart and nerves. It is only if the reader will grant some credence to this fact that he will with any sense of urgency interest himself in our next ques-tion: if the univocal is such a disease, what then is anal-ogy? Only cultures capable of locating their diseases will be interested in remedies.

THE UNIVOCAL MAN

We shall be in a better position at the end of this first section to summarize the general spirituality and tempera-ment of the univocal man. It is sufficient for the moment, in order that the reader may quickly identify and locate the kind of soul and temperament we are talking about, sum-marily to describe the univocal man. He is, emotionally, full of extraordinary energies—in fact, a kind of energy seems to be the mark of his whole character. He has a genius for unilateral passion, and is, therefore—and always has been —a passionate center of good and bad in human civilization. In the orders of thought, logic, calculation, planning, he is notably a simplicist, clear in his conclusions but also unin-volved. Superficially, then, he resembles the religious genius, and if we were to go no further in our analysis we would be guilty of this frequent but unfortunate identi-fication. It is only by exercising great analytical caution that we will avoid this profound mistake, and will refrain from giving this character the veneration that is not his due. What, then, is the origin of the univocal mind and what, in the order of the human concrete, are some of its operative qualities? These two questions are the concern of the following section.

THE UNIVOCAL IDEA

For very important reasons it is best to look at two modes of operation of the univocal idea; let us call them the ascending and the descending mode, accordingly as such an idea is moving out of or into what we have been calling actuality.

1. *The ascending mode:* A univocal idea or concept is usually described by the technical logician as one that applies in exactly the same sense to all its subjects. In order that this may be logically possible, the mind abstracts a common element from many things in a class, putting all points of difference and uniqueness aside and ending with a mental point of perfect unity. Precisely because we shall have serious reasons later on to emphasize the manner in which the analogical mentality handles the relations of the same and the different, the points of unity and uniqueness, it will be helpful to indicate with a simple diagram how this problem is handled by the univocal idea:

The common element x in a class of subjects is abstracted in such a way as to form the meeting ground for all of them (x being the univocal idea), and in such a way that the unique and differentiating qualities of each subject (contained under the numerals 1, 2, 3, 4, 5, 6, etc.) in no way enter into the constitution of x. What must be stressed is the complete externality of the resulting relation between the points of unity and difference. The result, as with purely logical operations, is illuminating but simplistic. Reality is organized and reduced to unities, it is made increasingly intelligible (after a fashion). In the presence of such unifications, the mind, escaping the mixed travail of the confusing real, settles into increasing points of relaxation. It has indeed simplified reality but, and this must be noted, *only a part of it*. It is only by externalizing from itself all the points of difference which lie at the heart of this muddy actuality that it has achieved even this goal.

This is not said in a critical or pejorative sense. When the univocal mind operates on the level of logic, the sciences, or mathematics, indeed wherever it operates in the world of pure essences and forms in such a way as to recognize that its own laws and its own final forms are either pure constructs or decidedly limited versions of reality, this mentality must be acknowledged for what it is: a perfectly valid, valuable, natural, and spontaneous function of the human mind. It is not an evil or a disease, rather it is a thing of man. Some of the greatest conquests of the human spirit have come from the workings of this faculty.

It is only when the logical mind, or the univocal spirit, or the character that fastens on the order of the pure forms, returns to the actual world and tries to impose its laws on the latter that we must begin to be gravely concerned. We then confront the descending mode of the univocal mind.

2. *The descending mode:* As it ascends to the discovery of many points of sameness in the real, the univocal has created many relaxing points of mental unity. It is partially but importantly true to stress that these are *mental* unities, emerging from the deep-rooted, instinctive, rational drives of man, from his abstractive and organizing sense. The laws of the human *ratio,* or reason, are not the total laws of the actual; the two can never be *wholly* identical; there are enormous gaps between them, and the one, the ontological, cannot be entirely reduced to the cognitive forms of the other. Certainly there is an ineluctable drive in every form of intelligence to become one with the being it confronts, and the degree of dignity in each form is measured by the degree of unity it achieves with reality. The conception of mind as a mirror simply reflecting reality is indeed superficial, for the mind, like the heart, has its own desires, desiring *to be* what it sees, and not merely to reflect it. It is in fact the whole medieval tradition to declare that the mind not only *becomes* its object, but *is* its object, by one of the most fascinating forms of unity in the universe. In God

this unity and identity are complete, absolute and perfect; in man the achievement is only partial, and within the level of the human intelligence the achievement of unity by the ratio, or univocal reason, is poorest of all. Not for nothing has the human "reason" been called the *ratio abumbrata,* the reason of shadows.

Thus it is well here to note the important paradox that characterizes its whole nature: in itself, its forms are certainly the clearest, the most defined, the best formed of all the modes of human cognition; but as images or points of identification with the real, they are the most distant, the most shadowy of all the human modes of intelligence.

Because of this paradoxical character of clarity and obscurity within the univocal idea, it is important to note certain pretensions of the univocal character to powers which do not at all fall under its governance. These pretensions lead it again and again, under many different guises, to return to shape the real, the truly human orders according to its own forms and single-minded passions. And it does this without judging itself, that is, without being able to see its own limits and limitations, without recognizing its own effective but inferior place in the hierarchy of all the cognitive powers of man.

As a consequence, the univocal mind often poses as the exclusive organizer and interpreter of a highly concrete, pluralistic and individuated world. What was a legitimate process as it rose out of this world to create its own forms of sameness, by eliminating and externalizing all the points of concretion and individuation, now becomes not only illegitimate but dangerous as well. Now it not merely isolates and externalizes; its whole temptation is to reduce everything, like and unlike, to a flat community of sameness —all in the name of an intelligibility and type of order that does not and cannot belong to the real world. Instead of trying to handle the difference or submitting it to other faculties that might discover intelligibility in it, it tends in various ways to eliminate the unlike, the different, the pluralistic, as a kind of intractable and even hostile material.

If I might hazard a few summarizing sentences, they would be these: 1. The univocal man has no respect for reality; he is either contemptuous of it, or destroys it, or distorts it, or flattens it—or he refuses to take up responsibility in the face of it. Apparently a man of decision, actually he is the very reverse. His decisions are taken outside of time, and even here he apes the saints. He is the true dogmatist, and here liturgically he apes the Church with a secular effigy of true dogma. 2. The univocal man is not free. He is rigid, unbending, fixed. One can understand the fixity of the ideas of logic and essences, but *his* fixed ideas are born of a fixity of all the forces in his personality and a refusal to remain open to existence. He is simply not free, and in saying this we locate the one point where he can no longer ape the saints. For they were ultimately and completely *free*. And this is one of the most beautiful adjectives in our language or our liturgies.

In the following section, materials are brought briefly together from two different types of human speculation and action to illustrate the actual working of the univocal mind on specific problems. The problems are located in the fields of metaphysics and the literary imagination. Neither of these is entered into in any elaborate or exhaustive way, for our intention is only to clarify and locate a mentality by deliberately scattered examples of its general tendencies and habits.

METAPHYSICS

The classical example of the univocal mind in metaphysics is Parmenides. We must not make the easy mistake of underestimating this man, for he is the first metaphysician of western civilization and, despite the rigorous criticisms of him by both Plato and Aristotle, his genius is curiously but firmly acknowledged by both.

The reason for this acknowledgment is simple: it was Parmenides who first discovered the Being of the philosophers. If we decide that his prime intention was simplistic and primitive, we shall altogether miss the point; if, on the other hand, we shall see that this intuition of his must be calculated among the great moments of human insight and that he stated a truth which is still the great problematic fact for all metaphysics, we shall have sensed the magnitude of his talent. And as extrinsic evidence that this is so, we need only realize that a very large part of the work of Plato and Aristotle is only an enforced commentary on the world picture given us by Parmenides. I say "enforced," because until they accepted the insight of the latter and succeeded too in evading the major dilemma set up for all future philosophy by the great Eleatic, they could never have moved forward to their own extraordinary achievements.

The central insight of Parmenides is that everything *is,* all things *are,* and this "is" which characterizes all things is *one and the same being* in all. Things are not simply themselves, in separate, locked-in, atomic existence; rather the world is somehow one. It is astonishing how this insight was so often lost by a history of brilliant minds between the Eleatic and the days of Plato and Aristotle. And of this collapse of the initial vision I give two examples: 1. The later Atomists: they were indeed Parmenidean in their fidelities, yet they insisted that each atom *is itself,* and the "is" of any x or y is in no way related, save by certain purely external relations of magnitude and position. Being, therefore, is nothing but a tautology; a thing is itself. 2. Almost a hundred years after the stroke toward unity executed by Parmenides, Plato himself had to fight against a new form of pure atomism, this time an atomism of human language and thought, as it was offered by certain "friends of the Forms." To put the matter simply, these would reject all the unities and relations projected by any sentence: it is wrong, for example, to say that "the horse is white," for a horse is a horse, and white is white, and that is the end of the discussion.

Not so with Parmenides, for the unity of all things in Being is very real and a great mystery, discoverable not by the treacherous senses but only by the mind ("nor let ordinary experience in its variety force you along this way, [*namely, that of allowing*] the eye, sightless as it is, and the ear, full of sound, and the tongue, to rule; but [*you must*] judge by means of the Reason [*Logos*] the much-contested proof which is expounded by me").[1]

Here is the first classical putting of the relation of the evidence of the senses—multiplicity, difference, division—and the evidence of the mind—unity—as a dichotomy and a contradiction. It will require an elaborate metaphysics of participation and analogy to solve this apparent dichotomy, and even yet we wrestle with the problem. Nevertheless, that is not in any way to diminish the achievement of Parmenides in discovering the world of mind and insisting that its unity is matched by the unity of reality ("For it is the same thing to think and to be").[2] Thus, he saw that if we say "x *is*" and "y *is,*" then both x and y and all other things are englobed within the same being.

His great mistake lay in the second major step he now

took: After his first declaration that "Being is," he then steps into a morass, from which he will never be able to extricate himself, by a further declaration that *non-being is not, is impossible.* This means that there are forms of non-being in the universe, non-being is unthinkable and is not. And it is precisely this affirmation that leads the philosophy of Elea into all the hopeless difficulties of the univocal mind. Indeed it will also have set up as the great task of the future for Greek philosophy the problem of resolving the many modes in which non-being can exist or can be inserted into being. In fact, I shall suggest in later pages that the principal metaphysical importance of Plato and Aristotle was to consist in the meaning and place they finally carved out for the Nothingness Parmenides could not even think about.

What is the relationship of this problem to the operations of the univocal mind in metaphysics? The best way to answer that question is to watch the descending mind of Parmenides as it invades our common day light world.

The phrase by which he describes the Being he has discovered, "a Whole all together. One, continuous," is most indicative of its structure, and our conclusion must be that it is reality without any inward structure. If one part of it were here and another part there, in such a way as to create an inter-related organism, this would indeed be structure. But wherever Being is, it is altogether there ("Thus it must be absolutely or not at all"). If it were any kind of multiple, divided fact—such as we know our world to be—then it would be partly in each sector, and partly *not.* One part would surely *be,* but also would *not be* another part. Everywhere not-being would be intruding itself as a strange effigy of reality, but this is impossible. This Being, therefore, so invades reality as necessarily to wipe out all difference, all boundaries, lines, separations, individuations ("Nor is Being divisible, since it is all alike").

Let us pause here for a moment, for we have come to the point of critical difference between two modes of the mind invading reality, the univocal and the analogical, and it will be important for our later discussions to accentuate the point without developing it. The Parmenidean and univocal unity wipes out all difference as it advances; the analogical mode of unity, as we have already noted, *generates difference at the very heart of its unity as it progresses.* There is the central opposition between the two processes. There is a majesty and power in each process, but today we are come to a crossroads and must choose between forms of power. The majesty of the univocal echoes in all the great liturgical phrases of Parmenides:

For nothing else either is or shall be except Being since Fate has tied it down to be a whole and motionless; therefore all things that mortals have established, believing in their truth, are just a name: Becoming and Perishing, Being and Not-Being, and Change of position, and alteration of bright colour.

There cannot be change or history in such a world. Nothing new can come to be for that would mean it once *was not;* it cannot die, for that would mean a passage into a fabulous and impossible non-being. Being is fixed; Fate has fixed it, motionless, altogether everywhere, triumphant;

Justice has never released (Being) in its fetters and set it free either to come into being or to perish, but holds it fast. . . . But it is motionless in the limits of mighty bonds, without beginning, without cease, since Becoming and Destruction have been driven very far away, and true conviction has rejected them. And remaining the same in the same place, it rests by itself and thus remains there fixed. . . .

THE UNIVOCAL IMAGINATION

The qualities of the univocal imagination altogether resemble and repeat those of the univocal *ratio* or reason. But by analyzing some of these qualities in their concrete operations we shall secure a firmer grip on our subject. It is my hope that at the end of this present section of distributed examples all of us may be able to say: I know what the univocal is and how it works, though I can give no single concise definition of it.

In our brief sortie into metaphysics we were confronted with a problem which cannot be resolved by the univocal intelligence: the difficult relations between being and non being. In the case of the imagination we shall begin our analysis with another but related problem, that of the one and the many. For, more professedly than the pure intelligence, the imagination's trade is to deal with the very multiplicity, divisions, colors, sounds, and complications of actuality itself. These are, as it were, its very business, and one might therefore wonder how a faculty that operates a the very heart of multiplicity could possibly fall into some of the same difficulties as does the *ratio,* or reason.

We saw that every univocal consequence occurs for the *ratio* when it proposes a purely extrinsic relation of being and non-being, when it cannot succeed in getting the second *into* the first. The same difficulties occur for the imagination when it can only produce an extrinsic relation between the many image materials that are its life-blood and the unity it ambitions to produce out of any particular complex of images and events.

Let the act of the imagination we call didactic, or allegorical, or moralistic be our simplest case in question. Whatever insight is present to such a literary work can be located and stated, purely, perfectly, and completely, at some single point of the organism (in this case a dubious "organism") created by the artist. All the other materials that are employed by the imagination, its metaphors, images, symbols, events, are reduced in function to the levels of illustration and example. These are themselves reduced in their content to what is purely relevant to the original, isolatable insight of the imagination. Thus they are stripped of their own actuality and uniqueness. This actuality is in no sense explored in order to produce any insight; rather the vision is imposed from above, and in such a way as severely and precisely to delimit the nature of any further vision. Of this kind of act we may therefore say that the essential work of the imagination is accomplished at its first stroke; everything else is no more than an illustrative addendum. All will be seen to be quite the contrary with the analogical imagination. *Its thinking will not be done until the last metaphor or the last event is inserted into the literary vision.* The univocal work is, thus, no true organism at all, for *the one* in it can be perfectly abstracted, and the other elements constituting *a many* stand in a thoroughly extrinsic relation to it. I have tried to show that this is the way the "theological imagination" of Eugene O'Neill operates. Aesop's fables are, of course, a charming, innocent example.

Like everything else, purely allegorical, didactic vision has its place; it would be ridiculous to take any other position. But its vision is limited, its work is facile, and the more it extends itself as any kind of high model for the literary man or for that more general act of the imagination we call culture, the more we shall suffer from its general mechanisms and attitudes toward reality. These are, principally, a leveling of the real, a manipulation of it in the interests of the One, and a foreshortening of the insights that can come only from a richer penetration into the more complicated materials present in actuality itself.

The word "manipulation" has been used, and "exploitation" of the real is another word that might well go with it. These are words, we may point out, which belong to the will and not to the mind. And so it is, at least partially, with the allegorical imagination. In a particularly brilliant piece of criticism, Allen Tate has noted the remarkable affinities that exist between this allegorizing tendency and a kind of cult of the will in literature, which, I may add, has its own powerfully univocal instincts.[3] Somewhere along the line poetry and literature were abandoned as possible sources of *cognition*, the whole possibility of which was surrendered to science. Well, if the imagination cannot be used as at least a partial instrument of cognition, then it can be turned into an instrument of power, and can at least *use* reality in the effort of the will, through vague thrusts, to transcend the order of cognition and true contemplation. The will of itself wishes only to get to its goal; nor will it be very discriminating about the means, and will in fact reduce everything to a means, never caring cognitively for the thing in itself, but always using it as an instrument. Now it is precisely in this quality that "the imagination of the will," if I may so term it, shares in the univocality of the mechanically allegorical imagination. Both are exploiters.

It is quite ironic that the very mystique of so much Romantic art, which was generated out of a distaste for and rebellion against the allegorical and the close paralleling of the latter with the *ratio*, should finally adopt the virulently univocal methods of the allegorical it had always rebelled against.

Let me add three further examples of the operations of this univocal imagination. They will be drawn from: 1. Kierkegaard's classical description of the aesthetic man; 2. Scobie, the man of pity in Graham Greene's *The Heart of the Matter;* and 3. Dr. Rieux, the hero of Camus' novel *The Plague*, who proposes a new modern priesthood in a univocal fight against pain.

1. *The aesthetic man.* The first two stadia or levels of life are called by Kierkegaard the aesthetic and the ethical, and it is necessary to understand what he means by the latter if we are to comprehend the univocal habit behind the kind

of world view which he has termed the aesthetic.[4] If we may return to a word already used several times, the ethical is like reality itself in that it is *articulated;* in this world one thing is not the other; in the case of ethical articulation, there are profound sources of differentiation which we call good and evil. There are other but related terms in which the conditions of existence associate themselves with the conditions of the ethical. For in a sense it is existence itself in all its actual conditions that determines the ethical. The woman a man loves for the whole of life is this one woman whom he has met, known and chosen; it is not the all-englobing idea of woman. The duty of a man is not an abstract idea that is rendered either harmless or infinite by its abstraction; rather, it is determined, enlarged and limited by the concrete circumstances within the range of a man's talents and obligations.

Let us insist, at any rate, on the notion that the ethical is, for any man, articulated and defined. It forces choices of the actual over the actual, the concrete over the concrete; it compels a man to choose *his* concrete. But not so with the aesthetic man, as he is understood in the dialectic of Kierkegaard. This man imposes a blanket of "the beautiful" over this field of articulation, thus wiping out the lines and distinctions of the latter in one magnificent stroke. Given the right technique, the right moment, the right magic, "beauty" can equalize or abolish good and evil, can eliminate the necessity of choice, can smash the Ixion wheel of struggle. And any alleged *choice* by the aesthetic man, any election for a moment of one beauty over another, is neutralized by a veritably scientific art of knowing how to illuminate such a moment to careful fullness without attachment or commitment. In the name of infinite possibility one must be cautious not to commit oneself to the finite; to do so is unscientific, vulgar and actual. It is a violation and a loss of freedom. The actual is a narrow gate, and who ever heard of entering heaven by a narrow gate?

Fundamentally and finally, there is no difference between the obliterating or neutralizing march of the Parmenidean intelligence and the march of this kind of beauty.

2. *The man of pity.* Here we touch an even more delicate subject than that of the passion for an undiscriminating beauty. For the sense of pity comes closest to being the best of human instincts and, if we keep an eye on the Christian story, pity brings man very near to the divine action itself.

Yet even this virtue, like everything else, has its dangers if it too becomes a univocal blanket that covers the lines of being. On the surface there is a great conflict today between forces of pity and cruelty, with the latter emerging as an almost diabolical force on the contemporary scene of history. But there is a sense in which even the cruelty has been, professedly, derived from a kind of heresy of univocal pity, a war against all poverties and class-structures. As such it will tolerate any methods to gain exalted ends. Thus we have suggested that we are faced with an enemy who in his tactic and freedom of movement is like an agile dancer in infinite space, again wiping out, this time with his fascinating and revolutionary pity, all the differences of the finite. On the other hand, we of the West, at least in principle, are dedicated to the laws of the finite, their smallness, narrowness, their apparent weakness, apparently a David against a Goliath, another version of the many debates between the way of the finite and the way of the infinite which this book is discussing.

But this is only by way of preface to a few remarks on a smaller and literary example of the heresy of univocal pity. Scobie, in Greene's *The Heart of the Matter,* is a classical example of the defeat and radical torment of our nature and its preoccupation with the problem of pity. In this book the last vestige of the decisive dance of Dante is dying. There is no verve left in us for his magisterial encounter with the forms of good and evil, for the slow building up of the partial forms of the good in our souls, and the expression of these choices in the great symbols of the finite. Dante had seen human life as a journey, with articulated stages of growth, with stages of insight, with advances and deviations, the lines of the will always trying to match the lines of the real; there was nothing univocal in it; each moment required new decision and caused new insight; everything in it was concrete and limited. And the poem of David Jones, *The Anathemata,* commemorates the same idea of life as a journey, an odyssey:

> You that shall spread your hands over the things offered make *memento* of us
> and where the gloss reads *jungit manus* count us among his argonauts whose argosy you plead, under the sign of the things you offer.

> Extend your hands
> all you *orantes*
> for the iron-dark shore
> is to our lee
> over the lead-dark sea
> and schisted Ocrinium looms in fairish visibility
> and white-plumed riders shoreward go
> and
> THE BIRDS DECLARE IT
> that wing white and low
> that also leeward go
> go leeward to the tor-lands
> where the tin-veins maculate the fire-rocks.
> The birds have a home
> in those rocks.[5]

The *details,* the bewilderingly concrete but twisting, maneuvering details of this journey, might well be a scandal to the mind that seeks freedom through the infinite and the univocal. The ship and the journey are so different from the vague ship bearing Tristan and Isolde on their vague journey. Again, in *The Anathemata*

> Christ was raised
> on this hill
> at a time's turn
> not on any hill
> but on this hill [6]

But in *The Heart of the Matter* this kind of movement has been superseded by the compulsions of a univocal pity for our state. The wife is to be pitied and the other woman is to be pitied, and, therefore, both are, without choice, to be chosen. Scobie cannot stand the idea of giving pain to either. Then he cannot endure the torture this dilemma causes in God, and offers to Him the holocaust of his suicide which wipes out the need and the agony of all partial and analogical choices of the good.

3. *The attack on pain:* The hero of Camus' *The Plague,* Dr. Rieux, would form a new priesthood, dedicated to an assault on pain in all its forms in this universe:

". . . When I entered this profession, I did it 'abstractedly,' so to speak; because I had a desire for it, because it meant a career like another, one that young men often aspire to. Perhaps, too, because it was particularly difficult for a workman's son, like myself. And

then I had to see people die. Do you know that there are some who
refuse to die? Have you ever heard a woman scream 'Never!' with
her last gasp? Well, I have. And then I saw that I could never get
hardened to it. I was young then, and I was outraged by the whole
scheme of things, or so I thought. Subsequently I grew more modest.
Only, I've never managed to get used to seeing people die. That's
all I know. Yet after all—"

Rieux fell silent and sat down. He felt his mouth dry.

"After all—?" Tarrou prompted softly.

"After all," the doctor repeated, then hesitated again, fixing his
eyes on Tarrou, "it's something that a man of your sort can understand most likely, but, since the order of the world is shaped by
death, mightn't it be better for God if we refuse to believe in
Him and struggle with all our might against death, without raising
our eyes toward the heaven where He sits in silence."

Tarrou nodded.

"Yes. But your victories will never be lasting; that's all."

Rieux's face darkened.

"Yes, I know that. But it's no reason for giving up the struggle."

"No reason, I agree. Only, I now can picture what this plague
must mean for you."

"Yes. A never ending defeat." [7]

Again and again the brilliance and sanctity of such fervent
goals are at least a momentary obstacle to understanding the
univocal drive behind such sanctity. Who will dare to criti-
cize such a saint? I have a very great respect for Camus,
who is much less of a rationalist than Sartre and who writes
with an intensity of conviction about the terrors of the finite.
The Plague is a parable, but written with great feeling and insight, a parable about the insertion of man into a cosmic
and limited situation from which he cannot escape. The
novelist calls for a holy act of rebellion against all the forms
of pain in men; it is therefore a rebellion which really asks
that all other causes, all other zeals and purposes, be liqui-
dated down into the form of this single crusade. There are
ideas, ideals, decisions, fidelities which mingle or oppose one
another; their very interactions and oppositions cause pain;
in the name of some of them it has always been traditionally
necessary, especially in the name of the ethical and the
sacred, actually to choose pain. But to raise the single flag of
the opposition to pain would flatten out this whole human
world, with all its pluralisms and profound oppositions.

Here, as elsewhere, what we are confronted with, in the
logical order, is the imposition of a single, inflexible form
upon the real. When the deeper orders of the emotional and

spiritual life are invaded by the univocal soul, the result is a rebellion without condition against the painful conditions of the finite itself. Therefore, no matter which the operation, whether it be the *ratio* of Parmenides, the Beauty of the aesthetic man, the Pity of Greene, or the Pain of Camus, two qualities seem always to be subsumed under it: the univocal man aspires to the condition of an angel and he is a rebel. (How much easier to say this if we all concede that we are caught in the problem.)

Another contemporary passion, the polar opposite of the univocal, is the passion for *autonomies,* for insisting that every fact, every science, every art, be allowed to have its own autonomous existence and structure. Thus, many an artist and social scientist resents the "intrusions" of philosophy and theology because he believes both to have qualities and ambitions which are alien to the idea of literary autonomy.

THE EQUIVOCAL

This defense of autonomies can have either one of two motives behind it. The first motive can be highly honorable, valid and without question. It would be a defense of the actual order and a demand that the latter be permitted to emerge in all its clarity, without distortion by any blinding of the eyes or without dilution by any nominalistic system, before it is unified with anything else. Thus each science has its autonomy from every other according to its subject matter and proper object; thus the real imagination instinctively insists that each human character in a story emerge in its own perceptible terms; or the psychologist will tell us that the mechanical laws of the emotional unconscious have their reality and must be reckoned with in any total moral view of man. Only a very foolish man would protest any of these insistences on autonomy.

However, there is often another mood behind the latter which is certainly more questionable, a view which is somewhat akin to one we have seen as characterizing a good deal of contemporary tragedy. It is not so much a love of the clarity and light that comes from the completely projected, independent, autonomous structure of any autonomous thing; nor is it the joy that comes out of the sharp *haecceitas* or "thisness" that is created by the mind of a Scotus or the imagination of a Gerald Manley Hopkins; it is much rather the love of the darkness and pain that is present to some minds in the fact that no one thing seems to be truly connected with anything else.

This kind and degree of autonomy are what the metaphysician calls the spirit of *the equivocal*. It is a mentality which believes that in the whole world of reality and being no two beings *are* in the same sense; everything is completely diverse from everything else. With the univocal idea we saw how sameness crushed the reality and diversity out of being; with the equivocal, difference, and only difference, reigns everywhere. Everything is a private world; everything is a solipsism. All is absurd, lonely, a private hell.

If this is true for the mind, what must the passion for the equivocal do when it reigns in the imagination, the sensibilities, the most intimate bloodstream of man. It is a terrible thing, and yet there *is* a secret love for it in many souls, and he who does not accept it is accused of a failure of nerve. This seems to me nothing more than another version of the age-old, pretentiously strong, Pelagian elite-artist telling the weak among the people to go to the devil if they are weak.

There is, for example, the *acte gratuit* of André Gide. This is the act of an artist who wishes to be wholly ready for the next moment of imaginative sensibility. But this readiness really involves a freedom of the imagination that must be absolutely "equivocal." It must be completely and separately *available* for every new and separate adventure; therefore it must not be committed to or polluted by any other previous or accompanying dedication, lest the new moment be not altogether purely caught. Gide even quotes scripture for his own purposes; he does violence to the words and spirit of Christ by calling this species of imaginer (who wants the new to be related to nothing) the poor man of the Gospel, the naked, spiritually free man who has left all in order to be ready for all. "Happy is the man who is attached to nothing on earth and who carries his fervor unremittingly with him through all the ceaseless immobility of life. I hate homes and families and all places where a man thinks to find rest . . . I hold that every new thing should always find the whole of us wholly available." [8]

NOTES

1. Plato, "Parmenides," frags. 7-8, numeration and trans. from

Kathleen Freeman, *Ancilla to the Pre-Socratic Philosophers* (Cambridge: Harvard University Press, 1948), pp. 42-44.

2. *Ibid.*, frag. 3.

3. Allen Tate, "The Hovering Fly," pp. 159-160.

4. A summary of the stages of life and the religious spirit will be found in Jean Wahl's *Etudes Kierkegaardiennes* (Paris: Aubier, 1949), pp. 136 ff. Let me say here that over against pure Hegelianism we are all attracted by the strongly Christian flavor of Kierkegaard's thought; but it would take a long study to clarify the presence of what I believe to be categories and leaps in him that are basically blind acts of the will.

5. David Jones, *The Anathemata* (London: Faber & Faber, 1952), pp. 106-107.

6. *Ibid.*, p. 53.

7. Albert Camus, *The Plague*, trans. Stuart Gilbert (New York: Alfred A. Knopf, 1948), pp. 117-118.

8. André Gide, *The Fruits of the Earth*, trans. by Dorothy Bussy (New York: Alfred A. Knopf, 1952), pp. 65-66.

6 The Analogical

The analogical imagination insists on keeping the same and the different, the idea and the detail, tightly interlocked in the one imaginative act. As its idea or pattern descends into the images of reality, it adapts itself perfectly to every detail or difference, without ever suffering the loss of its own identity. And the theme is always on the inside of the images. It is always eminently positive and is always creating difference and autonomy. The Oedipus Rex and Riders to the Sea are analyzed as analogical.

Analogy means ana-logon, "according to the measure." The literary imagination should grasp the human reality (which is always the same) not univocally (for it is also always different), but according to the measure of its every dimension, according to the measure of all its definiteness, according to the measure of its time phases, according to the measure of tragedy, comedy, and every other human facet. Thus, not only this chapter but this book takes its shape from analogy.

SOMEWHERE in between the two forms of the imagination we have been discussing (the univocal as a pure unity or sameness and the equivocal as a pure, ununified diversity) lies analogy and the analogical imagination.

This chapter will move toward a dialectical discussion of the nature of analogy although it may be hard for some to believe that such a development in our explorations has any real relevancy for the life of the imagination. We will be substantially involved in a metaphysical debate over the relation between the contrarieties of unity and difference, structure and detail, the same and the different, in a way that may somewhat shock some students of the literary imagination. Therefore it may be well to begin with a few pages on the relevancy of this discussion for literary criticism. The point of this introduction will be that the most thoughtful analysts of the literary imagination have been just as deeply embroiled as the metaphysicians with this problem of contrariety and have been caught in as difficult a vocabulary.

CREATIVITY AND THE CONTRARIES

The relation of the contraries is not an issue that is specific for metaphysics as some kind of science isolated from reality. It is a recurrent problem for the whole world of the real. And the same is true of the forms of actuality as they are fictively reported by the literary imagination. Coleridge tells us that the major function of the latter is esemplastic or unitive, that is to say, it must give organized and unified vision.[1] But how does it organize, and how unify? How does it put its many and its one together? Here the critical discussion still goes endlessly on; all the critics take their separate shots and invent their own vocabulary, their own dialectic. Actually, they are as dialectical and as vocabularistic as the pure philosopher. And they are as involved as he with the key issue of *structure*. They become fascinated with the word. One after the other tries his hand at it. The poem becomes an organism, and every last metaphor is fitted brilliantly into it. Or it becomes a thing; therefore "a poem should not mean but be." Then, as Robert Penn Warren notes,[2] we get not one, but dozens of versions of "pure poetry"; it must be so tightly organized by its own magic—would that we could put our finger once and for all on whatever the devil it is—that the marvelous awareness of its own autonomous intensity magically excludes whatever does not belong in it. The true poet knows what is *his* "one," and that is all there is to it. *He* will not be didactic, logical, rational, philosophical, ethical, or historical, because *his* is a unique world, the only point of complete and relaxing unities which climb above all our world of struggle and fragmentation. Or he will develop a psychologistic unity, according to the needs of which he will reject the bothersome detail of the relation of the soul to details and to belief; he will use plural objects for his own purpose; they will create "objectless beliefs" in the interior of man and thereafter will no longer be objects.[3]

But they will have unified the conflicting drives of the soul.

My point is not meant to be in the least discourteous or critical. Indeed, all I am trying to say is that the finest talents among our literary and critical people never leave off all the minor tortures of tackling the same problem in their field as do the philosophers in theirs. The centuries are not too long to work at the business, and each writer can make only his own little contribution to the dialectic of the situation (I certainly feel very much the same about this book though I may often seem to speak with a certainty beyond the possibilities of the subject).

My second point is that the literary theorists fall into as many dilemmas or create as many dilemmas and dichotomies for themselves as have the philosophers who have tried to work out the difficult relations between the one and the many, the same and the different.

The critical combat, with its own issues, is not without even its purely Parmenidean attempt to obliterate the whole action and division of the sensible world, and to try, in its stead, to start all over again and get hold of a world of pure being in the shape of the poem. Mallarmé tries to do it by sleep, by night, by death, tombs, empty vases, silence, virginity, immobility. Rimbaud tries it and, because it can never quite be done (poetry, like matter, always retains some opacity, thickness, "hostility" to eternity), he flies in despair to a distant land. So many of the talented French follow Poe in the search for a night which will dissolve all differences into the perfect, poetic dream.

Or there are those who will admit that we have two worlds on our hands but try resolutely to fight off a real dichotomy between them. There is surely a one and a many, the subject of a poem and its images, the structure and the detail. But Henry James comes out for an artist's mind that will not be violated by separate ideas, and Eliot insists that the ideas always, somehow or other, get into the poetry. Robert Penn Warren says there must be no rational statement that is not poetically earned.

But there are also those who come terribly near to accepting the dichotomy; they come almost to the point of accepting a situation of irrelevance between the structure and detail of a poem. I say "almost" because, despite the fact that the word "irrelevance" itself is used, I cannot believe they quite mean what they say. I believe that these men actually begin with some kind of confused notion of the metaphysical

structure of reality itself, as if there were in the latter some
kind of central structure of "meaning" and, somehow added
on, a periphery of fact and detail. Or better still, though
somewhat in caricature of their position, they think there is a
center of inviolate logic and a fringe of inviolate detail.
But this they can be forgiven, for many a teacher of analogy
thinks that an analogical idea is a common abstractable fact
which is to be applied in a sense partly the same and partly
different to all its subjects.

As an example of this kind of critic for the life of the
imagination, let us take John Crowe Ransom. Ransom has a
passion for two things that are unadulteratedly good and
healthy for poems or any other form of being. These two
things are (1) structure and (2) freedom or unpredictability
of detail. He wants these two good things, but he cannot put
them together.

> Total intention is the total meaning of the finished poem, which
> differs from the original logical content by having acquired a de-
> tail which is immaterial to this content, being everywhere specific,
> or local, or particular, and at any rate unpredictable . . . Poetic ex-
> perience is only to be had by disrespecting whatever kind of logical
> content we start with . . . In it (the poem) the relation of the meter
> to the meaning is that of a texture to a structure; this texture is
> adventitious, and irrelevant to the structure, but highly visible, and
> to the innocent reader like a curious increment of riches that had
> not been bargained for . . . the word "precision" is dangerous. The
> freedom does very well; the freedom is unpredictability, and the
> unpredictable or free detail cannot be precise in the sense that it
> was intended, that it unfolds logically according to plan. To have
> an unpredictable experience is not the same as treating experience
> with precision.[4]

But, in all justice to so fine a critic as Mr. Ransom, we
must note that his dialectic, or vocabulary, must not be
taken with complete seriousness. In using it he is certainly
doing himself an injustice. For he is not an equivocal critic
in the final analysis. Else why in the same breath is he
asking such questions as: "What are the sorts of texture that
will go along with a given structure? And what structure permits a given texture?"[5] These are not the questions of a
man who accepts irrelevance, or a dichotomy between the
one and the many. It is the skin of Esau, but the voice of
Jacob.

And there are worse forms of dichotomy than that created

by Ransom (some of which I am grateful to Mr. Warren for collecting). Here is the striking version of Frederick Pottle:

> . . . the element of prose is innocent and even salutary when it appears as—take your choice of three metaphors—a background on which the images are projected, or a frame in which they are shown, or a thread on which they are strung. In short, when it serves a structural purpose.[6]

Robert Penn Warren's succinct comment is: "Apparently, not only does the showcase bear no relation to the jewels, but the jewels bear no relation to each other. Each one is a shining little focus of heightened consciousness, or pure realization, existing for itself alone." [7] And this is a rather accurate reproduction of our own analysis of the equivocal.

So far, then, we see that:

(1) There are some creators and theorists whom we can only judge to be anxious to get the senses as far as possible out of the poem and to reach as purely as possible to the pure idea of things. Their final difficulty seems to be that they find the thick and diverse plural world intractable to such an absolute purpose; the purpose of their art and theory is not to handle but to remove the intractable and unattractive part of our dichotomy. We must be honest enough to realize that this is not only a tendency which fairly decisively marks this school of the imagination, but that it is also one which resides somewhere in the soul of every man.

(2) We come, secondly, across a kind of critical dialectic which is willing to accept dichotomy or irrelevancy between the one and the many, the structure and detail, of a work of the imagination. One cannot help but think this group is of the opinion that irrelevancy and the brilliant emergence of the adventitious or the free detail is the major quality of real poetry. At any rate, it is certainly some of its members who would be most averse to the right of the religious mind to be given any status in criticism or creative writing and who come out most resolutely for courage, the facing of the facts, and all that sort of thing. It is a temperament which has been rigorously dealt with by Lionel Trilling in *The Liberal Imagination*. Mr. Trilling believes that in America the writer has been most guilty of a thorough passivity in this business of reporting facts and refusing all those active processes of the imagination which might give whatever consolations might come from the discovery of unity. And there

are of course the existentialists, with practically a worship of the absurd and of the "authentic act," an act which had at its heart a contempt for all irrelevant systems behind which responsibility might try to hide.

(3) Finally there is a group which may not have a completely effective metaphysic or dialectical vocabulary at its command, but whose instincts are true. In operation this group tries manfully after an interpenetrative relation between the one and the many. They see the main enemy as that moment of dissociation in our history when sense and sensibility became separated into the different camps of science and imagination; their desire is to restore an intimate unity between these two. They know that, because of what has happened through this hostile separation of the modes of thought, we are sick and fragmented human beings, in the hands of a technology without sensibility or a sensibility without sense. They do not believe that a separated logic or a separated religiosity can help us out of our present intense encounter with facts and impulses. In the concrete of poetry and all the works of the imagination they will not tolerate a situation where the rationality of ideas and the power of images have their separate autonomies. And in saying these things they sometimes say things which do not please some Catholics, who believe that "ideas" and some strange version of dogma they have themselves concocted are the only things that matter. These Catholics believe that the saving of souls is the only thing that really matters, and that is true enough; but by the saving of souls they mean, without knowing it, the saving of the top of the head, and they are in danger, without knowing it, of themselves concocting a new doctrine of ideas without sensibility, even one of salvation without works.*

God knows we must always fight for the purity of dogmatic truth, but even here we must not be ourselves guilty

---

* Throughout this book I have been referring to a "transcendental" use of dogma and theology, and have been using the word "transcendental" in its pejorative sense. One synonym for such a use would be the word "irrelevant." Another would be the epithet "intellectual," but only, of course, as it occurs in some weak, Cartesian sense. As often as they are really understood, dogma and the science of theology need no defense. What might be in order is a more than occasional analysis of the human relevancy of both. The great dialectic of the Nicene Creed or that of the Council of Ephesus is also a great defense of man and of human civilization and of more than the conceptual life.

of that dichotomy which would make dogma reside in the pure mind and give it no relation to human reality, to sensibility, or to all the mighty energies of the imagination's bloodstream. If we do this, if we put all our eggs into saving the "intelligence" over against the aberrations of the intellectuals, then the cultural engineers—we have said it before—will take over the rest. And the people, having been given half a Christ, will be left to live in a hell of sensibility—without knowing it. At this point we can surely waive examples. We need only spend a day before television (*there* is a task) to realize what a hell that will be. Throughout that whole day we will not have *sinned* at all; but neither will we have what the heart desires or what the sons of God have a right to. If we have a right to God Himself, then our imagination has a right to its share too. Nor need we think that some day, many years from now when we have won our fight, we must finish a good day with the prayer of the Calvinists: "Nice day, but we'll pay for it."

But these theological subjects are best left to our final chapters. I hope that we are now in a better position to begin our brief summary of some of the historical bases behind the development of the metaphysics of analogy, and that our present pursuit of this theme seems less irrelevant to the various situations of the contemporary imagination.

A PRE-HISTORY OF ANALOGY

We have begun this chapter with the suggestion that the operations of analogy and the analogical imagination lie somewhere in between the univocal (as a pure unity of sameness) and the equivocal (as a pure, disunified diversity).

The first and consistently important thing to note about the *analogical* unity of the one and the many, the same and the different, is that it will no longer be possible or necessary to abstract the one from the many or the same from the different. The reader will be tempted to say that the analogical idea is indeed, therefore, an "obscure" idea, and he would be quite correct in this evaluation. But it is not obscure in any pejorative sense; rather it is so in the sense that it is not a "clear idea" as the latter has been understood in the technical history of philosophy. The clear idea has always been defined as one with absolute boundaries and limitations, such that it is not invaded or obscured by the character or quality of any other idea. It glories in a certain kind of precision and intelligibility, though this precision, when seen through, exists on the level of the primitive and not the sophisticated periods of philosophy. Thus we propose that if the idea we have of a one-many or of a same-different organism is that of a crude and separable intermixture of the components, we have such a clear idea, one which keeps perpetually insisting that the boundaries of its member parts are always potentially or in fact recognizable. After all, the task of real thought, and of the imagination too, is to organize the diversity of reality in unity, but in such a way that the diversity, which is a fact, still remains. But if one orders the real in such a way that the one, or point of unity, is still really outside the many, or the like outside the different, nothing very important has been accomplished. If this is all we want in putting the contraries together, we want very little; and it does not matter what you call the result; a mixture of two univocal or clear ideas, or a mixture of two equivocal ideas; you still have that with which you started; the contraries still stand outside of each other, and not all the juggling in the world of "clear ideas" will put them together.

What then is necessary if the mind is to put *diversity together,* while retaining diversity, and if the imagination, in its own tasks in all the arts, is to do the same? I should say that we must achieve some kind of *interpenetration* of unity and multiplicity, sameness and difference, a kind of interpenetration in terms of which the two contraries become one and the same thing—but "become" this only because existentially they always have been it.

And it is precisely this which is the achievement of the metaphysics of analogy. But our final, rather brief explanation of this achievement will be better grasped if we preface our explanation by some sketch of the debate on the relation of the contraries to each other as it was handed to us by the early philosophers.

GREECE AND THE CONTRARIES

One method of finding an intelligible structure in the history of Greek philosophy is to regard it as a series of engagements with this tortuous problem of the relations between the contraries, and a series of victories over the problem by way of gradual approximations to the perfect idea of interpenetration. This statement makes it clear that a mature theory of metaphysical analogy, as it finally emerged, did not spring suddenly and unprepared from the head of Zeus, but required much slower fermentation as its components were being slowly articulated in earlier periods of western civilization.

Being and non-being. The major problem of Greek philosophy from its inception was that of associating being and non-being * in one interpenetrating and associated act. All its major issues had been created by an early establishment of a dichotomy between the two, and by a number of consecutive failures to bridge that dichotomy. One of the central importances of both Plato and Aristotle to metaphysics is that each was responsible for substantial contributions in the solution of this impasse. For when they finish their work, non-being no longer lies on the outside of being. And the same will be true of all the other sets of contraries.

As we have already seen, Parmenides had created both the first great success of philosophy and the first turbulence over the life of the contraries *vis à vis* each other. He declared that only being is and that non-being simply and altogether is not. There is no sense in the name of non-being. But if this is so, how can you explain the validity of all negative judgments (in all of which we are constantly saying that that which is has some quality of non-being)? How can you explain the phenomenon of plurality (for any one thing in the world *is not* anything else)? And how can you explain the phenomenon of change or motion (for thereby things become what they once *were not*)?

Thus Parmenides is right, for surely all things *are,* and are contained under the unity of being. But he is also wrong, because by his logic he has made certain *facts* impossible— and that is one of the pretty ways in which pure logic has often dealt with facts. Later the neo-Parmenidean Atomists enter the scene, seeking a courteous correction of their master. They admit the diversity of the actual; they also admit the mysterious existence, in some way, of non-being. But they place the latter as a void in between, and therefore outside of, the many separate atoms which they postulate. By virtue of this void the atoms can indeed be multiple, and can change, not inwardly, but only by an external change

---

* I take the liberty of looking at these as a pair of contraries, and not contradictories, because the non-being to be considered is not absolute non-being.

in their relation to each other. The individual atom is thus given as only another smaller version of the total Parmenidean cosmos. It is eternal and unchangeable, and there is nothing *in it* by which it can relate itself to anything else. There is still no possibility of a true dialogue between beings.

As a result, the plural has been discovered but has not yet been made possible by a logic of a non-being that would reside at the heart of being itself. And in the bargain the original unity of Parmenides has been lost. The philosophical mind, while trying to be more faithful to experience, would seem to be worse off than ever. No help is really supplied by a group to follow, whom we may call the physical philosophers. They all find ultimate forms of unity, whether it be water, earth, air or fire, but they cannot explain how all that proceeds from these things is still in any way the same thing out of which it proceeds. And many of them discover principles of difference and unity, whether strife and love, or the unlimited and the limited, but all these principles continue to exist outside of each other.

THE ADVANCE OF PLATO

The achievement of Plato is itself a progressive one. He had been handed all the elements of the impasse between being and non-being, the one and the many, the same and the different, by his predecessors, and his first attempt at a solution had been almost as awkward as theirs. He had decided that there must be a multiple and pluralistic quality to the world, for how deny it and remain in any degree a realist? He had also decided, for linguistic, ethical, and epistemological reasons, that there must be unities in this multiple world. But it seems to me that, in common with those who had been before him, he could not at first endure the problem of contrariety. So that he first solves it in a famous but unfortunate way, by the early doctrine of the Ideas. According to this theory he would seem to have suggested that there are indeed elements of likeness and unlikeness in any sensible fact; that ultimately we cannot tolerate this incompatibility; that the matter is solved if you suppose the element of sameness (or oneness) to derive itself from a transcendent idea of sameness, and in like manner for the quality of diversity.

But this is to say that, if we are to make sense of the universe, we must construct a logic of being, or a set of concepts, according to which the one is purely and separately one, and the many, many, and never the twain shall meet, except in the sensible order and dubiously even there. In the world of the senses (and of poetry!) there is an horrendous problem of intermixture; but not so in the world of Ideas; there all is startlingly clear; the boundaries of each Idea are sharply and comfortably cut off from every other; by means of the latter, we will have created an instrument to explain the simple unities of words (a rose is a rose is a rose) and of our clear internal concepts (which seem to represent only one quality of reality at a time). But we will not yet have explained the everyday, workaday world where a rose is red and many things besides, but still a rose, both many and one.

The later work of Plato (especially in the *Parmenides*) is far more complicated, and indicates far more finesse. He now sees that he has sidestepped the real problem. An extraordinary attempt follows to put the one and the many together in the world of a logic of being, and then to return to the sensible world to put them together there in logic, where they had always somehow or other been together in fact.

The result amounts to this, as clearly as I can put it in so short a space: [8]

Rather than have each order of things be marked by different situations, the sensible order by the unresolvable presence of contraries, that of the eternal or transcendent by the sorted out and pure separation of the contraries, each with its own sharp demarcations, Plato now sees that both orders are marked by the same structural problems. Wherever you have anything that is truly a one, whether it be a sensible, a number, a concept or a transcendent idea, you have two qualities, oneness and manyness, which must finally be resolved into a true *one*. This he achieved by his theory of "participation," according to the terms of which, only oneness, the principle of unity, truly *is*, while the many members of this unity derive themselves from this principle. Thus, in a reality of the sensible order (and this goes for any literary organism), there is an absolute fact called the one and a fact called the many which has everything it has by participating in "the one."

Thus it is no longer true that there are two contraries existing on the same level of being which demand to be put together by some bond or chain external to both. The *one* is not a dead, monotonous fact; it only becomes itself by articulating itself into many jointings and members, and it has not become itself until, in its advance, it has created the last member, the last jointing of itself. If it does not allow each member to become fully itself, then it does not itself become itself. And if it does not allow all the members of the unity to take up a certain intricate relationship among themselves, the same consequence will develop. But under no circumstances must we any longer suppose that there is a central core of content which is the unity structure, and a number of details which are irrelevant to that unity.

The one and the many are, therefore, one and the same thing. However, this does not allow us to suppose that *any* group of details can make a one. Nor must we conceive that the principle of unity descends as a unifying blanket over a set of details which already exist and which only need this rather dubious process of being unified. It is the one, the structural and structuralizing principle, which is fashioning and determining its own membership out of its own inward and creative resources.

And there is a sense in which the absolute point of unity in a thing is entirely and completely present in every detail. Let me suggest a metaphor for what I mean. Let us suppose that the human principle is scattering and making itself through the whole of a man. When it comes to the eyes, they are fully human eyes—the eyes of the Mona Lisa. No semi-human principle has shaped such eyes. Nothing else but humanity, and no mere fraction of that, could have produced the hair of Botticelli's Venus. And so with a pair of hands in prayer. And so with the helplessness of the assassinated figure of Marat as painted by David. Only the fully human could have produced so full a death, and this kind of helplessness.

That is, I think, why it is that the detail can explode with so much fullness in literature and can stagger the heart as though it were not only itself, but the whole of man. A movement of the finger or the lips can reverberate through all the levels of awareness of man because it can tell of all of these levels as they are present in the finger or the lips. There are lines in Synge's *Riders to the Sea* where the men are carrying the dead body of Bartley in on planks, and the water from the body leaves a line of wet upon the floor. It tells, as other lines do not, the whole pitiful story of the human race against all great bodies of water, and it gives us in a visual instant the story of all tragedy, of that which cannot be done by the finite when it confronts an infinite.

One may especially notice that there is no blurring of detail in an art that has such articulating causes and desires behind it. It has none of that blurring which Mr. Empson has noted as a quality of so many of the writers of the nineteenth century who were overwhelmed with the desire to produce a taste or an atmosphere ("They admired the poetry of previous generations, very rightly, for the taste it left in the head, and, failing to realize that the process of putting such a taste in the reader's head involves a great deal of work which does not feel like a taste in the head while it is being done, attempting, therefore, to conceive a taste in the head and put it straight on their paper, they produced tastes in the head which were in fact blurred, complacent, and unpleasing").[9] Plato himself would have been even more succinct; he would have said (and did) that we must not go too fast from the many to the one. And the saints would have known what all this means; for example, St. Ignatius, in whose case Father Jean Danielou suggests that much of the substance of his life might be contained in the phrase *ne negliger rien*, to neglect nothing. Finally, there is a magic half line in Canto XI of the *Purgatorio,* where in a blurred way ("like the oppression that a dream may breed"), Dante is reviewing the procession of the proud; suddenly the blur dissolves into clarity with the extraordinarily articulating phrase: "Each in his proper pain."

There are people who are afraid that the pattern, the taste, the atmosphere, will suffer from the emergence of the detail. But how can it if detail is the life of the pattern and is the pattern itself, and if every detail can in its own way sing with the whole of the pattern? There are those, reversely, who are afraid the detail, the freedom, the exalted unpredictability of the world and of the imagination will suffer from the pattern. E. M. Forster, in his *Aspects of the Novel,* has this worry very much on his mind. But who is to judge the nature and breadth of patterns save the genius of the individual writer (and after him the reader, of course)? Who is to judge of irrelevancy by foreordained rules? Some pedagogues do, but these are people who wish to keep the world as small as themselves; indeed, we would all like to do that, but we may as well put up with the brutal fact that it cannot be done, and it is the function of the writer to keep telling us exactly this. If he does this, he will be doing no more than delivering to us the constant message of tragedy, that we are not the measure of the real; and he will, though very often blindly and rebelliously, be repeating Dante ("In his will is our peace," not in the detail *our* rigid patterns insist upon).

If we not only admit but insist upon all this, then we very much have the right, on the other hand, to warn the imagination that it cannot break through into the full vision of reality by violence. This means, in the concrete of our present point, that we cannot break through to the ultimate secret of things by smashing away with a kind of hysteria at any single area of an organic, imaginative statement. We have said that any fragment can echo with the total meaning of a thing, but that does not mean details do not also have their limitations. We do not lessen the possibility of insight by respecting the latter; actually, we increase it. For this intense smashing away at detail only bruises the total intelligence, and is an obstacle to that suppleness of attack which is necessary for vision. The intent stare of the madman seems to penetrate right into the heart of the world. But actually we never say of him that he has imagination. He is fixed on one point and cannot free himself. The same is true of the scrupulous person.

The same is deadly and monotonously true of so much Hollywood art, in which the ten-minute closeup makes us hate the face we might have liked were it not for the desperate insistence of the director. Nor, obviously, is there anything wrong with the biological level of love. But to concentrate on it alone is to prevent again the total vision of love. So that here we must note a very fascinating principle. It is that sacrifice is more than a negative and ascetical principle of theology; it is also a very positive principle for epistemology and criticism and creativity. Surely the artist can seize totally upon our imaginations, as Poe can, with some clever intensity or violence, but then we will be like men who are not listening to the rest of what you say. The writer must first give up his grip before the reader will. "He who loses his soul shall find it" would seem to be a very good creative principle. It is also a fundamental principle of the analogical imagination.

ANALOGY

We have not been waiting for this deferred moment to say something about the analogical mind and imagination.[10] Rather, we have been picking up threads and strains of it as we have been moving along through this limited historical discussion. And we shall be paying no disrespect to Aristotle if we seem to skip him as we close the history and get to our goal. It seems to me that it is a grasp of his metaphysics which would be (more than the Poetics) of help to the artist or critic. But these are sufficiently contained or sublimated in the work of the later analogists to justify our not delaying on the specific contributions of Aristotelianism. Whereas the positive poetic theory of Plato has been very much neglected, or taken from unimportant places in the corpus of the dialogues.

Analogy is a metaphysical explanation of the structure of existence, indeed of all that exists. Let us suppose that we are being asked by it to watch the act of existence descending to shape the real world, to make it precisely what it is, down to the last bit of mud in actuality, down, the artist for his part might say, to the line of water that exploded into a flood in *Riders to the Sea*. By "act of existence" I mean nothing more—though that is everything—than that in the guts of a thing which makes it actuality itself and more than possibility.

As existence descends in the initial creative act and in all its later dynamic processes of becoming through space and time, it is articulated, jointed, membered, shaped according to all the forms of all the things that can be, of all the possibles. So many of these things we know already. But what yet shall be we do not know; that is only limited by the ocean of possibility itself, as the history of existence shall touch it in the unguessable days to come.

The act of existence descends analogously, *ana-logon,* "according to a proportion." The degree of existence is always measured by the degree of possibility, by the degree of fullness of being any possibility may receive. The form of a mouse can receive only so much. No one yet knows how much the form of man can hold. But the proportion is always one and the same and altogether unvarying. It is always a proportion of "existence is according to possibility." That has always been, and always shall be. It is an absolute invariant. All being is therefore one and the same, completely predictable and with a decision which never changes as it advances in its processes.

But let us closely examine the invariancy of this analogical idea of being over against the invariancy of a univocal idea. As the latter descends in its shaping and organizing function, it must eliminate everything in the members of a class

which make them really many and diverse. Or else it must
forfeit its invariancy, its sameness. Let me take the liberty of
repeating the diagram which described its operations.

The numbers represent the sum of differences in each
subject of a class which make it uniquely itself and mark it
off from every other subject. These numbers cannot enter into

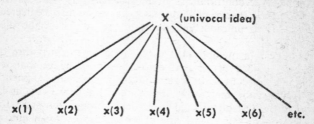

the constitution of the master point of unity, the univocal
idea of X. They are an intractable material for the latter.
There is nothing in the univocal which has to be changed in
order to take care of the entry of a new member into the
picture. Such entries do not force upon it any adaptive or
creative process. Its invariancy and type of decision are absolute.

But existence, as it descends, is analogous. It is never the
same act of existence. It is a completely new fact; it must be
new; for it must adapt itself completely to the new materials
which it confronts, adapting itself in its bone and heart to
the bone and heart of each new subject of being, each new
part of the total organism. So too with an analogical idea,
with our inward thinking about being. The work, the thinking
of it, is never done. The process of adaptation is eternal. We
can never come up with one logical core and say it will satisfy
the requirements of all the subjects. Only the proportion is
the same; but the two parts of the proportion are always
changing. The act of existence is always different; so too is
the possibility, the material into which it enters.

In other words, in an analogical organism of unity and its
epistemological counterpart, an analogical idea, every thing
in the subjects is altogether the same, and every thing altogether different. There is no "logic" or universal statement in
it. Its thinking is never done until the last member is found.
The new member obscures the total previous situation because it must be included in the idea on terms that are entirely personal to itself. Yet this new thing, with all its

differences, can be reduced to the terms of the proportion, and that without eliminating a little finger of it. In analogy, therefore, the process may be described by some such diagram as this:

With the line of unification adapting itself everywhere to the differentiating numbers. The consequence is that in the whole of this kind of cosmic pattern, in every step of it, there is absolute sameness and absolute diversification.

Now it is here that we come to a critical moment in the character of analogical thought. The critical question for us in this whole discussion has been: what is the relation of the contraries? How stands the same over against the different, the one over against the many? It is easy to see that in the case of univocal thinking it is a relationship of unqualified externality. But in analogy the relation is one of unqualified interpenetration. To put the matter tersely, the "same" contains its differences and does not have to go outside of itself to find them. Allow me to give an example. We may, but perhaps not too rigorously, define consciousness as an awareness of self. In the case of God, Who, being infinite and perfect, can have no divisions in Himself, the mind which knows in the act of self-consciousness and the mind that is known imply no separation of any kind into subject and object, no act of reflection or true bending back upon oneself.

But in human consciousness there is certainly some such division, no matter how shadowy the introspective act which grasps this inferior way of knowing or being present to the self. But here let us look intently, for here is the crux of the matter. What is this separateness and division in man of self as subject and self as object which differentiates his self-consciousness from that of God? It is precisely consciousness. It is the one original, *unifying* form which now steps in as the *differentiating* factor. The same and the different are caught up in one and the same act, whether the act be that of being or that of thought.

It is this identity of act between the contraries in analogy which makes both for its obscurity and its glory. Its obscurity: for it is impossible to abstract the same from the different so that they become two clearly demarcated univocal ideas. Its glory: for it is through this obscure but actual interpenetration that by living in the world of men, with all its weaknesses, we can live with knowledge in the world of God. We need not utterly change our ways and thoughts to know Him; we need not utterly jump out of our skins to get to Him. If analogy is a fact, then we need have no religious or imaginative resort to Manichaeanism. And the lines of Keats (Ever let the fancy roam/ Pleasure never is at home) begin to make much nonsense.

ANALOGY AND THE IMAGINATION

I do not wish to make any statement either apodictic or provocative about any smooth or unqualified transitions that may be made between analogical theory as it exists in metaphysics and as it may operate in the carved-out structures of the imagination. It is difficult not to hope that, for example, the work of the literary imagination will turn out to be not a propaedeutic to but a department of metaphysics, discovering or making analogies of being within the total structure of the analogy of being. But as these essays are unashamedly exploratory, I will leave it to far more knowledgeable metaphysicians than myself to scout out, confirm, or minimize the possibilities of these relationships. Actually there is no need to be concerned over the final, technical determination of this question. For one can always be certain that the literary man has much to learn from a truly existential metaphysics of analogy, and that the reverse is also true, even if philosophy may have to purify the findings or the makings of the artist.

Nevertheless, there *is* one technical point to be clarified before we go on. Philosophers who understand analogy are in the habit, correctly too, of insisting that analogy is not metaphor; on the other hand, I take it that there is a whole bevy of literary theorists who insist equally that poetry is a language of metaphor, and that metaphor is its very heart beat. Should we let this settle the issue, and should we therefore admit that literature is not analogical, or is, at any rate, in its metaphorical method, only one of the weakest forms of analogy? I think not.

For the debate should be held on more substantial grounds than this. The reason for saying this—a very brash reason, perhaps—is that I for one do not believe that metaphor is the very heart of poetic structures—unless we severely limit the idea of poetry. But for the sake, not of a quarrel but of fruitful debate, let us suggest here that metaphor may be the last and the least of the forms of the imagination. If it were the whole or the center of the latter, then the status of analogy in literature would be clear, but weak. For we know quite well that a metaphor, no matter what its power, is that kind of "same but different" relation to another thing in which the same can be quite clearly blocked off from the different. My God may very well be a mighty fortress, as the Lutheran hymn declares, but we also know very well that He is not a mighty fortress. Whereas when the analogist says that he knows with his mind and from his mind that God has a mind, he is not at all saying, despite the infinite differences, that it is of course also clear that God does not have a mind. It is this which makes the analogical imagination infinitely free in the distances it can cover with the forms it chooses and quite decisive in its fidelity to the forms chosen. Freedom and rigidity, the capacity for explosion into distance at the same time that there is an increasing articulation and actualizing of the exploding image. Mr. Tate has put the matter very rightly. Poetry *is* a matter of the creation of the widest extension in terms of the deepest intension. The only possible contribution I have suggested for his work here is the addition of some metaphysical notes which may give such critical ideas a further philosophical support.

With a substantial number of other people who know far more about the problem than myself, I should like to take the position that *action* is the soul of the literary imagination in all its scope and forms, and that metaphor either springs out of action as one of its finest fruits, or is itself one of its many forms.[11] It only remains to be added that the literary action gets farthest and goes deepest when it proceeds by way of analogy. It seems to me that I would go even further than Francis Fergusson in this direction—though I am not sure, so often do I have to correct myself about apparent small limitations in his putting of things. Therefore, in this spirit let it be said, for one thing, that it is difficult to understand his insistence that the distinction between plot and the deep human action of a play is fundamental. It is true enough that "plot" is *only* the literal level of the drama, and that it may be looked upon as a mere external level of movement, to be deepened by the insights proceeding from other and deeper levels of action. Yet it is also necessary to remember that, when all these other levels have been gained or added, it is the literal itself, that is to say, the plot, which has been deepened and illuminated for the content it always had, at least in potency. In saying this we are really laying the ground for the discussion, in our final chapter, of the fourfold level of biblical exegesis and for the most crucial point in that latter method. For I am convinced that according to its terms it is undoubtedly true that there are four levels of insight, the literal, moral, allegorical, and analogical, but that, even more importantly, there is also only one, and that the literal, which has been brought to complete illumination by the minds marching through all its possibilities, by marching indeed through a finite, according to the whole thesis of this book. We anticipate entirely therefore, but with good reason, if we now suggest that the fundamental problem still to be explored by the theologians, critics, and imaginative writers is the co-existence and identity of the four levels in the single literal level, *in una littera*.[12] But, as we shall see, medieval biblical exegesis was a version, within theological and historical areas, of analogical theory; so that we can afford to go on with our present subject: the prime fruitfulness, for the imagination, of proceeding by way of action, and analogical action.

In the *Oedipus* the plot seems quite simple, but is ultimately quite complicated. It *seems* to have a central core of action (the ironic search of Oedipus for the truth about him-

self) which seems to be illuminated, as from the outside of
Oedipus, by a corresponding search into themselves of other
characters. This is both true and not true. It is true. For
Oedipus the king is indeed searching for the pollution in the
land which is himself. He proceeds unknowingly to knowledge, as Dante does in the *Purgatorio,* through deadly sins
and movements of his own soul. Anger, suspicion, fear, pride
bring him closer and closer to a goal he would not, as they
brought Dante to a goal he would. At last comes the terrible
illumination of the meaning of his original actions, an illumination that is created by action as the heart of the poetic
process and further lighted by metaphor and song. But it is
also supported, this central coming to vision, by parallel and
analogous processions to self-knowledge. The idea of ironic
passage into insight, by means one would to an end one
would not, passes into the full reality of each sub-situation
and character and act without distorting the actuality of any
of these and without losing its own identity or face. Indeed,
it is by the dynamic interplay of these primary and secondary passages that the primary irony of Oedipus grows yet
greater, and reversely.

Not only does Oedipus look at an original friend (his early
acts and fortunes) and see now a horror and an enemy; but
so does every character in the play, within the exact cir-
cumference of his own intentions, character, and feelings.
The messenger from Corinth can at last look at his friendly
garrulity and see it for what it is and for what it has done;
the shepherd can see the horrible dynamism of his original
pity; Jocasta looks with what eyes now upon her courage
against the gods and upon her marriage-identity, and this occurs entirely according to the psychology of a woman; the
children see of whom they are the children, and they see as
children see, with their special pain and insight. "Each with
his proper pain," and irony. Each is a different and separate
world, but the differences have not moved out of the one
same ironic form by as much as an iota. It is a procession of
the same by creating differences out of the resources of
analogical difference. Therefore there is a double sense in
which we can use the old phrase, "the plot thickens." It can
be used in the sense of the pure external craftsmanship of
Scribe and Sarcey: The plot must get really tangled and move
toward real suspense. Or it can be used in the sense of
analogical thickness: the plot form moves into the differentiating thickness of reality.

Thus it is true that one vision re-enforces another, and this is the art of the *Oedipus*. A truly analogical idea crackles with light and makes other things crackle with the same and yet with their own light. Bring the ironic self-knowledge of Jocasta back to Oedipus and his own insight will burn more terribly still. Bring these two forms to the children and they will crackle with the immeasurable terror of a child. Mr. Fergusson has put the matter brilliantly with his analysis of the play within a play of Hamlet. By itself it is the most fragile, surface, melodramatic kind of plot, but bring it in touch with each conscience on the stage and it seems to have the infinite capacity to light up the special detail of each crime's conscience in a special way.

Thus analogy tests the conscience of all being, and its own action produces a similar but unique movement in everything. I would ask the reader to make the test of bringing the crushed heart of the mother Maurya in *Riders to the Sea* in close contact with that line of water on the floor. Until that moment of meeting, or in any other play, it is a dead thing, or at most a metaphor of the sea awaiting the reception of the life of action, and analogical action. But test this conscience with the presence of this heart and it immediately becomes all the seas of the world crushing all the women of the world who have ever borne a child. Or even if it is a moment of complete, inactive passivity, as in that moment in Camus' *The Fall*, when the conscience has not heeded the cry of a soul upon a bridge; let it then be confronted with any counterpart of that passivity, that dead, irresponsible no, and the non-being will lash back at the conscience with the most savage action known to man. What incredible ironies there are in this novel for those who wish to see. Really, it is a strong, almost bitter satire by an existentialist on a type of "system" and language, on excessive uses of "the human condition" and "we are all in the same boat," united in sameness at last, in a sameness of sin by which we overcome our difference, our lowliness, and therefore our sin, and thus recover our romantic pre-eminence through winning to the status of judge-penitent of the whole world. If we were to use the language of this chapter, *The Fall* seems to be an ironic use of analogy to destroy the principle of difference and the conscience. To escape its sin, it applies its sin to the conscience of every friend, and the sins leap out.

But in the end it has not worked, this attempt to lose our unique sin in the sameness of all sin; the cry on the bridge has not been overcome. If Camus himself, who is an honest man, were to use the language of analogy, he might say that we cannot, if *we* are honest, so lose ourselves in the same as to lose difference. We cannot win the game by anonymity; we cannot win it by becoming somebody else; we cannot by power or dream make the done deed be undone. We cannot accept a system of universal guilt in which the individual and individual sin do not survive.

It is no small wonder that it is in Christ we come to the fullest possible understanding of what analogy means in the fullest concrete, the facing relentlessly into the two poles of the same and the different and the interpenetrating reconciliation of the two contraries. He who is the Lord of all things is the lord of the imagination. As a good artist, and not an aesthete, he therefore knew what he was talking about when he said: If I be lifted up upon the cross (in complete isolation and differentiated uniqueness, without anonymity, without friends), I shall draw all things to me (in sameness, in love, in a universal Church). It is the universal teaching of the Church that it was itself born, not out of the Greeks, not out of the anonymous mind, not out of the chameleon imagination, but out of His blood, at a set hour, in a set place.

In that place and hour was brought about the wedding of the altogether unique and different Thing (down to the last drop of blood) and the ultimate society of the Church (the same). These two things, by virtue of a very great mystery, cannot be separated from each other. And this, their common mystery of identity, stands as the model for every analogical act of the imagination. On the highest plane of history it gave us complete warrant for thinking that we can advance into all the wells of specialty, the definite and the free, without for one moment abandoning society or unity. Philosophy can only speculate about things already done. Theology and Christ can act, and thus give us the ground for all later analogizing. Let us turn to these two—Christ, and theology.

NOTES

1. It is often said that it was the great task of the sensitive genius, critical and poetic, of Coleridge to bring these opposites together, to effect a real *reconciliatio oppositorum*, a unity of the same and different; yet one reads Coleridge and a great hesitation must remain. We cannot be quite sure what he has given us, whether it is a truly esemplastic and analogical im-

agination or whether it is not finally some "lonely center of consciousness," living apart from the learning, growing drive of the whole personality into reality, rechanging all realities to the frighteningly isolated genius of this separated corner of the soul. Let me cite here a section of Donald Stauffer's introduction to *Selected Poetry and Prose of Coleridge* (New York: Modern Library, 1951), p. XXVI:

Always there is this lonely center of consciousness, with vastness beyond. . . . The child at the center (or the damsel or the wanderer) is Coleridge, or his shaping imagination. This intention shapes the image of his secret thought: a living, sometimes frighteningly piteous, focus of consciousness, filled with the desire to concentrate the universe, vast shifting phantom though it is, within that one focus.

May I call the attention of the reader to somewhat the same problem as it occurs in the attempt of the modern poetic consciousness to reduce all the different historic points of *time* to the basis of its own secret genius.

The question must again be asked about Coleridge: With what metaphysical support is he warranted in saying the following, "Imagination . . . reveals itself in the balance or reconciliation of opposite or discordant qualities: of sameness, with difference; of the general, with the concrete; the idea, with the image; the individual, with the representative; the sense of novelty and of freshness, with old and familiar objects"? *Biographia Literaria*, II, pp. 254-255. The reader may wish to take advantage of the bibliographical note given for this critical text from Coleridge by Wimsatt & Brooks (*op. cit.*, p. 396, n.2). Perhaps it is legitimate to suggest here that the emphasis in the 18th century on the idea of the reconciliation of opposites (cf. Wimsatt & Brooks, p. 395) is not at all an original romantic construction but a weaker attempt to do what had been handled long before and with much more metaphysical nicety by a long philosophical tradition of the West. The attempt of the latter to "reconcile" or unify the mind and the thing is also just as valiant as the work of romanticism in this direction.

2. Robert Penn Warren, "Pure and Impure Poetry," *The Kenyon Critics,* ed. John Crowe Ransom (New York: World, 1951), pp. 17-42.

3. For a bibliographical note on this phase in the critical position of I. A. Richards cf. *Critiques and Essays in Criticism 1920-1948,* ed. Robert W. Stallman (New York: Ronald Press, 1949), p. 333, n.3.

4. John Crowe Ransom, "Ivor Winters: The Logical Critic," *The Southern Review* (Winter 1941), pp. 562-569.

5. *Ibid.*, p. 582.

6. Cited by Warren, *op. cit.*, p. 33. Cf. Frederick A. Pottle's treatment of the problem of pure poetry in his chapter "Pure

Poetry in Theory and Practice," *The Idiom of Poetry* (Ithaca, N.Y.: Cornell University Press: 1946), pp. 89-107.

7. Warren, *op. cit.*, p. 33.

8. These pages are a partial summary of an argument of my own on the meaning of Plato's *Parmenides: An Approach to the Metaphysics of Plato through the Parmenides* (Washington, D. C.: Georgetown University Press, 1959), pp. 235-250.

9. William Empson, *Seven Types of Ambiguity* (New York: Meridian, 1955), p. 22.

10. It is so difficult within the space of this section to try to buttress our analysis of analogy by references to texts and technical commentaries that I have decided to insert a special bibliographical supplement on the problem at the end of the book.

11. Against the idea of the essentially poetic imagination as one of action, it is difficult not to yield to the temptations of citing the following from Gertrude Stein:

. . . what is the vocabulary of which poetry absolutely is. It is a vocabulary entirely based on the noun as prose is essentially and determinately and vigorously not based on the noun. Poetry is concerned with using, with abusing, with losing, with wanting, with denying, with avoiding, with adorning, with replacing the noun. It is doing that always doing that, doing that and doing nothing but that. Poetry is doing nothing but using, losing, refusing and pleasing and betraying and caressing nouns. That is what poetry does, *that* is what poetry has to do no matter what kind of poetry it is. And there are a great many kinds of poetry.

When I said
"A rose is a rose is a rose is a rose." And then later made that into a ring I made poetry and what did I do I caressed completely caressed and addressed a noun. Now let us think of poetry and poetry all poetry and let us see if this is not so. Of course it is so anybody can know that.—

Lectures in America (Boston: Beacon, 1957), p. 233.

12. Cf. Walter J. Burghardt, S.J., "On Spiritual Exegesis," *Theological Studies* (March 1950), pp. 78-116, especially p. 105.

7 The Theological Imagination

At this stage of our investigations we begin to make explorations into other possible dimensions of the literary imagination. Now we raise an important question: does the literary imagination have a theological dimension? The important thing is to keep our minds open to the possibility. Otherwise we are not free.

Our thinking and imagining will be more fruitful here if we remember two things: 1. over against every naïve and romantic assumption to the contrary, there is no such thing as a purely spontaneous and autonomous literary image, absolutely "creative" and free of metaphysics or theology; 2. theology itself is not transcendental in the pejorative sense. For it, the "short way" and the "long way," the absolute specificity of human experience and the "meaning" of it all, are not two different things. Theology gets into the interior of our images and is not an exploiting appendage.

In this chapter we introduce the vocabulary of "levels of being." The collapse of such an idea has often been disastrous in the order of subjectivity and literary sensibility. We analyze three different major images on different levels, all the way from the immediately human to the theological: the image of man, the image of time, the image of ritual movement. An attempt is made to describe the unfortunate results for the imagination when it introduces various acts of dissociation into these levels.

The Four Quartets is a special subject. Apart from every purely conceptual and formally theological idea, its two central images of immobility and intersection are found to be eminently theological in their dimensions.

THIS HAS BEEN an attempt at an inductive analysis, probing for clues as to the possible dimensions of the imagination, not first on grander supernatural levels but rather on the plane of those immediate images which are the stuff of literary sensitivity and which challenge the latter for a reaction, for a dead giveaway of the personality, the spirituality and the instinctive theology lying underneath them.

Thus I have proposed testing the literary imagination against the definite and limited images of human life; against the image of time; against the ultimate seriousness of the tragic moment and the funny moment of comedy; against Prince Hal and Falstaff, the void, the night, silence and Hollywood. And we have been asking one constant question. How stands this imagination against the fact of limitation? For, after all, this matter is crucial; we limited human beings have no other problem twenty-four hours of the day. In reply we have been trying to say that, far from our limits being only *a problem and a concern* for the imagination, they are also its *center,* to be seized upon as a fruitful and a generative thing.

I should like now to discuss the relation of theology to the imagination in a more specific and formal way.

THE "AUTONOMOUS" IMAGINATION

There is an important sense in which the life of every imagination is compact with theology, that is to say, with some theology or other. We like to think that there are such things as pure images, issuing forth from the spontaneity and creativity of the artist's mind, and we often insist that these creative images have their own autonomous rights, rights which are prior, at least in time, to any extrinsic insertion of the "thinking" mind into them as a buttressing or critical force.

But this doctrine of a purely creative image, unadulterated by any form of metaphysics or theology, is a very dubious one. John Crowe Ransom, in his essay "Poetry: a Note on Ontology," has taken one of the purest little poems of Imagism (a poetic practice which thought it could reduce the image or the thing to pure thingness) and has indicated that the strictest attempts in this direction are unsuccessful.[1] T. S. Eliot, speaking in a somewhat different vein, has expressed a similar doubt: "The process of increasing self-consciousness—or, we may say, of increasing consciousness of language—has as its theoretical goal what we may call *la poésie pure*. I believe it to be a goal that cannot be reached. I believe that poetry is only poetry so long as it preserves some 'impurity' in this sense: that is to say, so long as the subject matter is valued for its own sake." [2] This statement is used for our own purposes, but let it be hoped here that our analysis of analogical thought has been helpful with the eternal problem of "subject-matter." If there is no such thing as a pure poetic image, neither in any important sense is there such a thing as pure ideas in poetry, ideas which would not have to shift and zigzag and proportionalize themselves to images and actions, or at least take a special life from their birth out of the latter.

This may be all very well and good, many a reader will say, and all one would have to do by way of countering the relations we have been exploring is to admit with Freud that it is quite difficult to get over the persistent theological neurosis of the whole human race. Moreover, the objection might continue, with all this chatter about the theological penetration of our images, the theological imagination ends up in an insuperable dilemma; for it destroys the very possibility of autonomy and the somehow autonomous existence of every fact in this world. A rose is a rose is a rose and that is all there is to that. Except to add that such autonomy is not only a subjective passion of the contemporary intelligence but also has a profound factual and ontological foundation. If we cannot keep theology out of things anywhere, might run the climax of the charge, then we are ourselves Manichaeans and are discarding the very substance of the achievement of contemporary civilization.

We must not blink at the fact that this is a very strong and healthy position, and that, if anything, our own paraphrase of it has diluted rather than magnified its strength. The only real trouble is that it is generally too content to remain within its points of power. The idea of autonomy is a real and great achievement. We all realize that it has been an incalculably serviceable weapon in the development of science, literary criticism, psychology, and has even been of tremendous help in such a more theological domain as that of Church-State relations. But if the autonomous mind and imagination are content to stay within the present limits of its achievement, it will take on all the vices of the equivocal mind and imagination, and will continue to generate diseases which otherwise it would not.

Let me begin the elaboration of this criticism of the *present* status of the passion for autonomy by choosing to remain for the moment within the area of "subjectivity." By this I mean to suggest that it is better not to rush too quickly at the perennial philosophical debate which revolves around the question of the levels of being, the levels of a rose or any other "fact." Plato, I take it, was the first to speculate to the effect that for every level of cognition there is a corresponding level of being that is known. If he were speaking the later language of an analogical thinker, he might tell us, for example, that there is a fact called "society" or community, but that this fact has a gradated existence; there is a society which exists on the simplest human level of the biology and the tissues of sex; there are widening and horizontal forms of society, which achieve their existence out of the stuff of familial, economic and political life; there are also vertical forms of the same fact which drive the soul into higher and higher (or, if you will, deeper and deeper) expressions of communion.

The highest or deepest of all these you may call union with God, but I call it the Church, because the Catholic imagination does not force me to imagine that at the end I must free myself from all human society to unite myself with God. Rather, it helps me to imagine that once I have embarked on a good thing with all its concreteness (here it is society), I can and must carry it with me all the way into the heart of the unimaginable.

On the other hand it is hard to think otherwise than that the Protestant imagination sometimes seems to conceive society to be a necessary evil, to be endured on all the lower levels of being, good to the next to the last drop, but to be abandoned with indecent haste before true insight or the face of the living God. It stands over against the theological imagination as Mallarmé stands to poetry (*his* goal was to destroy it). The Protestant seems, at any rate, to wish to stand in nakedness before God outside of society and often seems to make God a silence and an abyss. But He is not a silence; even *He* could not know Himself save through the Word; and are we better than God that we can know Him save through Christ; but the Church is Christ. If some unity among men is not the final word, we may as well give up all imagining and all poetry now, and love with it. For in this hypothesis we should have to take off all imagining at the end in His presence, as Jacob took off his shoes, and love would be an end but not a way. No, the mysteries of Christianity are too complicated for that kind of simplicity. We do not use the finitude of man as a final jumping-off place for our contact with the infinite; we enter more and more deeply into man, into the fact of society until we come to that depth or height which is Christ; this we can call the Christic point of society, beyond which we need not go farther. For God's "imagination" from the beginning could not and did not go farther.

Admittedly, then, there are levels of being, and certainly each level has its right to separate expression. Here the idea of autonomy can very well take an unalterable stand. But let it not then create the terms for a specious debate in terms of which it would fight monotonously for facts over against merely verbal and allegorical extensions of facts as executed by a "celestial" theology. It is true that a fact is a fact is a fact, and a rose is a rose is a rose. But the true debate is: what is the fact and what is its true dimension? We have insisted that the mysteries of Christianity are a penetration deep into the fact of man, all the way into his Christic center; and that where many dig into the same center a Church is made. It is not at all a matter of constructing levels outside of the fact. The levels are proposed as deeper borings into actuality. If the maturer biblical exegetes of an earlier age were using our language and had our controversies on their hands, they might very well have said that every spiritual exegesis of a fact is not an extrinsic appendage but a deeper boring into the literal level of exegesis. But we will have more of that problem in the next chapter. Our business now is to recall that we agreed to a temporary abandonment of the real truth of the levels of the Christian mysteries. The question we might first ask ourselves is this:

What happens, we might say in a purely clinical way, if, in effect, every theory of levels of being is surrendered? What are the results in the way of pure subjectivity? What are the subjective diseases generated by this new situation?

What first happens—and it has already happened—is a flattening out of the orders of human sensibility, the orders of what we might call human reaction to facts. "Flattening out" is a mild phrase, for some critics have described the new situation under the words *no sensibility* or *no reaction at all*. It was this condition which Eliot undertook to project in *The Waste Land*. There is much talk in certain sections of that poem, but the talk is (deliberately) chatter and mean-

ingless. There is "the hot water at ten./ And if it rains, a
closed car at four." And there is "nothing again nothing,"
no knowing and no remembering. And there is again the lady
who indulges in the biology and the tissues of sexual society; sensibility is dead in the upper levels of her soul; the
once deeper fact is not there to delight or torture her with
its echoes in other levels of her self. "When lovely woman
stoops to folly and/ Paces about her room again, alone,/
She smooths her hair with automatic hand,/ And puts a
record on the gramophone." And there is the immersion in
time: *Hurry up please it's time*.

THE SURFACES OF LIFE

In the remaining pages of this chapter I shall ask the
reader to share my musings over various aspects of the flat-
tened-out fate of three broadly important "facts." They are:
1. the general image of man himself, whether he is a multi-
dimensioned reality or no; 2. the phenomenon of time, and
how slowly we should fly to "eternity" before we give up the
probing of the levels of time; and 3. the phenomenon of
ritual movement, whether again we do not abandon this natural instinct for ritual with indecent haste in the name of
the dubious glory of isolated sensibility. I fervently wish
that other writers would explore the status of other facts
among us. This kind of task must be as endless as life and
facts themselves, and I have only chosen these three as
examples, though they are rather central. To go on from
there, with detail and insight, would seem to me to be one of
the important functions of a creative criticism that could get
very close to being poetry itself.

1. DISSOCIATION IN MAN

It is with complete deliberation and forethought that I
choose in the following pages to deal with the dissociative
habit in so far as it occurs in two *Christian* writers like Eliot
and Greene. For we who believe in a Christian way are a
little too apt to think that the problem of dissociation and
the inability to move in a related way through the various
levels of being occur only outside ourselves. I would hold
that this is somewhat naïve and that we will be helped rather
than hurt by an increased awareness of the degree to which

we are ourselves vulnerable to the rather overwhelming imaginative ills of our time.

As for Eliot, there is one central point at which I am compelled to question him, and this is done with as much grace and courtesy as a great writer commands. For he has himself tried notably to reconstruct our damage in his later poetry, and there is the suspicion abroad that he has failed in several notable respects. But grace is demanded in saying this for the simple reason that we have all failed. (Allen Tate, for one, has noted how much Catholic poets have also broken down in the face of the problem of sensibility.)

In *The Waste Land* Eliot was giving us an ironic picture of the desert of our time, but in *The Cocktail Party* it has seemed to me that he is unhappily giving us a bit of a waste land of his own. My criticism is somewhat indirect and amounts to saying that this is a good play but it would have been nice if the author had written an entirely different piece. At any rate, my suggestion is that the play has as its problem the desert of human love, and there are two solutions to two human thirsts in it. One woman is sent back by her psychiatrist to the monotony and dross of her human love, and the other takes up a divine and contemplative vocation. But the psychiatrist speaks truer than he knows in saying that each is but another form of loneliness, an inferior and a superior desert. One is tempted to wish that it had been the same woman who had taken up the two vocations in the one act and the one situation.

One has no right seriously to ask that the writer should have written another play, but this second would have been the real problem of the people; we do not have the right to give to the latter a solution which is only tolerable, if deceptively, as a solution for intellectuals. As levels of being the finite and the infinite are very frequently in dissociation among us, and we do not help the matter by introducing a Christian act of dissociation.

Or let us look at the case of Graham Greene. We have earlier seen that in *The Heart of the Matter* Scobie is a classical example of the defeat and radical torment of man. All Scobie does is stand outside of the finite, totally outside of himself, and desperately pray that God will accept his damnation as a pleasing gift. But then came Greene's novel *The End of the Affair*. In *The Heart of the Matter* he had been sketching the situation of much of the modern imagination, not his own. Now, however, he seems bent on a recoup, and that in Catholic terms, and he too fails to put things together (again, who are we to accuse him? but analyzing him may help us to understand ourselves).

In this novel we were given a subtle if unconscious demonstration of the Manichaean way. I would briefly suggest that in it there are two decisive halves, one which represents the failure and breakdown of human love, the other its achievement on the divine plane and without any relation to the human. The divine love is in no way achieved in the same act as the human; the latter does not lead to the divine; the divine, once achieved, does not fortify the human. This is said despite the difficulty that the affair is adulterous and of itself has no such relation. For the tones of the book are such that the liaison is not primarily adulterous, but to be taken as the attempt of man as such to find love. The second half of *The End of the Affair* is consumed by a long Augustinian dialogue with God on the part of the woman. This is a solution, indeed, this divine love, but it is not a solution which passes through the eye of a Beatrice, or the life of time. It leaps out of time. It is not a human way. One has the feeling that Greene has written a Catholic novel that is more Catholic than Catholicism.

2. DISSOCIATION IN TIME

One lesson we can draw from all this is that, in all our attempts to analyze and correct the gradations of the collapse of sensibility in our time, we must all appraise ourselves lest, always partially blind to our own involvement in the contemporary story, we overshoot the mark. Dissociation is not helped by anything but true association, and we always have to question exactly when we have the latter. And as it is possible that we are only at the beginning of the way up, we may not get it very often. In talking of the *Four Quartets*, let us turn from the problem of human relations to that of time and human sensibility about it. The remarkable imagination of Eliot is now dealing with this very sharp area of trouble. No one is better equipped to reproduce the problem for the bloodstream of the mind through the resources of poetry. The problem seems to be that we are immersed in time and are flattened down to its dimensions:

Time past and time future/Allow but a little consciousness.
To be conscious is not to be in time . . .
Distracted from distraction by distraction.

Men and bits of paper, whirled by the cold wind
That blows before and after time,
Wind in and out of unwholesome lungs
Time before and time after.
Eructation of unhealthy souls
Into the faded air, the torpid
Driven on the wind that sweeps the gloomy hills of London . . .

Ridiculous the waste sad time
Stretching before and after.

. . . as, when an underground train, in the tube, stops too long
          between stations
And the conversation rises and slowly fades into silence
And you see behind every face the mental emptiness deepen
Leaving only the growing terror of nothing to think about;
Or when, under ether, the mind is conscious but conscious of
          nothing—

Men's curiosity searches past and future
And clings to that dimension. But to apprehend
The point of intersection of the timeless
With time, is an occupation for the saint.

Or else the poet knows also that men are already swept, in
the temporal sequence of their diseases, into new generations
who have the taste of the abyss of anxiety, who know the
terror of a larger time, the time of the sea and the time of an
incredible history of the race before and after:

  The distant rote in the granite teeth,
  And the wailing warning from the approaching headland
  Are all sea voices, and the heaving groaner
  Rounded homewards, and the seagull:
  And under the oppression of the silent fog
  The tolling bell
  Measures time not our time, rung by the unhurried
  Ground swell, a time/Older than the time of chronometers . . .

These are some of the problems of the poem, the flatness of
the small time and the terror of the new; and the question
of the poem, though it is not a conceptual question, seems
to be, what about it, what shall we do, what else is there,
what else is there?

If I at all question the answers (they are not conceptual
answers, but come from the refined bloodstream of a great
Christian poet), it is not before considerable hesitation. For
the time of Eliot is most certainly not the time of Baudelaire,
of Proust or Poe. His sense of time is ever so much more
subtle. He knows that only through time is time conquered. He knows that the moment, as lived by men for
good or evil, is more than an isolated moment; rather, it
carries the weight of tradition and all the past and future,

> Not the intense moment
> Isolated, with no before and after,
> But a lifetime burning in every moment
> And not the lifetime of one man only
> But of old stones that cannot be deciphered.

He knows that time is the preserver, and that if we know
more than the past it is the past we know for all that.
Like St. Paul ("Leaving behind the things that are past")
he also has the sense that all things are new,

> Fare forward, travellers! . . .
> You are not the same people who left that station
> Or who will arrive at any terminus . . .

And the nature of language itself, and of poetry, must par-
ticipate in the same surge of the same history, so that Dante's
figure of Casella can also be seen in this modern version of a
divine comedy, chasing the poet relentlessly on and away
from his momentary conquest of time:

> Every phrase and every sentence is an end and a beginning.
> Every poem is an epitaph. And any action
> Is a step to the block, to the fire, down the sea's throat
> Or to an illegible stone: and that is where we start.[8]

But here perhaps is the beginning of my difficulty. For it is
hard to say no to the impression, if I may use a mixture of my
own symbols and his, that the Christian imagination is
finally limited to the element of fire, to the day of Pentecost,
to the descent of the Holy Ghost upon the disciples. The revelation of eternity and time is that of an *intersection*,

> But to apprehend
> The point of intersection of the timeless
> With time, is an occupation for the saint—

It seems not unseemly to suppose that Eliot's imagination (and is not this a theology?) is alive with points of *intersection* and of *descent*. He seems to place our faith, our hope, and our love, not in the flux of time but in the *points* of time. I am sure his mind is interested in the line and time of Christ, whose Spirit is his total flux. But I am not so sure about his imagination. Is it or is it not an imagination which is saved from time's nausea or terror by points of intersection? [4] There is his concern for

> . . . the hardly, barely prayable
> Prayer of the one Annunciation.

There is the dubiously temporal fascination of the poem for

. . . the still point of the turning world . . .

I can only say, *there* we have been: but I cannot say where. And I cannot say, how long, for that is to place it in time.

To be conscious is not to be in time . . .

Everything that is good is annunciation and epiphany (and we may note here the altogether understandable poetic passion for epiphany in our day); there are

> hints and guesses,
> Hints followed by guesses . . .

> The moments of happiness—not the sense of well-being
> Fruition, fulfillment, security or affection,
> Or even a very good dinner, but the sudden illumination—

> right action is freedom
> From past and future also.

> Here the impossible union
> Of spheres of existence is actual,
> Here the past and future
> Are conquered and reconciled . . .

> For most of us there is only the unattended
> Moment, the moment in and out of time,

The distraction fit, lost in a flash of sunlight,
The wild thyme unseen, or the winter lightning
Or the waterfall, or music heard so deeply
That it is not heard at all, but you are the music
While the music lasts.

. . . This is the use of memory:
For liberation—not less of love but expanding
Of love beyond desire, and so liberation
From the future as well as the past.

There seems little doubt that Eliot is attracted above all by
the image and the goal of immobility, and that in everything
he seeks for approximations to this goal in the human order.
"Love is itself unmoving." There is the violin, and we are the
music while the music lasts, and the perpetual stillness of
the Chinese jar, and the caught measure of the dance that
does not seem to advance as the dance should. There is the
detachment, as this poem understands it, of St. John of the
Cross. Above all, there is this definition of love as "itself
unmoving." Now this latter definition may be all very true,
and capable of sharp substantiation from, let us say, St.
Thomas. But it is also only partially true, according to the
partialities of all human language, and capable of sharp addition, also from St. Thomas. For he tells us that God is act,
and that everything is perfect in so far as it is in act.

At this point one may very well ask what right we have
to impose an abstract metaphysics upon the spontaneous
images of the poet. But to this we have already given several
answers in passing. For in the first place there is no such
thing as an abstract metaphysics; it is composed of images,
but these are *composed* according to the metaphysics of the
analogy of being; in the second place and more importantly,
I do not believe that there is such a thing as a purely spontaneous poetic image, free of the participating creativity of
metaphysics and theology. Actually, there is no point in the
soul so innocent that it is untouched by metaphysical and
theological instincts and conflicts; therefore, our images are
always and already going one way or the other. There is only
a doubtful refuge from this fact in the aesthetic of modern
poetry.

The readers of Eliot will have to find out what shapes and
directions their own imaginations take. One hypothesis I would
lay down about his is that, with relation to time and its prob-

lems, his own poetic images show a tendency to keep bouncing and leaping off this line in the direction of "eternity" and all its analogues. It does not evince a native inclination to pursue the possibilities of the line itself. Some possible evidence has been adduced for the validity of this impression. With a little less certainty on the writer's part, one last item will be suggested. Though in another context the poet tells us that here and now does not matter, he tells us even more strongly, and in a more conclusive part of the poem, that our precise place and moment are the precious thing. Nothing more than this would seem to come closer to some of the main propositions of our own essays.

> There are other places
> Which also are the world's end, some at the sea jaws.
> Or over a dark lake, in a desert or a city—
> But this is the nearest, in place and time,
> Now and in England.
>
> Here, the intersection of the timeless moment
> Is England and nowhere. Never and always.

It is the word "nearest" that is interesting here. What does it mean? It could possibly mean that this place and time where we stand are nearest to us. But this would surely be a tautology, pretty much like saying that the nearest is the nearest is the nearest. Very likely what is being said is that it is the nearest to "eternity." Whereas, if we accept a dramatic and constructive view of time, it would seem much truer to say that it is nearest to the next moment in time. This is not meant to be subtle or ironic, for the matter is as simple as can be and as simple as that. But, you might very well say, is it not better to leap off the line into any approximation of eternity, or at any rate meet it vertically at the point of the line, than to continue on our horizontal pain with the rest of the "time-ridden faces"? Perhaps it would be, but actually it is impossible. And here I would recall some of the poem's opening lines,

> What might have been is an abstraction
> Remaining a perpetual possibility
> Only in a world of speculation.

No, what we must do is go along with the time-ridden faces. For they are at least on the right track and dealing with the right fact. We are constitutionally committed to the structures of temporality, and the major reason for most of the pain therein, for the boredom and the terror, is that at the moment we are historically committed to but one level of it. Jumping out of our human facts will not help at all, and will produce nothing but further strains. The only answer, as in every case, would seem to be to deepen the fact and its possible levels, to enter more deeply into it. And that will be done only by adding the dimension of Christic time. What that means may be gathered from the materials suggested in an earlier chapter about the identity of process involved in the humanistic and Christic penetrations of time throughout the *Spiritual Exercises* of St. Ignatius.

The phases of the life of man are the mysteries of man. The phases of the life of Christ are the mysteries of Christ. But it is the time of man which He re-explored. As St. Gregory tells us, the first Adam was constituted in grace and insight *at the point of achievement* of both, but the new Adam takes as his instrument, not the point of achievement, but the whole temporal process. Eliot says that the poetry, the process, does not matter, but the poetry and the process do matter (we have said that poetry is an action) and, like the age of Christ itself over against the first age of man, it must be considered a superior instrument. God is ironic, and He will not be beaten at His own game, and His game is time.

Thus his victory over Satan is internal and complete, not a victory that is extrinsic and Manichaean. His Son is the Sun, but the course of this Sun is through man. Above all, He is a bridegroom (*et ipse tamquam sponsus procedens a thalamo suo*) and an athlete (*exultavit ut gigas ad currendam viam*) running with joy (*desiderio desideravi*) through the whole length and breadth of the human adventure (*a summo caelo egressio ejus usque ad summum ejus*). He marches to the ultimate of the finite (*usque ad mortem*). Wherefore he has been exalted and every knee shall bow to Him, of all the things that are in heaven or on earth or under the earth. And this is not merely a mark of an external reward for suffering and obedience; it is the perfect sign and accomplishment of the mysteries or stages of human life, that they are, on a level much more intense than ever before, an intrinsic path to the infinite. We miss the point if we only say that Christ is the gate and do not also add that man is the gate. It is our recurring mystery of more than one level in the one act and in the one fact. The single taste is the only taste which can water the waste land. Dissociated tastes, examples of which I have earlier essayed in the case of Eugene O'Neill, and here in the case of Eliot, can only produce on the one hand a further disgust for the mysteries of man and on the other the most tenuous gnostic contacts with the mysteries of God. We have begun to settle for this kind of contractual arrangement.

But John Donne had not yet so settled. This is the way he contemplates the sick room where he may die:

> I joy that in these straights I see my west;
> For though their currents yield return to none,
> What shall my west hurt me? As west and east
> In all flat maps (and I am one) are one,
> So death doth touch the resurrection.[5]

And he reaches great identities in one single taste, the taste of the sweat of man and the blood of Christ:

> Look Lord, and find both Adams met in me;
> As the first Adam's sweat surrounds my face,
> May the last Adam's blood my soul embrace.[6]

3. DISSOCIATION, RITUAL, AND RITUAL DRAMA

Let me give a third example of a fact which, if reduced to but one level of existence, can produce the most disturbing repercussions in the human person. I am thinking of the instinctive drive in the soul toward ritual. This drive toward common movement and ritual existence is one of the most powerful movements in the soul of man. If it is choked off and denied on the deepest and religious levels of existence, as indeed it has been, it will concentrate the whole of itself on the most superficial levels of life, the immediately social, and will end in becoming an absolute, a parody of itself and of its own dignity. Whereas, if we were really united at the bedrock of our natures, most of the pressures toward the kind of conformism that all men really hate would be enormously lessened.

The fact is that these pressures come from the inside of us and are not really being satisfied at the more vital points of the soul. Romantic rebellion is always the too obvious counterpole to the kind of cheap, overgrown ritualism which besieges us, but it is no solution; in fact it only intensifies the difficulty. The thought I have in mind, not at all a reproachful but an analytical thought, is that it has been the collapse of the idea of the Church in our civilization that has driven us into our present social rites. Gimmick ritual has necessarily been substituted for the real thing. But this process is true not only of the world of technology and the mass media; it is also terribly true for many developments within the contemporary literary imagination as they occur within the souls of the intellectuals.

One thing we may be sure of. The achievements and the distortions within man's search for common movement will go on to the end of time. And so will the conversation about and the work toward a religious and ritual theatre. None of us, I dare say, can really believe any longer the facile judgment that ritualism was an early and primitive beginning for the theatre in the West, that we know too much, now feel too much, are now too human, have too great a burden of sophistication, to recover earlier situations. We are all getting a bit weary of settling essential matters by mere tricks of vocabulary, and this use of words like "primitive" and "sophisticated" happens to be one of the tricks. The rhythm of the facts changes too easily for that. What was primitive becomes sophisticated a generation later, and vice versa.

The historical fact not often enough noticed is that *Quem Queritis,* the simplest and earliest piece in the liturgical theatre of the tenth century, was already surrounded by a context of symbolism, movement and architecture that had taken a thousand years of sophistication and toil for the West to produce. Now we have somewhat the opposite general situation: our plays are for the most part highly "sophisticated" pieces that appeal only to the "intellectual" areas of society, but they could hardly have a more miserable and more primitive context, architecturally and socially, within which to operate. There is no general style of life, in the highest and best sense of that phrase, which the theatre can call upon outside of itself as one of its natural resources. So far as real movement and manners are concerned, our playwrights are completely on their own, for the simple but tragic reason that we too are on our own, unless indeed we wish to submit to the style of no-style—that there be no ritual in life.

An interesting example of the dramatist's problem is presented by *He Who Must Die*. My own reaction to this superb piece of craftsmanship was one both of admiration and deep uncertainty. It was more than uncertainty of the top of the head; it belonged more to the whole body, which found it difficult to enter into the movement and the action, into this powerful modern retelling of the life and passion of Christ and His friends. The more I searched out the reasons for the uncertainty, in the picture itself, in *The Greek Passion*, the novel by Nikos Kazantzakis from which it was drawn, and in *The Odyssey: A Modern Sequel*, Kazantzakis' remarkable rendition of the Ulysses theme, the more I felt that the collapse of movement was his, not mine. The action was being used in the name of ideas, and the two never quite came together. And the ideas themselves were both brilliant and fraudulent, always giving the impression of having been put together and manipulated by a *composer*. The top of the writer's head was in final command. The realism was powerful, but always black and white and therefore contrived.

The real is thus manipulated in the name of superficial parallels to the Gospel story. The priests are either martyrs or villains, the people either haves or have-nots. (I was confirmed in this interpretation when I read Kazantzakis' theory that the artist has the power and right to make, mould, manipulate, destroy reality, in Book XVII of *The Odyssey*.) In the name of Christ the immaculately "white" characters of the movie-book are always leaving the "black" characters, always desperately giving something up, abandoning it, leaving it, running, running, running. The final clue for both the movie and the novel must come from the brilliant poem. The clue is Ulysses, for Christ and the good priest, and all their friends, are Ulysses; not the Greek Ulysses trying to find his valiant way home, but the new Ulysses creating the new ritual of no ritual at all, breaking away from every father and every home, even from hope, and finally even from freedom itself. In the end all things indeed come home again: but into the home of the head of Ulysses whose head has created them all and receives them again, with compassion because even compassion is a nice idea. The religious drama ends in the perfect parody of ritual, in the lonely head of Ulysses. It is the brilliant rite of Narcissus. Nobody else is there. This is one of the great temptations of the intellectual as he tries to create a new ritual drama.

The thought occurs, before turning to Archibald MacLeish's
J.B., that one of the greatest obstacles to any possible effective
restoration of biblical-ritual drama among us is the constant
insistence on the imposition of "modern sensibility" within
the action. There is a good sense in which this can and must
be done, but the project also has its fraudulent senses, especially when it means, rather apodictically, that we are
what we are, we feel what we feel, and that is that and let
no one raise any questions. This is historicism at its purest.
Sensibility, *our* sensibility, is so precious a commodity that
everything gets used for its purposes and is to be reduced to
its shape.

Certainly in the case of *J.B.* the cart of sensibility and
thought is way out in front of the horse of the action. If almost to the point of parody one wanted an encyclopedia of
the thoughts and systems of modern man, Jung, Bergson,
Freud, Husserl, the existentialists, The Golden Bough, Joyce,
Dostoevski, Marx, he will find it all in the Ulysses-Christ of
Kazantzakis. The same thing goes on in *J.B.*, though in a
narrower and less competent way. The air is oppressive with
the thoughts and speculation of the author, who is using the
story of Job as a vehicle. It is a new Job we are given, a
thoroughly Romantic one, as many critics have pointed out.
In the contest with God he turns out much more handsomely
than God. Though nothing is left to him, there is Life and
Love, a few leaves of forsythia, his wife, and the potential
coals and fires of his own heart. So that thus far we have on
our hands the creative mind of Kazantzakis and the endur-
ing, understanding heart of MacLeish, both pretty much alone.
There is little room here for the choral dance or the choral
song.

I do not intend to quarrel here about the question of God,
who is doubtfully believed in but much talked about within
this religious play. My own concern is with the general assumption in the air that if *J.B.* is not very good theology it
does at least explore the human experience as the theologians
do not. If this were true we could all be critically happy about
the play because it is a reasonable certainty that an art which
really follows the lines of human experience will be following the lines of light and the Holy Spirit, and will willy-
nilly get to God. There were a few lines in the televised
performance of *Child of Our Time* in which the boy who has
just told the priest that he does not believe in God is given
the answer that the priest is not concerned with his present

disbelief but that if he will go and do everything the other boys in the home are doing for a few months the priest would then gladly discuss the problem. This would be something more substantial than the few forsythia leaves which alone are left in the ashes of civilization and which alone prevent the suicide of Mr. and Mrs. J.B. Mr. MacLeish is a very reputable fighter for ideas but in this case the ideas are too artificial to find a body. That man is magnificently best in his worst moments, that *he* can love if Reality cannot, that light can come only from the coals of our own heart, that man will go endlessly on, these are "splendid" ideas, but they cannot get a grip on reality, and the only ritual they will ever evoke is the lonely movement of thought in the head of an isolated poetry.

Even the language, therefore, gets tenuous and unsubstantial. Forsythias are not very much reality. Names like Mrs. Murphy and Mrs. Botticelli do not evoke real images, and surely neither of them is in the audience for such a play. There is a preciosity communicated even to the real things: "the time of the wild goats," "God the boiling point of water," "blond in all that blood that daughter," "you know Muff, my purple poodle," "sticks and stones and steel are chances," "can the seven bones reply." [7]

These "realities" mean something if and only if one knows what the writer is saying and thinking in the order of something that is almost pure argument. If one doesn't follow the argument—which is as likely as not—then he will find the greatest difficulty in locating the lines of significance of Mrs. Murphy and Mrs. Botticelli, the forsythia, or death as "a bone that stammers . . . a tooth among the flints that has forgotten." Do not believe for a moment in the new dichotomy that has been offered to us, on the one hand of a Christian theology that is transcendental and on the other hand a new poetic and non-theological experience that is in touch with reality. It is already a good number of years since Lionel Trilling did us the great service of pointing out that it is the liberal imagination which is transcendental and out of touch with the gripping lines of experience. Perhaps *J.B.* should have begun where it ended, with an exploration of the love of Mr. and Mrs. J.B., to see if it has the actuality of love uncapitalized.

It is not necessary to be complicated about this whole matter. Perhaps what I am saying is that we need a lot more dancing in common before we do any more thinking. We must also begin to ask the fundamental question, what makes a playwright and what should his basic training be?

Certainly he must make himself more than a "thinker," more even than a poet as we now understand the term. Such a restriction would be theatrically fatal. He should know a good deal, and this in terms of his own bloodstream, about the dance and ritual in the oldest and widest senses of these terms. He should be an actual man of the theatre, as Shakespeare probably was and Kazantzakis, MacLeish, even Eliot, probably are not. He should be a man who delights in the coronation of a queen or the inauguration of a President, who delights generally in a public style of life for man. He should know history and not think that his private mind can alone create a theatre. He should be deeply aware of the eternal rhythms of the heart of the *people*, the strength these rhythms have for salvation (as they were caught, for example, at the end of Cabiria). He must, finally, come to an intimate knowledge of the work of the choreographers and the musicians, and not leave his own skills in isolation from theirs.

Let us therefore end this discussion of ritual where we began. We could very well end by borrowing a term from the psychologists. The term is that of *displacement*. By every instinct in them men desperately need to think and move together, ritually. One of the sources of modern anxiety is surely that people get into too many situations where they do not know what people will think or do next. If these ritual needs collapse on the deeper levels of the body and spirit, then they will break out (and have) on the cheaper levels of both.

The solution should rather lie in the direction of the deepening of the fact, or the rediscovery of its levels. Here our case is ritual. The rhythms of a song are a ritual, but they are being reduced to a crooning dream, one of the cheapest of all gnostic creations. The rhetoric of great human speech is a ritual, but I have heard it too often torn to the tatters of "meaningful fact" by fine actors who were intent on showing that they could enter into each line and syllable and movement of the body, thus giving personality and modernity to every fact. The lines were no longer allowed to float out in the air as ritual victories. Judith Anderson has done this sad thing to Medea and Laurence Olivier has done it to both Oedipus and Richard III.

Afraid of the victory of conformity, we let it remain in

its present degenerate state, and we eagerly seek the recompenses of the victories of "personality" on the levels of art and the spirit. The artist becomes the isolated, romantic hero, instead of taking up the task of building, on those other levels of the fact, higher and deeper rituals wherein alone personality will be achieved and our cheaper conformities or etiquettes restore themselves to sense through not having to exhaust this magnificent energy at a single point. The dance is always formful, but David danced before the ark in freedom. It is an amazing fact that the rigidities of the perfect sonnet rhythms create the possibility of freedom for its individual musical phrases. Surely too, it is interesting that it is in the higher reserve of the divine liturgy that we have suddenly the sense of freedom, of having escaped from society. And let this last phrase be perhaps our last and best example of the truth that we have given up the penetration into all the levels of factuality. I should correct the words "escaped from society," but will not. Let them stand as they are, as a symbol that the language of the solipsist, of the romantic hero, has taken over in these highest matters, so that I as a Catholic am trapped into the use of them when I am talking of my most social, my most ritual, my freest moment. Not to speak of music, rhetoric, the dance, the sonnet, the liturgy, we hardly have the most ordinary vocabulary left in terms of which we might speak of fidelity to the forms of our literal human reality all the way through the whole line of being without abandoning these forms for some final gnostic and non-human temptation.

Perhaps it would be good to close this chapter with a brief remark on this problem of vocabulary. Is there a proper and satisfactory vocabulary we can use to clarify the whole import of that crucial question of levels of being which we have placed at the very center of the relations between theology and the imagination? Probably not, because the presence of such a satisfactory language among us would itself be an indication that we were in conscious possession of these critical dilemmas and of possible ways out of them. Nevertheless we must begin. We on our part shall begin with an outline of the vocabulary of the fourfold level of biblical exegesis, not with the great hope that it will resolve everything but with the confidence that, if interpreted rightly and for us, it does supply *some* clues for an escape out of what ails us. Furthermore, we should stress that, if the questions it helped the human mind to confront are far from dated, the language itself of biblical exegesis may be quite old-fashioned for the purposes of the contemporary imagination; it is in great need of adaptation. I think that we would be more sympathetically placed toward his vocabulary and his whole way of thinking if we were to suppose that the biblical exegete was trying, in so far as this was possible, to put himself in the place of God and to follow the operations of His "imagination" as the latter was working out a unique supernatural history for men.

NOTES

1. John Crowe Ransom, "Poetry: A Note on Ontology," *Critiques and Essays in Criticism 1920-1948*, ed. Robert W. Stallman (New York: Ronald, 1949), pp. 30-46.

2. T. S. Eliot, *From Poe to Valery* (New York: Harcourt, Brace, 1948), p. 26.

3. All poetic citations from T. S. Eliot are in:
   T. S. Eliot, *The Complete Poems and Plays 1909-1950* (New York: Harcourt, Brace, 1956).

4. I would call attention to this use of the intersection of time and eternity in Karl Barth, *The Epistle to the Romans*, pp. 29 and 60.

5. "Hymn to God My God, In My Sickness," *The Complete Poetry and Selected Prose of John Donne*, ed. Charles M. Coffin (New York: Random House, Modern Library, 1952), p. 271.

6. *Ibid.*, pp. 271-272.

7. Archibald MacLeish, *J.B.* (Boston: Houghton Mifflin, 1958).

8 The Christian Imagination

One final possibility and hypothesis is here dealt with: the possibility that there is such a thing as a formally Christian or Christic imagination, that there can be a Christian and Christic dimension for the literary image. So provisional, and, of course, so controversial, is this stage of our discussion that it should be kept apart from all the experiential findings of the earlier chapters. Nevertheless, one should not be afraid of the question.

In brief, the question can be put thus: in our terms of analogy the act of existence has descended and keeps descending into every created form and possibility, adapting itself to every shape and form and difference. Is it true or not that the natural order of things has been subverted and that there has been a new creation, within which the one, single, narrow form of Christ of Nazareth is in process of giving its shape to everything? To think and imagine according to this form is to think and imagine according to a Christic dimension. It would also make every dimension Christic. However, like analogy itself, this would not destroy difference but would make it emerge even more sharply.

This is not quite the same question with which our first chapter began. There we used Christology only as a model for the penetration of the finite and as a source for the energy needed in that odyssey.

Our present chapter is an attempt to interpret, in terms of some of our own literary problems, the medieval habit and theory of Christian and biblical exegesis according to four levels of images, the literal, the tropological, the analogical, the anagogical. A supplement of medieval texts has been added for the convenience of students and scholars.

WE HAVE WATCHED men constructing poems, and have taken it for granted that the poetry ends in and gives us insight. The critics have devoted a good deal of analytical energy to the work of locating the points, the details, the processes, of poetic insight. Let us now make a not-too-violent mental transfer and suppose that God, in the two Testaments, is describing a construction of his own which he has carved out in history and which leads to increasing insights for the human race, finally indeed to the insights of the resurrection. What are some of the simple methods and laws we can discover about this divine construct? How does God "imagine" through the lines of *this* poem, through the lines of this history he has made and is making? [1]

THE LITERAL AND ALLEGORICAL

In the first place there are the literal words of the biblical text. As St. Thomas insists, the function of words in the Bible is the same as in any other book. They are the signs of things, of realities other than themselves, and this referential meaning is to be gathered from the text itself and from its context. But uniquely in the case of the Bible, and this because of God's structural governance of supernatural history, the realities signified by the text have a referential relationship to other realities in history. The Jews of the Old Testament are liberated from Egypt and from the waters of the Red Sea. This is more than a word, it is also an historical fact. Yet, without becoming less of a fact, it is also a sign, a type, of another reality to come, the liberation of Christ from the dead. Yet it is more than an historical metaphor, or an artificial sign implanted in a fact, chosen at random to be related to something else. For it has the same concrete structure, though on a poorer and less important level, as that greater thing toward which it points. And the deeper one goes into the whole historical concretion of the earlier reality, the more insight there is into that which is to come (reality is no block to insight, as it is to so many forms of the romantic imagination). But the reverse is also true. If one brings the Resurrection back over against the liberation of this ancient people from the waters, that first act of liberation is illuminated as never before. There is a mutuality of forces for insight operating between the two events. Each is borrowing light from the other. Just when our insights are losing contact with the reality of one, we have the wherewithal to restore the vision through the other. We can imagine as God imagined, as He drew His people from the waters. He is already carving out the forms of His Son, according to all the possibilities of different historical materials. Yet the materials keep their full historical identity. God's imagination is not univocal.

We have used the phrase "according to all the possibilities of the material." That is true, but we should also add, "according to all the energy of the form that is entering into it." In our chapter on analogy, we saw that it was an act called existence which was descending deeper and deeper into the possibilities of the world to take on the proportions of these possibilities while retaining an identity. Nothing stopped it from remaining the same; no difference was lost through being organized by it. This is the action of creation, and of the endless dynamisms set in motion within the created world. What the end shall be, what the next minute shall deliver us to, we do not know. And yet we know. The determining form is rigid *and* unpredictable. It was only such an action as existence that could enter into the possibilities of everything.

Yet there has been a second and a new creation. And now the form which shapes it is no longer an existence which becomes different in everything it touches, leaving only the proportion the same, the proportion between the act of existence and the possibility of the essence. Now the action is Christ, rigidly one person, born in that place, at that time, with all those specificities, with this body. How energetic (and esemplastic) will he be, how malleable to him will the world be? The Greek mind and the pure intelligence is at home in the first creation. So is the chameleon faculty of the romantic imagination, for they both love to follow and take on the forms of all the possibilities of nature. Though neither of them likes to deal with time; it is such an unpredictable, such a surd, so irrational. But even more, how can they deal with so exact a person, such an "irrational" as Christ? How can this Nazarene be imagined through as the form of a new creation? He will be no scandal to existence, no scandal to the Greek or romantic imagination, if he submits to being one of their forms, one of their possibilities. But he refuses this role and insists on turning the tables. He proclaims himself the master of the Sabbath (which in our discussion is to be translated "the imagination"). He the single Jew proclaims that he can do better what existence alone once did. It is now demanded of a new imagination that it use this "hopelessly rigid" form as a new analogical instrument with which to enter into the shapes of all things without cancelling them out. One clue for suspecting that there has been no cancelling out is the greater importance of a finger or a toe nail in Christian art, or the greater importance of a cry in the night on a bridge. I am not at all arguing that Christic materials have to get into our arts in any formal way; but they are there for all that; at some point or other they began to push the details of creation even further into our faces, and to make it even more impossible not to listen to any cry on any bridge in the world. Again, in *The Fall* of Camus, the narrator tells us that Christ felt guilty because of the children who were murdered in His name. It would be objectionable on our part to object to this fine mind continuing to feel and think this problem out, but surely we have every right at this point to repeat that He misses the issue of the relationship of the new imagination to the old. The children cried, within this history, because they suffered, as much as children can, within the cries of Christ. A man can only *cause* pain to somebody outside of himself. Christ's cries are wider than we think and grow more actual through the body of our own.

Here let me say a related word about the matter of belief and poetry. It is fashionable among some critics to say that belief is not essential to the act of poetry (whether the act be that of the reader or the writer), or that the belief of the reader need not duplicate that of the writer; we may sum up this view by saying we can read Dante without believing as he did.

There is so much indirect truth, obviously, in this possibility that even our firmest Christian writers are perfectly willing—and understandably so—to grant the point in all poetic generosity. Maritain, Fergusson, Auden, Eliot could all be cited to this effect, though some like Empson and Winters express their objections. As for others who are not so firm, one would sometimes think, so far has the psychologistic aesthetic gone in our times, that it is not necessary to believe or know anything, much less Christianity, in order to read poetry. About such an aesthetic Winters speaks in a properly caustic tone when he says that "One might as well demand poetic rights for those who cannot read or speak, or poetic rights for idiots." But more usually the substance of ordinary human sensibility and of some metaphysical sense is admitted to be necessary to the reader, and the line is only drawn, sometimes rather fiercely, at that point where Christian belief begins.

The argument amounts to this, that there is no need to believe theologically in order to believe poetically; poetic belief is able to reduce everything, including theological structures, to its own purposes and its own types of insight. And this position does not differ very much from that of the modernist theology of the nineteenth century, in men like Loisy and Sabatier, who thought it a mistake to commit theology, much less poetry, to reality-beliefs. It would seem not too much to say that these views stem from the built-up conviction of the last century that the aesthetic is an absolutely unique and isolated faculty, and that its object is an extraordinarily unique thing called Beauty. It is then easy enough, having moved into this position of vantage, to claim that poetry has the right and power to push everything univocally into its own forms, and into its own forms of belief. All this it does in the name of its own autonomy, its own act of self-consciousness. But this is an autonomous act in the name of freedom which is quite capable of defeating the real autonomy of poetry, and its freedom to be completely itself. After the fashion of a metaphysics of analogy, it should rather allow itself progressively to enter into every level of belief, into all the levels of the possession of objects and of self, borrowing its poetic strength from their already potent and hierarchical poetic strengths, and nowhere needlessly limiting its own powers.

But in the case of the Christian imagination an even more crucial issue is at stake. For Christ, we have said, is not another item of the first creation, to be used as any other item by the old imagination. The real point is ever so much more crucial. For he has subverted the whole order of the old imagination. Nor is this said in the sense that he replaces or cancels the old; rather, he illuminates it, and is a new level, identical in structure with, but higher in energy than, every form or possibility of the old.

The biblical exegete of the late Middle Ages—and the ordinary literary man of the time—was certainly no match for the modern line of poets in craftsmanship and the mature spiritual possession of poetic technique; but he did clearly see the dimensions of the problem of the reorientation of the imagination. First of all, Christ, before he universalizes himself, is unique. This uniqueness also attaches itself to some of the special events of pre-Christic history. The exegete

was cautious about finding too many such events, for by this
time there had been a sharp veering away from the old
Alexandrine habit of finding Christic correspondences
everywhere in actual events. But this is only a temporary
hesitation until the absolute specificity of Christ and of the
dramatic line of history which generated him is suffered to
emerge. He shall have his narrow personal march from Bethlehem to Calvary, but he is already having his great march,
by dramatic generative analogies, through history. It is only
progressively, after it has the unbreakable confidence that
there is some essential Christic development in supernatural
history, that the new imagination begins to assume the order
of creation and to lift it into its own vitality. Thus Christ
is water, gold, butter, food, a harp, a dove, the day, a
house, merchant, fig, gate, stone, book, wood, light, medicine, oil, bread, arrow, salt, turtle, risen sun, way, and many
things besides. And in this process there is another clue to
the difference between the two imaginations. We have seen
that there is a good deal going on today in the direction of
reducing all the planes of life, including those of theology
and history, to the plane of the poetical spirit. But what is
happening with the Christic imagination is quite the reverse:
the old realities and metaphors of nature are being raised
to the level of historical commitment, and are therefore
surcharged with new poetical power, not less. And there is
less temptation, at least there should be less temptation, to
reduce them to thin metaphors whose thickness might get in
the way of vision.

Thus, then, we already have two Christs, one taking on
the dimensions and the concreteness of an actual life, the
other the dimensions and concreteness of human history. The
dimensions of a human life seem never enough for the
imagination which is after insight. It must also go to the
larger thing called history, as well as to human society. With
Christ this will be the Church which is Christ. Or it will find
him in a drop of wine. The same yesterday, today and forever, but always completely different. The imagination loves
these transformations, and it has always been the business of
the poet too to accomplish them dramatically, earnedly, truly.
Sometimes it is all accomplished in a single speech. We stay
with one of our examples, *Riders to the Sea*. There are the
drops of water. There is the story of Bartley and Michael.
There is the dead line of dead sons, which is history. There
is all of us, which is society. So that Maurya at the end, as the

result of a rhythm no one would question, can move into the lines of a high priest:

> (puts the empty cup mouth downwards on the table, and lays her hands together on Bartley's feet). They're altogether this time, and the end is come. May the Almighty God have mercy on Bartley's soul, and on Michael's soul, and on the souls of Sheamus and Patch, and Stephen and Shawn (bending her head); and may He have mercy on my soul, Nora, and on the soul of everyone left living in the world. (She pauses, and the keen rises a little more loudly from the women, then sinks away.) [2]

On the literal level, it is the simple story of Bartley and Michael, surrounded by the present literalness of their lives and their deaths, the dripping water, the socks, the shirt. You do not run away from these things to get to the other planes of the fact, those of history, society, eternity. It is by digging deeper into the facts that you get there. There is a certain ambiguity about the unidentified shirt, and the very ambiguity creates the presence of endless bodies done in by the sea; for "aren't there great rolls of it in the shops of Galway, and isn't it many another man may have a shirt of it as well as Michael himself?" [3] And there is the detail of the coffin nails, the nails Maurya has forgotten. The forgetting sweeps us into history, for "it's a great wonder she wouldn't think of the nails, and all the coffins she's seen made already." [4]

THE ANAGOGICAL AND THE LITERAL

There is, then, the literal sense of things, and one climbs through it, not around or above or below it, to the allegorical sense of history and society. But the exegete did not use the word "allegorical" in our weaker sense. He moves through that density of the Old Testament which Marcion could not stomach, not to ideas, but to the other realities of Christ and the Church. And there is the anagogical sense, the world of complete insight, the world of eternity and Christ in glory. It is not a jump to a Manichaean moment, conqueror of time. It is the end, the last moment of time, an end effected by time itself, both natural and supernatural, and it produces the anagoge in its moment of final exhaustion: "An old woman will soon be tired with anything she will do, and isn't it nine days herself is after crying and keening, and making great sorrow in the house?" And Maurya says, "Michael has a clean burial in the far north, by the grace of the Almighty God. Bartley will have a fine coffin out of the white boards, and a deep grave surely. What more can we want than that? No man at all can be living forever, and we must be satisfied." [5] But where is the anagoge ("So death doth touch the resurrection")? Well, it will take generations of exploration of these our literal scenes to find out where it is, especially at these many points of death. But in all of them we would do well to remember what the literal and what the anagoge were at the point of Christ's death. We should remember that the inner life of the Trinitarian God is the total communication of self by different Persons to one another. And that on the literal plane of his earthly life Christ communicated himself completely to us, down to the last drop of his blood. There are two forms of the death wish, as there are two forms of death in and for poetry. In the one there is a death which is a desert and a wish for it; and this, we know, may occur for poetry too, where some of our poets have wished to reduce it to silence, the night, a false virginity.[6]

But there is another form of death, which is the most positive and creative of all the moments of life, a communication of self to self to the last drop. This is the creative wish of St. Paul, "I wish to be dissolved and to be with Christ." Two bloods meet and dissolve into each other in the Chalice of the New Testament, that of the Church and that of Christ. And who shall call this a desert or a night of non-being? We can very well let the anagoge and the fuller insights take care of themselves if we will see that to get to them we need to explore endlessly the little literal concretions of love.

Again, we come back to the character of Camus' *The Fall* who knows that this is true. The cry of the woman on the bridge is always there, and he wishes that the chance of the conscience might only be relived, that he might be able to throw himself into the literal water. But there is no easy way to beauty. The water would be so cold! It is no joke, nor a dream, this thing called beauty. We can jump into the desert in a moment, but the way of the literal is longer, and there are no shortcuts through it or around it. This is true even of the Christian wish for either death or poetry. Blessed Robert Southwell went to England with a passion for martyrdom, but when he got there he found that he was too busy with the manifold shapes of the literal to die too quickly. Even in death, therefore, we must not go too quickly from the many to the one. For it has many drops to be explored. This, then, is something of what might be said regarding the relation of the literal to the anagoge, with the healthy understanding, of course, that many things have at this exact point been not repeated and left unsaid, especially all the things that could be repeated about the comic elements in the literal! After all, neither death nor love is always serious.

THE TROPOLOGICAL

There is another, a fourth sense of biblical texts and realities, the tropological or moral sense, which we have thus far omitted because it is frequently and disastrously misunderstood. Ordinarily when we think of the ethical sense of texts, we think of a moral and didactic lesson which can be drawn from them. This sense is in poor reputation among us, and we keep averring, because of our over-refined understanding of the autonomous status of all art, that it has nothing to do with poetry. There is an intense debate going on among us about the right to freedom which the arts have over against the moralist; the insistence is that the latter must at best be kept within the role of an extrinsic policeman who will see to it that the autonomists, while in pursuit of the magnificent autonomy called beauty, will do no harm to little children who are not quite up to the game. But this debate makes sense only if the ethical is meant according to a minimal sense and if the word *beauty* is given its recent isolated sense—isolated, that is, from the profound meaning of the truly moral. One is almost tempted to think it necessary to scrap this whole vocabulary, thus understood, of beauty and the ethical, and to restore these two concepts to broader existences before this unnecessary debate will cease.

For what else is the moral, when properly conceived, save the very life and shape of the soul itself? It is the shape of the soul, as Plato saw in *The Republic*. It is also the inner moving life of the soul, as Dante saw in *The Purgatorio*. It is a highly definite movement and passage, and this is why it is so much attached to the idea of decision. But poetry—and this is what Aristotle saw in his famous definition of tragedy —is an imitation of this movement; it too, therefore, is in its best forms full of decision and judgments and is prophetic. But the decisions are not extrinsic, the judgments are not conceptual; the decisions involve the very substance of the poetry, and the judgments involve a logic of sensibility and awareness which is deeper than the conceptual. Thus understood, it surely makes much sense that poetry, if it is to reverberate in the soul and is to reach that order of subjectivity toward which modern poets lean so strongly, must pass through the ethical if it is to achieve the thing called beauty. It is true that beauty, whatever it is, is of a nonconceptual and immediate order of awareness. But it cannot be had save by a real passage through the orders of literal facts, history, society and the ethical life of man. This is what Kierkegaard saw and said, that the first order of immediate sensibility, the pejorative order of the purely aesthetic man, must pass through all these other worlds if it is to reach to a second order of immediacy and vision, that of a man.

The non-conceptual vision of the ethical existed for the biblical exegete on the highest plane of immediacy. For he meant by the ethical that the form of Christ is extended, not only into history and society and Eucharistic *things* but into the very marrow of the soul, so that all the levels of the latter might reverberate with it and become identical with it according to all its variegated possibilities and differences. "I live, yet not I, but Christ in me." Maritain has been using the superb word "connaturality" to indicate the shapes which poetry gives the soul in relation to existence. It is a good word for the old imagination, but it falls short of the needs of the new. For the new creation can only be satisfied with a word which comes nearer to "identity."

What more is there to say?

NOTES

1. For a set of documents and texts which will supply the reader with basic information on the foundations of these pages in biblical exegesis see Supplement III.

2. John M. Synge, "Riders to the Sea," *Five Great Modern Irish Plays* (New York: Modern Library, 1941), p. 189.

3. *Ibid.*, p. 182.

4. *Ibid.*, p. 189.

5. *Idid.*, p 189.

6. Mario Praz, *The Romantic Agony,* trans. by Angus Davidson (New York: Oxford University Press, Meridian Books, 1956), pp. 31-36.

S upplements

SUPPLEMENT I

ON THE DEFINITE

As a case in the *architectural* imagination, Erwin Panofsky postulates a striking relationship between Gothic art and medieval philosophy. Both systems depend on the articulation of a kind of infinite through definite links and parts, the one articulating space, the other human thought.

As High Scholasticism was governed by the principle of *manifestatio,* so was High Gothic architecture dominated—as already observed by Suger—by what may be called the "principle of transparency." Pre-Scholasticism had insulated faith from reason by an impervious barrier much as a Romanesque structure conveys the impression of a space determinate and impenetrable, whether we find ourselves inside or outside the edifice. Mysticism was to drown reason in faith, and nominalism was to completely disconnect one from the other; and both these attitudes may be said to find expression in the Late Gothic hall church. Its barnlike shell encloses an often wildly pictorial and always apparently boundless interior and thus creates a space determinate and impenetrable from without but indeterminate and penetrable from within. High Scholastic philosophy, however, severely limited the sanctuary of faith from the sphere of rational knowledge yet insisted that the content of this sanctuary remain clearly discernible. And so did High Gothic architecture delimit interior volume from exterior space yet insist that it project itself, as it were, through the encompassing structure; so that, for example, the cross section of the nave can be read off from the facade.

Like the High Scholastic *Summa,* the High Gothic cathedral aimed, first of all, at "totality" and therefore tended to approximate, by synthesis as well as elimination, one perfect and final solution; we may therefore speak of the High Gothic plan or the High Gothic system with much more confidence than would be possible in any other period. In its imagery, the High Gothic cathedral sought to embody the whole of Christian knowledge, theological, moral, natural, and historical, with everything in its place and that which no longer found its place, suppressed. In structural design, it similarly sought to synthesize all major motifs handed down by separate channels and finally achieved an unparalleled balance between the basilica and the central plan type, suppressing all elements that might endanger this balance, such as the crypt, the galleries, and towers other than the two in front.

The second requirement of Scholastic writing, "arrangement according to a system of homologous parts and parts of parts," is most graphically expressed in the uniform division and subdivision of the whole structure. Instead of the Romanesque variety of western and eastern vaulting forms, often appearing in one and the same building (groin vaults, rib vaults, barrels, domes, and half-domes), we have the newly developed rib vault exclusively so that the vaults of even the apse, the chapels and the ambulatory no longer differ in kind from those of the nave and transept. Since Amiens, rounded surfaces were entirely eliminated, except, of course, for the webbing of the vaults. Instead of the contrast that normally existed between tripartite naves and undivided transepts (or quinquepartite naves and tripartite transepts) we have tripartition in both cases; and instead of the disparity (either in size, or in the type of covering, or in both) between the bays of the high nave and those of the side aisles, we have the "uniform *travée*," in which one rib-vaulted central bay connects with one rib-vaulted aisle bay on either side. The whole is thus composed of smallest units—one might almost speak of *articuli*—which are homologous in that they are all triangular in ground plan and in that each of these triangles shares its sides with its neighbors.

As a result of this homology we perceive what corresponds to the hierarchy of "logical levels" in a well-organized Scholastic treatise. Dividing the entire structure, as was customary in the period itself, into three main parts, the nave, the transept, and the chevet (which in turn comprises the fore-choir and the choir proper), and distinguishing, within these parts, between high nave and side-aisles, on the one hand, and between apse, ambulatory, and hemicycle of chapels, on the other, we can observe analogous relations to obtain: first, between each central bay, the whole of the central nave, and the entire nave, transept or fore-choir, respectively; second, between each side-aisle bay, the whole of each side aisle, and the entire nave, transept or fore-choir, respectively; third, between each sector of the apse, the whole apse, and the entire choir; fourth, between each section of the ambulatory, the whole ambulatory and the entire choir; and fifth, between each chapel, the whole hemicycle of chapels, and the entire choir.

It is not possible here—nor is it necessary–to describe how this principle of progressive divisibility (or, to look at it the other way, multiplicability) increasingly affected the entire edifice down to the smallest detail. At the height of the development, supports were divided and subdivided into main piers, major shafts, minor shafts, and still minor shafts; the tracery of windows, triforia, and blind arcades into primary, secondary, and tertiary mullions and profiles; ribs and arches into a series of moldings. It may be mentioned, however, that the very principle of homology that controls the whole process implies and accounts for the relative uniformity which distinguishes the High Gothic vocabulary from the Romanesque. All parts that are on the same "logical level"—and this is especially noticeable in those decorative and representational features which, in architecture, correspond to Thomas Aquinas's *similitudines*—came to be conceived of as members of one class, so that the enormous variety in, for instance, the shape of canopies, the decoration of socles and archevaults, and, above all, the form of piers and capitals tended to be suppressed in favor of standard types admitting only of such variations as would occur in nature among individuals of one species. Even in the world of fashion the thirteenth century is distinguished by a reasonableness and uniformity (even as far as the difference between masculine and feminine costumes is concerned) which was equally foreign to the preceding and to the following period.

The theoretically illimited fractionization of the edifice is limited by what corresponds to the third requirement of Scholastic writing: "distinctness and deductive cogency." According to classic High Gothic standards the individual elements, while forming an indiscerptible whole, yet must proclaim their identity by remaining clearly separated from each other—the shafts from the wall or the core of the pier, the ribs from their neighbors, all vertical members from their arches; and there must be an unequivocal correlation between them. We must be able to tell which element belongs to which, from which results what might be called a "postulate of mutual inferability"—not in dimensions, as in classical architecture, but in conformation. While Late Gothic permitted, even delighted in, flowing transitions and interpenetrations, and loved to defy the rule of correlation by, for instance, overmembrification of the ceiling and undermembrification of the supports, the classic style demands that we be able to infer, not only the interior from the exterior or the shape of the side aisles from that of the central nave but also, say, the organization of the whole system from the cross section of one pier.

—ERWIN PANOFSKY, *Gothic Architecture and Scholasticism*. (NEW YORK: MERIDIAN, 1957), pp. 43-51

The predicament of the *musician* faced with the demands of nothing but the limited to work with and the desire to be free is described by Igor Stravinsky. If his position is valid, then the situation of the composer corresponds remarkably with that of the literary artist.

Let us understand each other in regard to this word, "fantasy." We are not using the word in the sense in which it is connected with a definite musical form, but in the acceptation which presupposes an abandonment of one's self to the caprices of imagination. And this presupposes that the composer's will is voluntarily paralyzed. For imagination is not only the mother of caprice, but the servant and handmaiden of the creative will as well.

The creator's function is to sift the elements he receives from her, for human activity must impose limits upon itself. The more art is controlled, limited, worked over, the more it is free.

As for myself, I experience a sort of terror when, at the moment of setting to work and finding myself before the infinitude of possibilities that present themselves, I have the feeling that everything is permissible to me. If everything is permissible to me, the best and the worst; if nothing offers me any resistance, then any effort is inconceivable, and I cannot use anything as a basis, and consequently every undertaking becomes futile.

Will I then have to lose myself in this abyss of freedom? To what shall I cling in order to escape the dizziness that seizes me before the virtuality of this infinitude? However, I shall not succumb. I shall overcome my terror and shall be reassured by the thought that I have the seven notes of the scale and its chromatic intervals at my disposal, that strong and weak accents are within my reach, and that in all of these I possess solid and concrete elements which offer me a field of experience just as vast as the upsetting and dizzy infinitude that had just frightened me. It is into this field that I shall sink my roots, fully convinced that combinations which have at their disposal twelve sounds in each octave and all possible rhythmic varieties promise me riches that all the activity of human genius will never exhaust.

What delivers me from the anguish into which an unrestricted freedom plunges me is the fact that I am always able to turn immediately to the concrete things that are here in question. I have no use for a theoretic freedom. Let me have something finite, definite —matter that can lend itself to my operation only insofar as it is commensurate with my possibilities. And such matter presents itself to me together with its limitations. I must in turn impose mine upon it. So here we are, whether we like it or not, in the realm of necessity. And yet which of us has ever heard talk of art as other than a realm of freedom? This sort of heresy is uniformly widespread because it is imagined that art is outside the bounds of ordinary activity. Well, in art as in everything else, one can build only upon a resisting foundation: whatever constantly gives way to pressure constantly renders movement impossible.

My freedom thus consists in my moving about within the narrow frame that I have assigned myself for each one of my undertakings.

I shall go even farther: my freedom will be so much the greater and more meaningful the more narrowly I limit my field of action and the more I surround myself with obstacles. Whatever diminishes constraint diminishes strength. The more constraints one imposes, the more one frees one's self of the chains that shackle the spirit.

To the voice that commands me to create I first respond with fright; then I reassure myself by taking up as weapons those things participating in creation but as yet outside of it; and the arbitrariness of the constraint serves only to obtain precision of execution.

From all this we shall conclude the necessity of dogmatizing on pain of missing our goal. If these words annoy us and seem harsh, we can abstain from pronouncing them. For all that, they nonetheless contain the secret of salvation: "It is evident," writes Baudelaire, "that rhetorics and prosodies are not arbitrarily invented tyrannies, but a collection of rules demanded by the very organization of the spiritual being, and never have prosodies and rhetorics kept originality from fully manifesting itself. The contrary, that is to say, that they have aided the flowering of originality, would be infinitely more true."

> —IGOR STRAVINSKY, *Poetics of Music in the Form of Six Lessons.* (NEW YORK: VINTAGE, 1956), pp. 66-69

There is one line in the following text and comment on Blake by Herbert Read which the reader is asked to contemplate. It is: "Leave out this line and you leave out life itself." It is a singular expression of the place of the finite in the *painter's* imagination.

But the clearest expression of his principles comes in that *Descriptive Catalogue* which he [Blake] wrote for the first exhibition of his tempera painting of the Canterbury Pilgrims. Is this the creed of a "romantic" artist?

"The character and expression in this picture could never have been produced with Rubens' light and shadow, or with Rembrandt's, or anything Venetian or Flemish. The Venetian and Flemish practice is broken lines, broken masses, and broken colours. Mr. B.'s practice is unbroken lines, unbroken masses, and unbroken colours. Their art is to lose form; his art is to find form, and to keep it. His arts are opposite to theirs in all things.

"The great and golden rule of art, as well as of life, is this: That the more distinct, sharp, and wiry the bounding line, the more perfect the work of art; and the less keen and sharp, the greater is the evidence of weak imagination, plagiarism, and bungling. . . . The want of this determinate and bounding form evidences the want of idea in the artist's mind, and the pretence of plagiary in all its branches. How do we distinguish the oak from the beech, the horse from the ox, but by the bounding outline? How do we distinguish one face or countenance from another but by the bounding line and its infinite inflections and movements? What is it that builds a house and plants a garden but the definite and determinate? What is it that distinguishes honesty from knavery but the hard and wiry line of rectitude and certainty in the actions and intentions? Leave out this line and you leave out life itself."

There is one further point to make, both in relation to Blake's art and to Gothic art. If Gothic art is living form, it is not, on that account, representational form. There is no necessary relation between the energies which the inspired artist seeks to embody in definite form and the limitless and indefinite forms of nature. A "living" line or form is not necessarily "life-like"; it is merely "lively." Indeed, all epochs of original art have recognized a divorce between the forms of reality and the forms of art—which are the forms of the imagination. The actual is simply the unimaginative, and there is no inspiration in it. And so we find Blake confessing that "natural objects always did and do weaken, deaden, and obliterate imagination in me." Imagination, "mere enthusiasm," was the only reality, the only value. Imagination is a vague term, and enthusiasm can be a disparaging one. Perhaps the fact that Blake rather defiantly adopted the badge of "enthusiasm" at a time when it was a term of reproach had led to a further misunderstanding of his genius. Mr. Burdett, in this sense, has called him "the Wesley of the arts"—an unfortunate witticism. Dr. Johnson defined enthusiasm as "a vain confidence of divine favour of communication," and by his devotion to the works of Lavater and Swedenborg Blake almost earned this opprobrium. If we had nothing but the poetical works to judge him by, and with the Prophetic Books in mind, we might almost concede the epigram—though it is rather hard on Wesley. But it is quite meaningless when we consider the paintings. Here Blake was not so nakedly original; he did abide by a tradition, though he went far to find it. He had a discipline, but it was self-imposed, self-discovered, not given by the society he lived in.

—HERBERT READ, *The Meaning of Art* (NEW YORK: PENGUIN, 1951), pp. 122-123.

Chesterton suggests that the *humor* of George Bernard Shaw becomes nomadic and inept when it loses its roots in ordinary human reality.

I have stepped on one side from the immediate subject because this is as good an instance as any we are likely to come across of a certain almost extraneous fault which does deface the work of Bernard Shaw. It is a fault only to be mentioned when we have made the solidity of the merits quite clear. To say that Shaw is merely making game of people is demonstrably ridiculous; at least a fairly systematic philosophy can be traced through all his jokes, and one would not insist on such a unity in all the songs of Mr. Dan Leno. I have already pointed out that the genius of Shaw is really too harsh and earnest rather than too merry and irresponsible. I shall have occasion to point out later that Shaw is, in one very serious sense, the very opposite of paradoxical. In any case if any real student of Shaw says that Shaw is only making a fool of him, we can only say that of that student it is very superfluous for anyone to make a fool. But though the dramatist's jests are always serious and generally obvious, he is really affected from time to time by a certain spirit of which that climate theory is a case—a spirit that can only be called one of senseless ingenuity. I suppose it is a sort of nemesis of wit; the skidding of a wheel in the height of its speed. Perhaps it is connected with the nomadic nature of his mind. That lack of roots, his remoteness from ancient instincts and traditions is responsible for a certain bleak and heartless extravagance of statement on certain subjects which makes the author really unconvincing as well as exaggerative; satires that are *saugrenu,* jokes that are rather silly than wild, statements which even considered as lies have no symbolic relation to truth . . .

As has been said already, there must be some truth in every popular impression. And the impression that Shaw, the most savagely serious man of his time, is a mere music-hall artist must have reference to such rare outbreaks as these. As a rule his speeches are full, not only of substance, but of substances, materials like pork, mahogany, lead, and leather. There is no man whose arguments cover a more Napoleonic map of detail. It is true that he jokes; but wherever he is he has topical jokes, one might almost say family jokes. If he talks to tailors he can allude to the last absurdity about buttons. If he talks to soldiers he can see the exquisite and exact humour of the last gun-carriage. But when all his powerful practicality is allowed, there does run through him this erratic levity, an explosion of ineptitude. It is a queer quality in literature. It is a sort of cold extravagance; and it has made him all his enemies.

—G. K. CHESTERTON, *George Bernard Shaw* (NEW YORK: HILL AND WANG, 1957), pp. 123-125

This is a summarizing passage from Allen Tate, who has been so vigorous in attacking the *angelic imagination.*

I call that human imagination angelic which tries to disintegrate or to circumvent the image in the illusory pursuit of essence. When human beings undertake this ambitious program, divine love becomes so rarefied that it loses its human paradigm, and is dissolved in the worship of intellectual power, the surrogate of divinity that worships itself. It professes to know nature as essence at the same time that it has become alienated from nature in the rejection of its material forms.

> —ALLEN TATE, *The Forlorn Demon* (PRINCETON: PRINCETON UNIVERSITY PRESS, 1953)

And the following is a sketch of an equally strong attack on the imagination of *the Symbolist poets*.

The first of these needs, directly implied by all his [Jacques Rivière's] criticism thus far is for the palpable . . . the work of art itself, just as its source in the material world, must even typographically be thick, long, "a cake of earth and stones," no longer haunted by "blank pages," nor built on "absence," or even "silence"; for these are not the things of man.

> —BRADFORD COOK, "JACQUES RIVIÈRE AND SYMBOLISM," IN *Yale French Studies* (SYMBOL AND SYMBOLISM), NO. 9, P. 109.

A good deal of controversy has been aroused over the value for the imagination of Eliot's *objective correlative*. Eliot proposes that an emotion, to be able to be eternally rediscovered through art, must be carried out in terms of a set of objects.

The only way of expressing emotion in the form of art is by finding an "objective correlative"; in other words, a set of objects, a situation, a chain of events which shall be the formula of that particular emotion; such that when the external facts, which must terminate in sensory experience are given, the emotion is immediately evoked.

> —T. S. ELIOT, *Selected Essays* (NEW YORK: HARCOURT, BRACE, 1932), pp. 124-125.

SUPPLEMENT II

On Time

Shakespeare did not begin with some univocal idea and reduce all the phases of time in his characters to it; rather he advanced into these phases and learned progressively from them.

. . . Among the things that dramatic action must burn up are the author's opinions; while he is writing he has no business to know anything that is not a portion of that action. Do you suppose for one moment that Shakespeare educated Hamlet and King Lear by telling them what he thought and believed? As I see it, Hamlet and Lear educated Shakespeare, and I have no doubt that in the process of that education he found out that he was an altogether different man to what he thought himself, and had altogether different beliefs. A dramatist can help his characters to educate him by thinking and studying everything that gives them the language they are groping for through his hands and eyes, but the control must be theirs, and that is why the ancient philosophers thought a poet or dramatist Daimon-possessed.

—W. B. Yeats to Sean O'Casey, *Letters,* Ed.
Allan Wade (New York: Macmillan,
1955), p. 741.

These lines on the image of time in Mauriac's work are offered here as a dubious solution for the question: they seem to say that it is the function of grace to release us from time, to help us transcend it.

In his description of the great moment of recall in the Guermantes courtyard, Proust outlines at length his subjective theory of reality which makes man in effect the creator of his own world. In the memories of Venice, Balbec, and Combray, past and present are merged by the creative imagination and the narrator attains ". . . the only environment in which he could live and enjoy the essence of things, that is to say, entirely outside of time."

This personal and relative interpretation of time is wholly foreign to Mauriac. Absolute time is a fundamental component of his world. His characters are poised between the ephemeralities of creatures and days that pass and the diuturnity of God and the eternal verities which do not pass. His brooding compassion for the human lot, which the serious reader quickly senses in his bleakest plots and most forbidding senses, is based on a conviction of man's subjection to suffering but it is rendered more poignant by his sensitivity to man's concomitant subjection to time. On the blank canvas of childhood, he insists, years and sorrows, equally inescapable, will sketch the outline and compound the colors of the final portrait. And this is as it should be, for the passage of time is essential to human destiny. For those who would escape it, especially for those women who would arrest its advance, Mauriac has no patience . . . They are delivered from every ordeal, even from the old age which is common to every living thing . . .

Those who would isolate themselves from time may do so, Mauriac makes clear, only at the expense of isolating themselves from life, for time is of the essence of human fellowship, of the substance of the human adventure . . .

He offers no possibility of man's withdrawal into an inner world where time is not and where the human spirit, freed from the limitations of time and space, impresses on the materials of sensuous recollection an order and character of its own choice. The dignity and the awesomeness of human life for Mauriac lie in the impingement of time on the timeless and of the timeless on time, in which process, far from achieving a mutual impenetration, each retains its own identity . . . Still the endless chain of ganglionic and muscular compulsion can be broken on the plane of time just as can guilt and retribution on the plane of the eternal, by the intervention of Grace. It is Grace alone which for Mauriac preserves man's autonomy and opens to him the possibility of escaping time not by immersing himself in it but by transcending it.

—MICHAEL F. MALONEY, "TIME AND FRANÇOIS MAURIAC," *Blackfriars,* APRIL, 1957, pp. 173-177

A noted Protestant theologian tells us that time and events fit, not as a problem but as an essential core, into the structure of Christian thought. It is this which distinguishes it from the Greek mind and from every form of gnosticism.

From this (Hellenistic) standpoint, in so far as the need of man for revelation and redemption is to be satisfied, it can take place only in the direction of timeless mysticism, which thinks in spatial concepts.

If today, in the prevailing attitude, the radical contrast between Hellenistic metaphysics and Christian revelation is often completely lost, this is due to the fact that very early the Greek conception of time supplanted the Biblical one, so that down through the history of doctrine to the present day there can be traced a great misunderstanding, upon the basis of which that is claimed as "Christian" which in reality is Greek . . .

The first apostasy from the Primitive Christian understanding of time . . . comes . . . in *Gnosticism.*

. . . in all Gnostic systems the following features go hand in hand:

1. Rejection of the Old Testament, both in its explanation of history as the creative action of God and in its claim that the history of Israel constitutes a redemptive history.

2. Docetism, which is not exhaustively presented in the theory that has given the name to this heresy, the theory according to which Jesus possessed only the semblance of a body but had no actual human body; its chief distinguishing mark is rather to be seen in its rejection of the judgment that redemptive history passes on the quite ordinary particular historical event that occurred in the incarnate Christ, and that includes the offensively ordinary fact of the death of the cross. Thus here also we have to do with the denial of the redemptive significance of an event that occurred in time.

3. Rejection of the Primitive Christian eschatological expectation, whose characteristic distinction in terms of time between the present and the future age is replaced by the Greek metaphysical distinction between this world and the timeless Beyond.

—Oscar Cullman, *Christ and Time* (London: SCM Press, 1951), pp. 54-56

The contrary of everything said in this book on the value of time to the literary imagination is said by Gertrude Stein. Perhaps she is right in her remarks about Proust and Joyce.

A saint a real saint never does anything, a martyr does something but a really good saint does nothing and so I wanted to have four saints who did nothing and I wrote the *Four Saints in Three Acts* and they did nothing and that was everything.

Generally speaking anybody is more interesting doing nothing than doing something.

—Gertrude Stein, *Everybody's Autobiography* (New York: Random House, 1937)

It looked very lovely and the movement was everything they moved and did nothing, that is what a saint or a doughboy should do they should do nothing, they should move some and they did nothing it was very satisfying.

—COMMENT OF GERTRUDE STEIN ON A PRO-
DUCTION OF *Four Saints in Three Acts,* CITED
BY ELIZABETH SPRIGGE, *Gertrude Stein, Her
Life and Work* (NEW YORK, HARPER, 1957),
PP. 189-190

. . . Americans wanted "no narrative to soothe"; everything has to be exciting, "to move as everything moves." She [Gertrude Stein] had already asserted in the earlier lecture *How Writing Is Written* that in the twentieth century events were so continuous that they were no longer exciting. People were not now interested in what happened but in existence, and so it was "quite characteristic that in *The Making of Americans,* Proust, Ulysses, nothing much happened."

—*Ibid.,* 195-196

If, as Gertrude Stein affirmed, much of the modern mind has lost its hunger for "meaning" in the whirlwind rush of event upon event, the following analysis of Biblical thought will help to measure just how tragic that loss is. For in the following excerpt Tresmontant demonstrates not only that events have meaning, but that the meanings resonate through several levels of being simultaneously.

I. CREATION

The sensible world is *created.* This proposition, which we are accustomed to, was profoundly revolutionary from the point of view of Greek metaphysics. It is still revolutionary for modern philosophies which preserve the principles of ancient metaphysics.

For Plato the sensible world proceeds from the intelligible world by an "imitation" (mimesis). The former is the shadow of the latter. In Platonism participation plays the role which creation holds in Biblical thought . . . but participation does not exhaust the content of the idea of creation. Creation is much more than a participation.

For Plotinus the sensible and the multiple proceed from the One by gradation, by a fall, a dispersion into time and into space. . . . For Hegel nature is an alienation of the spirit. We find again a theme of the "Kabbala," that of the "exile" of the *Shekhina,* the "imprisoned sparks" in matter, the gnostic theme, the echoes of which we also meet in Manicheanism.

In all these metaphysical systems [Plotinus, Spinoza, Leibnitz, Hegel] the genesis of the real, whether it be as fall, or as deduction which will be reabsorbed into an eternal unity, or as alienation, is never thought of as a positive creation.

To think of the genesis of the real as a creation, as an eminently positive operation, is an originality of the Biblical tradition. It is a total overturning of the point of departure of metaphysics and of the initial movement of human thought. . . . Its consequences are immense. Over this fundamental point from which all metaphysics proceeds, Hebraic thought goes exactly in the inverse direction to Greek thought. . . .

In considering the general movement which since antiquity makes philosophers treat the genesis of the real as something negative, and in modern times makes them reject the idea of creation for an idea of falling, inversion, alienation, we can wonder if there is not a constitutional incapacity of human thought (like a principle of Carnot immanent in our intelligence) which prevents the understanding of what creation is. . . .

There are two ways for the one to become many. A unity, a living organism, may become many by disaggregation, by decomposition: that is death. In this case the movement which goes from the one to the many is negative; it is a fall. Or a unity, a seed, may become many by fecundity, becoming an organism which in its turn will produce a multitude of seeds. In this second case, the passage of the one to the many is eminently positive; it is no longer a deficit, but a movement ascending towards more being; it is a genesis: more precisely an *anagenesis.* In the first case there is less after than before, less in the many than in the one. In the second case, on the contrary, there is *more* after than before, more in the many than in the one.

. . . It seems that by a natural pessimism the Greek philosophers have spontaneously related the multiplicity of living beings to the idea of a disaggregation, a pulverization of the One. Consequently this multiplicity of beings would represent only something negative, something like a fall. On the contrary, in the Biblical universe, the multiplicity of beings is a result of an action that is eminently positive. It is a creation, an excellent creation. At each stage of the genesis the Creator sees that it is "very good. . . ."

In a natural form of thought which attempts to explain the origin of evil, this cause of evil is spontaneously carried back onto the process of birth itself, and, in the absence of the idea of creation, this genesis is, ultimately, the fall of God himself. The fall and the birth are one and the same thing. The origin of evil and the origin of being are confused, and this original fall, as cause of the real, this division which has been the birth of the world, is situated in God. The many is degradation, the scattering of the One.

The sensible and multiple world, therefore, is by nature a place of exile, an alienation. The sensible, like a scapegoat, is charged with fault, with the origin of evil. It is "matter" which is responsible. . . .

Biblical tradition, at the same time that it involves the idea of creation, radically distinguishes creation and fall (in the same chapter of Genesis). The fall, or the origin of evil, is not tied in essence to the creation, to the origin of being. Creation is "very good." In radically distinguishing creation and fall, the Bible opens a new dimension for the problem of evil. The origin of evil is *situated* elsewhere than in genesis itself. With regard to the sensible, this results in an attitude profoundly different from that of Greek thought. It is not the sensible, "matter," "body," which are evil and defective. . . . Sin is of another order. Its origin is spiritual. . . .

To analyze these metaphysical positions of Hebraic-Biblical thought is to take account of that which is contained implicitly in the idea of creation; it is to distinguish it from that which is not creation (from fabrication, which is a "making" proper to the human being) and to develop all its demands and all its consequences. . . . If one does not accept all the implications in the idea of creation, one is led by logical necessity to jettison: *Time;* the idea of *Person,* since the many has not been engendered by a creative will, but proceeds from a purely negative individuation by "matter"; the idea of *love,* since the multiplicity of persons is nothing but the illusory or regrettable inverse of a Unity which alone is truly real. That which the pantheist would call love is only the return to the One.

II. TIME

Creation is not far removed from us, relegated into an inaccessible past. It continues today as in the beginning; or more exactly, today *is* also beginning. Genesis has not ended. It continues. We are in genesis. . . . The real is not a universe of fabricated objects, finished once for all. It is in the act of being created. It is proper to creation not to be a fabrication. This act of creation is a fact of experience, the most common, the most universal, and the richest of the teachings of metaphysics.

Time is a concept which signifies that all has not been given at once, but that there is a creation of new reality in a progressive and unceasing fashion, that the real is in the process of being made, in the process of being invented, little by little. It signifies that the new is continually being engendered. It is a concept derived from the real. It characterizes that aspect of the real which is to be still in genesis, in parturition. Time is a concept that the act of creation connotes, as one of its properties. . . .

We shall see . . . the importance of this sense of the temporal in the Biblical concept of the intelligence which is a dynamic intuition of Being in genesis, and in the Biblical notion of stupidity which is an inversion, a sin against creation, an infantile fixation to that which is bound and dead. . . .

In metaphysics where the world is only an image of the intelligible, from which it proceeds by a participation, there is not a real creation of new being, only imitation of the eternal Idea: time, in this case, is itself also only a moving image of eternity (Timeus 37d) . . . a movement of descent from the One . . . "the necessary deduction of the premises which enfold an idea." Then time is nothing, because a deduction . . . by an infinite mind, would be able to be effected instantly. . . .

There are several kinds of movement. 1) Displacement. . . , 2) Cyclical movement. . . , 3) The movement of evolution. This last is the movement of growth, genesis, maturation. It is irreversible. . . . It is movement par excellence, the most real. It is the movement developing organic wholes. The other movements, displacement and the cyclical, are derived from this one. The tree grows, life engenders species, the universe explodes in sheaves, the individual is born and grows—that is their primal movement. Displacement of a "thing" is only a secondary phenomenon, for the "thing" no longer participates in living genesis; it is a "falling off". . . .

The Cartesian universe is a universe of "things," which means basically a universe of fabricated objects. . . . Descartes confuses the organic and the mechanical, that is to say creation and fabrication. . . . The "thingism," the "shockism," are the result of a misunderstanding of physical or biological reality, which is always organic. In this artificial universe of dislocated "things," in this world composed of a dust of things, time itself is composed of a dust of instants. . . .

The Greeks seem to have been struck above all by cyclical movement, in the interior of a whole which is itself an evolution. They did not have the idea of this movement of creative evolution, cosmic or biological. As we said, *we* are in the process of discovering time; modern biology, paleontology, astrophysics, reveal to us that at all levels, in all species, we are not a cosmos, but in cosmogenesis. The Greek universe is a finished, arrested cosmos. In the movements they had before their eyes, the Greeks gave their attention to repetitive cycles, and on the other hand, to a movement of falling away, that of *catagenesis*. . . .

The Heraclitean *panta re* signifies rather that all passes, all escapes us, all flees us. . . . Time is an aging. The Greek future is pessimistic; it defines itself as a passage toward death. It assumes a negative sign: it is a descending becoming, a falling off. . . .

In the Biblical texts . . . creation is in the process of being made. Particularly in regard to man, something is in the process of being created. History is this *maturation*. . . . This history . . . admits of *stages* of "time," "moments." A property of Biblical history is that through the prophets it has become conscious of its sense or direction. The *nabi* is he who has the understanding of the sense of history, that which it signifies, where it goes. We can understand only simultaneously the significance of the historic event, its intentionality, that which it announces, that which it prepares. An historical event is a sign in so far as we can read in it that which is in the act of being made. . . .

"The understanding of times to know that which Israel must do" (I Chron., 12:33). . . . "The king appealed to the wisemen who had the knowledge of times" (Esth., I:13). . . .

A certain "plenitude of times" is necessary for each creation, for the harvest, for the birth, as for the Incarnation. . . . These movements of maturation of history are discoverable by intrinsic "signs," as the peasant discerns the degree of maturity of wheat and the proximity of harvest from the appearance of the ears: "Do not you say: There are yet four months, and then the harvest cometh? Behold, I say to you, lift up your eyes, and see the countries. For they are already white to harvest." (John 4:35.) "And from the fig tree learn a parable: When the branch thereof is now tender and the leaves come forth, you know that summer is nigh" (Matt., 24:32). "When it is evening, you say, It will be fair weather, for the sky is red. And in the morning: today there will be a storm, for the sky is red and lowering. You know then how to discern the face of the sky: and can you not know the signs of the times?" (Matt., 16:2.) "When you see a cloud rising from the west, presently you say: A shower is coming. And so it happeneth. And when ye see the south wind blow, you say: There will be heat. And it cometh to pass . . . you know how to discern the face of the heaven and of the earth: but how is it that you do not discern this time?" (Luke, 12:56.) Jesus has awareness of the time of a certain maturity, a certain "threshold" for the act of his life and his death to be accomplished: "My *kairos* is not yet come" (John, 7:6); "My *kairos* is not yet accomplished" (John, 7:8); "My hour has not yet come" (John, 2:4); "His hour had not yet come (John, 7:30; 8:20). At a certain "moment" Jesus declares: "My time, my *kairos* is near" (Matt., 26:18); "the hour has come" (John, 12:23; 17:1); "Jesus knowing that his hour had come . . ." (John, 13:1). Even as there is a "time" of Incarnation, so there will be a "time" of plenitude, a *plêrôma* of time: that of the final maturation of all creation, and of the final harvest. "The time is near" (Apoc., 1:3).

History is an unceasing invention where multiple liberties cooperate, the creative action of God and the co-creative action of man. History is not the unfolding in time of a pre-existing model where all would have been given in advance. This results in the fact that the hour of the end would not know to be known. "But of that day or hour no man knoweth, neither the angels in heaven, nor the Son, but the Father" (Mark, 13:32), "but the Father alone" (Matt. 24:36).

III. THE TIME OF ETERNITY

But the disinterestedness of knowing, its contemplative detachment is not, as in Platonism, exclusive of action. On the contrary, a knowing capable of embracing history in the unity of one apprehension is a taut knowing, creative, eminently active, but its action is free of practical concern. It is not a fabricating knowing, but a creative knowing: "Isn't it precisely the tension of duration of a knowing being that measures his power to act, the quantity of free and creative activity that he is able to introduce into the world?"

Time connotes the act of creation. Eternity is the point of view of the creator. There is, therefore, in Bergson a notion of eternity in the sense that all the past can be assumed by a knowing which is creative and free in an eternal present. . . . In Plotinus, eternity comprehends, *tota simul,* the past, the present, and the future. . . . "God so defined, has nothing all made; He is life incessant, action, freedom. Then the Absolute reveals itself very near to us. . . . He lives with us. Like us, but in certain respects infinitely more concentrated and gathered to Himself; He lasts."

In Biblical thought, as in Bergson, eternity co-exists with an inventive and creative time. Time is not the unfolding of that which was already given in the non-temporal, of such a kind that a glance freed from temporality could see at once that which was given one time for always. Time is in reality perpetual genesis, "unforeseeable newness. . . ."

The Biblical dialectic between time and eternity excludes all fatalism, all conception of predestination which would rest on the postulate that all is already made, finished somewhere, and that we only wind off a skein and a destiny already spun. Time, and history as well, would not have a direction if they were only the duplication, the progressive copy of an anterior model, much more perfect, where all was already given. . . .

In Biblical metaphysic, God created gratuitously. Time is creation in the act of being accomplished; eternity is the point of view of the creator. Their co-existence is that of the creative action of God and His sufficiency. This is the paradox of the gratuity of creation. The creative action of God co-exists with His repose, His Sabbath. . . . In God, this co-existence of His sufficiency and His Action opens a perspective, demands a hypothesis which the New Testament will come to confirm: God created by love. Thus the Biblical dialectic of time from eternity founds a metaphysic of liberty for human action, and a theology where the reason of all finds itself in love.

God has created beings who are creators. . . . Human action is creative; it co-exists with divine Action. The latter supports the former, engenders it and pushes it to the plenitude of its autonomy, its liberty: "You are Gods." There is an immanence of human action in the Action of God . . . and inversely immanence of divine

Action in human action; the Action of God operates all with regard to our action. . . .

The Biblical conception of liberty is the Biblical conception of
time. God has created the world, but the creation in its turn continues to be invented. Man, in particular, is creator of his life and
his destiny. . . . As he advances he separates the thorns to the right
and left, and his way is made in proportion. Vocation is apophatic:
it tells us, by defeat, boredom or chagrin, that for which we are not
made. God does not proscribe us a model all made that He suffers
to be followed with obedience. He requires us to be creators, original inventors of this unique way to which we are called. It is with
each one of us like Abraham, who, "being called by God, went out
without knowing whither he went" (Hebr., 11:8). Metaphysicians
who deny real time deny liberty also, because they misunderstand
creation, the power that man has to create his destiny in col-
laboration with God. . . . According to Leibnitz, the destiny of each
man is contained in a seed, implied in his substance, from the time
of his birth. . . . To Leibnitz development is an explication of a
mathematical kind: the notion manifests little by little its properties and its predicates. . . . The Biblical metaphysic is a metaphysic of dialogue. . . . The problem of time and eternity is parallel
to that of the free will of man and the prescience of God, of
free will and of Grace. . . .

What is fascinating in the Platonic universe for a lover of the
Bible is the doctrine of participation. . . . In Platonism, the sensible
participates in the Idea by a degradation. . . . In the Biblical universe, the sensible participates in the intelligible by creation . . . it
is at one time being and sign. . . . The Platonic symbol for represent-
ing and signifying a metaphysical or theological reality appeals to a
myth, to the unreal. The symbol is disincarnated. The sensible, the
concrete, is not suitable to carry the message. It is necessary to
construct a chimera. Only the unreal can play the role of allegory. . . .

On the contrary, the Hebrew uses daily things, communal reality,
history, to signify and teach the mysteries which are the proper
nourishment of the spirit . . . Never does he have recourse to myth,
allegory, legend. The existing contains enough in itself to signify the
mysteries to be known. . . . The advantage of the Hebrew method
of teaching metaphysics and theology by the *maschal* and the parable of concrete fact is its capacity for universality. The *maschal*
grows from the concrete, the most common, the most universally
human. It has no party tied to one particular culture and all its contingencies—its system of abstractions is often reserved for one caste.
In the Biblical mode of expression, it is enough to be human to
understand that which is proposed. The Biblical parable is as intelligible for the Galilean peasant as for the Corinthian docker in the
time of St. Paul, as it is for the worker in the factories of Paris in our
time. We must even add, by them above all. A Greco-Latin culture

is often an impediment to an understanding of these parables, which imply a sense of the real and of work, and such a love of the concrete element as seems a defect to a Platonic mentality; the latter is more or less unconsciously dualist, and too aristocratic to prove the depth and richness of the mystical content of these daily realities of working with the elemental. . . . The particular is the existant. Hebrew thought springs from the particular existant; the particular in the Biblical universe is neither negligible nor insignificant. It is a vehicle of sense.

God has chosen a particular people among the nations to manifest the truth. To do this He called a particular man who is named Abraham, at one particular time and in one limited place. The Incarnation is the choice of the particular, of the real with all its historical and geographic contingencies; a particular woman, a particular epoch, a particular with all its sociological contingencies. God Himself becomes someone particular for us, concrete, an individual with his name, country, his face, his history. The choice of the particular to manifest universal truth, to teach the truth which by right is universal, is without doubt the most profound intellectual scandal, the scandal par excellence for the Hellenic intelligence.

From the Greek point of view, there is too much of the particular in the books of Israel, too many proper names, too much geography, too many dates, and too much history to be a metaphysic. Too many contingent things: truth is necessary. Too many sensible things: the truth is abstract. Too many particular people: truth does not regard persons. Too much geography: truth is outside of space. Too much particular reality: truth is universal. Why this people, rather than those; rather than that man, why this man; why this time, this precise date, rather than another? All our intellectual habits, inherited profoundly from Greek thought, are opposed to this passage through the existing to teach a truth, to this birth of truth, this manifestation of truth in and by a particular reality, existing and concrete. This method—which is the method of the Incarnation—contradicts the profound dualism congenital to our thought: irreducible separation between that which is of the order of essences, the intelligible, and that which is of the order of fact, of the existing, which is contingent and absurd. There is in the scriptures, we say, too much history and geography, too many *facts* for a metaphysics.

—EXCERPTS FROM *Essai sur la Pensée Biblique* BY CLAUDE TRESMONTANT (PARIS: LES ÉDITIONS DU CERF, 1953). The translation is by Sally Appleton.

SUPPLEMENT III

ON ANALOGY: A BIBLIOGRAPHY

Anderson, James F., *The Bond of Being* (St. Louis, 1950).

Anderson, J. F., and Dom. A. Mark Pontifex, "Basis of metaphysical analogy," *Downside Review* (LXV, Winter 1947-48), pp. 38-50.

Aquinas: there is no specific treatise by St. Thomas on analogy. For materials cf. Anderson, *The Bond of Being,* p. 328. For a list of texts in St. Thomas on analogy, cf. A. van Leeuwen, "L'Analogie de l'être," *Revue néo-scolastique* (XXXIX, 1936), p. 495.

Aristotle: for Aristotle on analogy cf. bibliography in Anderson, *The Bond of Being,* p. 238; Owens, J., *The Doctrine of Being in the Aristotelian Metaphysics* (Toronto, 1951).

Balthasar, N., *L'abstraction et l'analogie métaphysique des êtres dans l'être* (Louvain, 1935).

——————, *L'Etre et les principes métaphysiques* (Louvain, 1914).

Bittremieux, F., *De analogica nostra Dei cogitatione et praedicatione* (Louvain, 1913).

Blanche, F. A., "L'Analogie," *Revue de philosophie* (XXX, 1923), pp. 248-70. "La notion d'analogie dans la philosophie de S. Thomas," *Revue des sc. phil. et théol.* (X, 1921), pp. 169-93. "Sur le sens de quelques locutions concernant l'analogie dans le langage de S. Thomas," *Revue des sc. phil. et théol.* (X, 1921), pp. 52-59. "Une théorie de l'analogie," *Revue de philosophie* (XXXII, 1932), pp. 37-78.

Byles, W. Esdaile, "Analogy of Being," *New Scholasticism* (XVI, 1942), pp. 331-64.

Cajetan (Thomas de Vio), *The Analogy of Names and the Concept of Being* (Pittsburgh, 1953).

——————, *Scripta Philosophica, De nominum analogia, De conceptu entis,* ed. P. N. Zammit, Institutum Angelicum, 1934.

Chollet, A., "Analogie," *DTC*.

Collins, James, "Przywara's Analogia Entis," *Thought* (XVII, March, 1942), pp. 119-35.

Euclid, *The Thirteen Books of Euclid's Elements* (tr. Heath), vol. 11, esp. pp. 112-117, 120-124, 131 ff.

Fabro, C., *La nozione metafisica de participazione seconde S. Tommasco d'Aquino*, 2 ed. (Torino, 1950).

—————, "Un itineraire de S. Thomas: L'établissement de la distinct réelle entre essence et existence," *Revue de philosophie* (XXXIX, 1939), pp. 285-310.

Feckes, K., *Die Analogie in unserem Gotterkennen* (Munster, 1928).

de Finance, Joseph, *Être et Agir dans la philosophie de St. Thomas* (Paris, 1945).

de Munnynck, M., "L'analogie métaphysique," *Revue néo-scholastique* (1923), pp. 129 ff.

de Solages, Bruno, *Dialogie sur l'analogie* (Paris, 1947).

Foote, E. T., "Anatomy of Analogy," *Modern Schoolman* (XIX, Nov. 1940).

Gardeil, Henri, "La structure analogique de l'intellect," *Revue Thomiste* (1926).

Geiger, L., *La participation dans la philosophie de S. Thomas d'Aquin* (Paris, 1942). (Esp. chapter on Being.)

Gilson, Etienne, *Jean Duns Scot, Introduction à ses positions fondamentales* (Paris, 1952).

Grenet, P., *Les origines de l'analogie philosophique dans les dialogues de Platon* (Paris, 1948).

Hayen, André, *L'Intentionnel dans la philosophie de S. Thomas* (Paris, 1942).

Heath, Sir Thomas, *A History of Greek Mathematics* (Oxford, 1921), Vol. I, esp. pp. 325-27, pp. 384 ff.

Horgan, J., "Aspects of Cajetan's Theory of Analogy," *Irish Ecclesiastical Record* (46, 1935), pp. 113-36.

Hubatka, "De momento analogiae entis in theologia dialectica Caroli Barth et Aemilii Brunner et in Thomismo," *Doctor Communis* (Rome, 1950), pp. 187-92.

Landry, Bernard, *La notion de l'analogie chez St. Bonaventure et St. Thomas d'Aquin* (Louvain, 1922).

Marc, P. A., *Cursus Ontologiae* (Jersey, 1937).

—————, "L'Idée thomiste de l'être et les analogies d'attribution et de proportionnalité," *Revue néo-scholastique* (XXXV, 1933), pp. 157-89.

Mascall, E. L., *Existence and Analogy* (London, 1949), Chapter 5, "The Doctrine of Analogy."

Owens, Joseph, *The Doctrine of Being in the Aristotelian Metaphysics* (Toronto, 1951).

Parente, P., "Quid re valeat humana de Deo cognitio," *Acta Pont. Acad. Rom. S. Th. Aq.* (1935), pp. 7-13; bibliography, p. 13.

Phelan, Gerald, *St. Thomas and Analogy* (Milwaukee, 1941).

Ryan, Columba, "God and Analogy," *Blackfriars* (25, 1944), pp. 137-42.

Souilhé (Père), *La notion platonicienne d'intermédiaire dans la philosophie des dialogues* (Paris, 1919).

Valensin, A., "Une théorie de l'analogie," *Revue apol.* (1921).

Van Leeuwen, A., "L'Analogie de l'être. Génèse et contenu du concept d'analogie," *Revue néo-scholastique* (XXXIX, 1936), pp. 293-320.

"L'Analogie de l'être. Précisions sur la nature de cette analogie," *Revue néo-scholastique* (XXXIX, 1936), pp. 469-96.

SUPPLEMENT IV

Medieval Exegesis:
Some Documents for the Literary Critic

Prepared by JOHN P. McCALL

In recent years students of literature and theology alike have shown great interest in the techniques of medieval exegesis and the fourfold method of interpretation. It is the purpose of these pages to illustrate some of these techniques, to show various contemporary reactions to them, and to focus attention on certain crucial issues so that new questions may be asked, and new solutions sought.

No attempt has been made to make this a definitive collection of documents, or to show an historical development of critical attitudes. Nor do I pretend to be simply a compiler. It is my own feeling that enough, and perhaps too much, has been said to draw clear lines of distinction between literalistic and symbolistic criticisms, particularly in medieval studies; it may very well be that each side is in the process of distorting the views of the other, instead of clarifying their mutual problems. Thus, if the documents have any particular aim, it is to affirm the values of both the "letter" and the "spirit" in the hope that we may discover more about the ways in which they nourish each other.

JOHN P. MCCALL
GEORGETOWN UNIVERSITY
OCTOBER, 1959

Contents
for Supplement IV

An early illustration of the fourfold method appears in the *Collations* of John Cassian (ca. 370–435 ....). He begins with the distinction between handicraft, or literal interpretation, on the one hand, and spiritual interpretation, on the other. The spiritual interpretation, though it did not allegory to the literal significance, enlarged or liberally displicated and enriched... literal significance. The implications of... it... to put the distinction together, but it should be noted that the conclusive passages, taken singly, once emphasized, discover... the narrative material, asking always... regarding importance of... each... of the historical... in keeping with the list of original passages.

I. THE FOURFOLD
METHOD OF EXEGESIS

1. JOHN CASSIAN

An early description of the fourfold method appears in the *Collationes* of John Cassian (ca. 370-435 A.D.). He begins with the distinction between historical, or literal, interpretation on the one hand, and spiritual interpretation on the other. The spiritual interpretation, then, is divided into allegory or doctrinal significance, anagogy or heavenly significance, and tropology or moral significance. The simple explanation of "Jerusalem" according to all four levels of significance helps to pull the discussion together, but it should be noted that the complete passage is neither simple nor mechanical. Moreover, the emphasis that the author places upon the importance of reality—of the historical fact—is in keeping with the best medieval exegesis.

But let us return to the exposition of knowledge which we mentioned at the beginning of the discussion. Practically speaking, as we said above, knowledge is drawn from many professions and studies. Theoretically it is divided into two parts, that is, into historical interpretation and spiritual understanding. For this very reason, when he had enumerated the manifold graces of the Church, Solomon added, "For all her domestics are clothed with twofold garments" (Proverbs, 31, 21). The kinds of spiritual knowledge, however, are tropology, allegory, and anagogy; and concerning these three Solomon says in Proverbs 22, 20, "Describe my doctrine to yourself in a threefold way, above the breadth of your heart." And so the history of past and visible things embraces an understanding of things which the Apostle describes in this way: "For it is written that Abraham had two sons, the one by a bondwoman and the other by a free woman; but he who was of the bondwoman was born according to the flesh; but he of the free woman was by promise" (Galatians 4, 22-23). They refer, however, to the allegory which follows because, on one hand, they truly existed [in history], and, on the other hand, they are said to have prefigured the nature of the agreement: "For (he says) these are the two testaments: the one from Mount Sina, engendering unto bondage, which is Agar; for Sina is a mountain in Arabia, which hath affinity to that Jerusalem which now is, and is in bondage with her children" (Galatians 4, 24-25). Anagogy, then, concerns spiritual mysteries and ascends to the loftier and more sacred secrets of the heavens. The Apostle puts it this way: "But that Jerusalem which is above is free, which is our mother. For it is written: 'Rejoice, thou barren, that bearest not: break forth and cry, thou that travailest not: for many are the children of the desolate, more than of her that hath a husband'" (Galatians 4, 26-27). Tropology is moral explanation and refers to the amendment of life and to practical instruction. It is just as if we understood these same two testaments as a practical and a theoretical regimen. Certainly we may understand Jerusalem or Sion as the soul of man, as when we read, "Praise the Lord, O Jerusalem: praise thy God, O Sion" (Psalm 147, 12). Therefore, the four above-mentioned figures may run together in this way, if we wish, so that the one and the same Jerusalem can be understood in a fourfold way: according to history it is the city of the Jews; according to allegory it is the Church of Christ; according to anagogy it is the city of God in heaven, which is the mother of us all; according to tropology it is the soul of man which, by this name, is frequently reviled or praised by God [in Sacred Scripture]. Concerning these four kinds of interpretation the Apostle says this: "But now, brethren, if I come to you speaking with tongues, what shall I profit you, unless I speak to you either in revelation, or in knowledge, or in prophecy, or in doctrine?" (1 Corinthians 14, 6.) Surely revelation refers to allegory through which those things that historical narration touches upon are revealed in a spiritual sense and meaning. It is as though we tried to explain how "our fathers were all under the cloud and all in Moses were baptized, in the cloud and in the sea," and how "all did eat the same spiritual food, and all drank the same spiritual drink of the rock that followed them; and the rock was Christ" (I Corinthians 10, 1-4). This account, which prefigures the body and blood of Christ that we consume daily, by comparison, contains the basis of allegory. Indeed, knowledge, which is recalled in a similar way by the Apostle, is tropology, by which we discern through prudent study all those things that refer to practical good conduct, whether useful or honorable. Take, for example, this case: when we are advised "to judge" for ourselves whether "it is fitting for a woman to pray to God with her head uncovered" (1 Corinthians 11, 13). This remark, as has been said, contains moral significance. In the same way prophecy, which the Apostle put in the third place, echoes anagogy, through which the discourse is transferred to the invisible and future [world], as it is here: "And we will not have you ignorant, brethren, concerning them that sleep, that you be not sorrowful, even as others who have not hope. For if we believe that Jesus died and rose again, even so them who have slept through Jesus, will God bring with him. For this we say unto you in the word of the Lord, that we who are alive, who remain unto the coming of the Lord, shall not prevent them who have slept. For the Lord himself shall come down from heaven with commandment, and with the voice of an archangel, and with the trumpet of God; and the dead who are in Christ shall rise first" (1 Thessalonians 5, 12-15). In this kind of exhortation the figure of anagogy is revealed. Indeed, doctrine clarifies the simple order of historical narration where nothing very hidden is understood, unless it re-echoes and is contained in words. Consider these examples: "For I delivered unto you first of all, which I also received, how that Christ died for our sins, according to the Scriptures, and that he was buried, and that he rose again on the third day, and that he was seen by Cephas" (1 Corinthians 15, 3-5); and "God sent his Son, made of woman, made under the law, that he might redeem them that were under the law" (Galatians 4, 4-5); or this, "Hear, O Israel, your Lord is the one God" (Deuteronomy 6, 4).

—TRANSLATED FROM *Collatio* XIV, CHAPTER 8 (*Patrologia Latina*, XLIX, COL. 962-965). The translation is my own.

2. HUGH OF ST. VICTOR

This selection describes how Hugh St. Victor, in the twelfth century, approached the reading of Scripture. It should be noted that Hugh is a traditionalist and not a revolutionary. He re-emphasized basic principles which extravagant allegorizers had been neglecting, namely, that the literal or historical meaning is the basis for figurative interpretations, that allegory is important—it is the "body of the doctrinal edifice," and that hasty, arbitrary allegorizations, which neglect reality, are dangerous.

The reader's attention is called to the recent publication of a scholarly translation of Hugh of St. Victor's *Didascalicon* by Jerome Taylor (New York: Columbia University Press, 1961) and to the appearance of the monumental study on the fourfold method by Henri de Lubac. S.J., *Exégèse medievale: Les quatre sens de l'écriture* (Paris: 1959, 1961, 2 parts in 3 volumes).

Hugh St. Victor distinguishes three senses of Scripture: the literal or historical sense, the allegorical sense, and the moral or tropological sense (*history, allegory,* and *tropology*). However, let us not always try to find these three senses at the same time in Scripture: that is, some passages ought to be understood only in a spiritual sense, others concern conduct particularly, others signify only history and facts; some contain history, allegory, and tropology all at once. And the reason for this richness of Scripture, which characterizes it with respect to secular [pagan?] writings, is that not only the words have significance, but the realities signified are themselves symbolic. . . .

. . . *History, allegory,* and *tropology* represent not only three senses of Scripture, but three distinct disciplines which are taught and studied separately, with particular methods. It is fitting to study them in order: history, then allegory, and finally tropology.

The first technique, the one which is the foundation of the two others, is *history.* This word has a double sense. It signifies first of all the account of things past, but . . . one may also understand by *history* the sense which appears in a text at first glance, that is, the literal sense. It is *history* understood in its ordinary and first sense which Hugh regards as the foundation on which all the structure of scriptural interpretation should rest. He insists that one study it seriously. In his opinion, one could not acquire great skill in allegorical interpretation except by first knowing *history* well, and he mocks those of his contemporaries who said that they wished to leave the fiction to the false-apostles, and to philosophize immediately, that is to come to the allegorical interpretation at once. This is like wanting to be called a grammarian before even knowing the alphabet.

Hugh St. Victor insists on this point in the *De Scripturis et scriptoribus sacris.* "Since the understanding of the mystical sense has for its foundation what the letter presents to us at first sight, I am amazed by the boldness of some who pride themselves in being doctors of allegories, even when they still ignore the first meaning of the letter.—We, they say, we "read" the Scripture, but we do not "read" the letter; we are not concerned with the letter; but we teach allegory.—And how can you "read" the Scripture without "reading" the letter? If one does away with the letter, what is left of the Scripture?—We, they reply, we "read" the letter, but we do not "read" according to the letter. For we "read" the allegory and we comment on the letter, not *according to the letter,* but *according to the allegory.*—But then Hugh replies, how can you comment on the letter without showing what the meaning of the letter is?—The letter, reply his adversaries, has two senses, one *according to the letter,* and the other *according to the allegory.* Thus the word *lion* understood *according to history* signifies an animal, but *according to the allegory* it signifies Christ." To this Hugh St. Victor replies with a great deal of finesse and pertinency that it is not the word *lion* which designates Christ, but the reality itself designated by this word is alone the symbol of the Saviour. A significant discussion and one which is an indication of a dangerous tendency; to rely, less and less, on the proper sense of the text, and to surrender to perfectly arbitrary allegorical interpretations. . . .

The knowledge of history is acquired; then it is time to look for allegories. Hugh St. Victor, comparing the teaching of the Scriptures to the construction of a building, says that *history* is the foundation, *allegory* represents the walls—the whole of the structure, *tropology* the roof and the ornamentation. By *allegory,* then, he means the part of the building which is erected after having put *history* at the base, but he gives no precise and clear definition. "There is allegory," he says, "when what is signified by the letter of Scripture symbolizes, in turn, another fact, present or future." In the spiritual sense not only the words, but things and events are signs. This definition does not clearly explain what the direct object of allegory is—considered as distinct from tropology. But one recognizes quickly on reading Hugh St. Victor, and the authors who talk about the allegorical sense, that by this they understand the doctrinal content of Scriptures.

Hugh of St. Victor insists a great deal on the difficulty which allegorical intrepretation presents; it is not within reach of slow and feeble spirits; it requires subtlety and prudence, a precise and clear knowledge of Christian truths; for it must always conform to doctrine, to the truth of the faith. Allegory is the construction, the body of the doctrinal edifice: but it includes, besides the foundation—the knowledge of history—the solid laws which are the rudiments of the faith. All allegories, to be acceptable, must be suited to, and not contradict, the fundamental truths of the faith. . . .

It is now time for moral considerations (*tropology*), which give spirit to the realities signified in Scripture. There is a natural goodness (*justitia naturalis*) in Scripture from which right and just moral conduct can arise (*justitia positiva*): "By contemplating what God has done, we recognize what we should be doing. All nature speaks of God. All nature teaches man. All nature gives birth to reason, and nothing in the universe is sterile." Nature, for Hugh, is more than a field for empirical investigation: it has meaning; one can grasp in nature the benevolence and the lessons of its divine Author. It induces man to look zealously for the purely physical explanations, but even more to find, in the interior itself of the natural order, a thought of God.

—G. PARÉ, A. BRUNET, P. TREMBLAY, *La Renaissance du XIIe Siècle: les écoles et l'enseignement* (PARIS AND OTTAWA, 1933), PP. 221-226. The translation is my own.

3. ST. THOMAS AQUINAS

The preciseness of St. Thomas' systematic approach to the fourfold method is evident in Father Spicq's account. But in addition to clear definitions, we can see that St. Thomas gives less value than his predecessors to spiritual interpretation. Like a number of his contemporaries he seems more interested in solid arguments from Scripture than in the spiritual reading of it. However, it is well for the modern critic to remember that medieval and renaissance humanists were not always as ready to question the value of spiritual reading; Erasmus, for example, could say that it is better to read pagan fables allegorically than the Bible only literally.

St. Thomas emphasizes the spiritual sense less than his predecessors; but his definition of it is a great deal more precise: "When the things of the Old Law may signify those of the New Law, we have the allegorical sense; when the things realized in Christ, or concerning the figures of Christ, are the sign of what we should do, we have the moral sense; finally, if we consider that these same things signify what concerns eternal glory, we have the anagogical sense." Like all the medieval writers, St. Thomas scarcely treats the anagogical sense in practice, and he is often content to contrast the literal sense with the mystical sense—the one which includes the three spiritual senses—according to the practice sanctioned by Stephen Langton.

Quodlibet VII, a. 15 explains in more detail: "The truth which Holy Scripture teaches by the figures of things is determined by two things, believing well and doing well. If it teaches doing well we have the moral sense, which is also called tropological. But if it teaches believing well, we must distinguish according to the order of things believed. Indeed, as Denis the Areopagite says: the condition of the Church is intermediate between the state of the Synagogue and the state of the Church triumphant. Therefore the Old Testament was the figure of the New; the Old and the New together are the figure of celestial things. Therefore the spiritual sense, directed toward believing well, may be established on this figurative method according to which the Old Testament figures the New, and this is the allegorical or typical sense; in this sense the events related in the Old Testament are understood in terms of Christ and the Church; or the spiritual sense may be established on this figurative method according to which the Old and New Testament together signify the Church triumphant, and this is the anagogical sense."

The reply to the fifth objection in this same article is still more developed. It gives the hermeneutic rule for the application of the spiritual senses—called for by Hugh St. Victor—through a

rational systematization of which St. Thomas is the creator. First
of all here is the principle of progressive finality and of scriptural
revelation: "The four senses are attributed to Scripture, not so
that we should give a quadruple intrepretation of all of its passages, but sometimes four, sometimes three, sometimes two, and
sometimes only one. In fact, *in Holy Scripture it is especially
true that what should follow in the order of time should be signified by what precedes it;* thus occasionally it happens in Holy
Scripture that what is said in the literal sense of what precedes
can be interpreted, in the spiritual sense, of what will come later;
however, the reverse is not true." The application of this principle follows: "But among all the things that are narrated in Holy
Scripture, the first are those which spring from the Old Testament, and that is why what is related according to the literal
sense in the deeds of the Old Testament may be interpreted according to the four senses indicated. In the second place come
the things which are related to the state of the present Church;
among these things, the first are those which concern the head
(Christ), those which refer to what concerns the members (the
faithful); for the true body of Christ himself, and what occurs
in him, are the figure of the mystical body of Christ, and what
happens in it; thus we should take the example for our lives from
Christ himself. Finally, future glory is prefigured for us in Christ.
The result of all this is that what is said in the literal sense about
Christ, our head, can be interpreted (1) allegorically, by referring it to his mystical body, and (2) morally, by referring it to
our acts which should be reformed to his example, and (3) ana-
gogically, in as much as the road of glory is shown to us in the
person of Christ. On the contrary, what is said of the Church in
the literal sense cannot be interpreted allegorically, unless, perhaps, we interpret what is said in this way of the primitive Church
in order to apply it to the subsequent state of the actual Church.
But we can give a moral and anagogical interpretation of these
facts. On the other hand, what is presented in the literal sense,
as pertaining to moral conduct, is usually interpreted only according to the allegorical sense. Finally, what refers to the state of
glory, in the literal sense, is not ordinarily interpreted in any other
sense, because it is not the figure of another thing, but on the
contrary all the rest figures it."

Therefore—and this is a considerable innovation—we cannot
arbitrarily apply any spiritual sense to a text of Scripture. Moreover, in spite of these exact limitations, the allegorical, moral or
anagogical interpretations cannot be derived from the text with
absolute certitude; a good deal of conjecture always remains; also,
we can propose these interpretations with confidence only in so
far as the truths that they express are clearly affirmed by the literal sense of other biblical texts: "Nothing is expressed by hidden meaning anywhere in Holy Scripture which is not expressed

in clear meaning elsewhere; thus a spiritual interpretation should always be supported by some literal interpretation of Holy Scripture; in this way the occasion of all error is avoided."

The answer to the subsequent objection makes it clear that if we cannot make an effective argument from the spiritual sense, it is not because it lacks authority but because it depends on a comparison; but there are so many possibilities for resemblances between things that we cannot with certitude refer this thing to that, more than to some other: "It is not because of the lack of authority that it is impossible to draw an effective argument from the spiritual sense, but because of the nature of similitudes on which the spiritual sense is based. For one thing can resemble many things; therefore it is not possible, when one thing is intended in Holy Scripture, to proceed from that one thing to some others in a fixed way; this is a fallacy of consequence. For example, the lion signifies Christ and the devil because of certain similarities; therefore, because something is said of the lion in Holy Scripture, we cannot reach either significance for arguing in Holy Scripture." We can add (according to II^a II^{ae}, qu. 1, a. 9, 10) that the authority of the Church will determine exactly the tenor of these spiritual senses.

—C. Spic, *Esquisse d'une histoire de l'exégèse latine au moyen âge* (Paris, 1944), pp. 285-88. The translation is my own.

4. DANTE

In the letter to Can Grande della Scala, Dante explains the fourfold method for biblical exegesis, and then for the *Divine Comedy*.

To elucidate, then, what we have to say, be it known that the sense of this work is not simple, but on the contrary it may be called polysemous, that is to say, "of more senses than one"; for it is one sense which we get through the letter, and another which we get through the thing the letter signifies; and the first is called literal, but the second allegorical or mystic. And this mode of treatment, for its better manifestation, may be considered in this verse: "When Israel came out of Egypt, and the house of Jacob from a people of strange speech. Judaea became his sanctification, Israel his power." For if we inspect the letter alone the departure of the children of Israel from Egypt in the time of Moses is presented to us; if the allegory, our redemption wrought by Christ; if the moral sense, the conversion of the soul from the grief and misery of sin to the state of grace is presented to us; if the an-

agogical, the departure of the holy soul from the slavery of this
corruption to the liberty of eternal glory is presented to us. And
although these mystic senses have each their special denomina-
tions, they may all in general be called allegorical, since they differ from the literal and historical; for *allegory* is derived from
alleon, in Greek, which means the same as the Latin *alienum*
or *diversum.*

When we understand this we see clearly that the *subject* round
which the alternative senses play must be twofold. And we must
therefore consider the subject of this work as literally understood,
and then its subject as allegorically intended. The subject of the
whole work, then, taken in the literal sense only, is "the state of
souls after death," without qualification, for the whole progress of
the work hinges on it and about it. Whereas if the work be taken
allegorically the subject is "man, as by good or ill deserts, in the
exercise of the freedom of his choice, he becomes liable to re-
warding or punishing justice."

> —THE TRANSLATION IS FROM THE TEMPLE
> CLASSICS, *The Latin Works of Dante* (LONDON,
> 1934), PP. 347-348.

5. BOCCACCIO

In his *Genealogy of the Gods* Boccaccio illustrates how
the fourfold method of Scriptural interpretation analogously
applies to pagan fictions. But at one point he makes an important distinction: although pagan fictions in Christian
writings could sometimes "be employed in the service of
Catholic truth"—that is, they could be used according to the
fourfold method—nevertheless, pagan fictions in pagan writings should be interpreted only according to physical nature
or natural morality.*

The first meaning is the superficial, which is called literal. The
others are deeper, and are called allegorical. To make the matter
easier, I will give an example. According to the poetic fiction,
Perseus, son of Jupiter, killed the Gorgon, and flew away victor-
ious into the air. Now, this may be understood superficially in its
literal or historical sense. In the moral sense it shows a wise man's
triumph over vice and his attainment of virtue. Allegorically it
figures the pious man who scorns worldly delight and lifts his
mind to heavenly things. It admits also an anagogical sense, since

* *Genealogy of the Gods,* XV, viii. Compare D. W. Robertson, Jr.,
"Some Medieval Literary Terminology," *Studies in Philology,* XLVIII
(1951), 678.

it symbolizes Christ's victory over the Prince of this World, and his Ascension. But all these secondary meanings, by whatever name, are essentially allegorical. For "allegory" is from 'άλλο, Latin *alienum,* and is so called being alien from the literal or historical sense. But it is not my intention to unfold all these meanings for each myth when I find one quite enough.

—*Genealogy of the Gods,* I, iii, TRANSLATED BY CHARLES G. OSGOOD IN HIS *Boccaccio on Poetry* (PRINCETON, 1930), P. *xviii.* A paperback edition of this text has recently been issued by the Liberal Arts Press, New York, N.Y.

6. NICHOLAS OF LYRE

This familiar quotation from Nicholas of Lyre (14th century) briefly and simply summarizes the four levels of meaning.

The literal teaches history, your belief is allegory;
Moral is what you do, where you go is anagogy.
(Littera gesta docet, quid credas allegoria.
Moralis quid agas, quo tendas anagogia.)

—*Patrologia Latina,* CXIII, COL. 28. The translation is my own.

7. NICHOLAS OF LYRE'S DISTICH EXPLAINED

The implications of the distich are described at length by Father De Lubac. He points out the sophistication, the logic, and the present value of the fourfold method when properly understood.

(1) *Littera gesta docet.* Scripture first gives us actual facts, the story of God's interventions in the history of humanity. This is the first thing to be learned, the foundation of all the rest. (2) *Quid credas allegoria.* Here we have the doctrine, the very object of faith, the "mystery," the ensemble of truths concerning Christ and His Church, prefigured everywhere in the Old Testament, presented in the New. It is the medieval idea: "materia sacrae Scripturae totus Christus est, caput et membra." (3) *Moralis quid agas.* Not just any moral instruction, but that which flows from

the dogma, from the mystery. The whole Bible is then a mirror, where man learns to know himself with his misery and his sin, and the perfection to which God destines and calls him; in the facts of Scripture we find the inward drama of the soul. (4) *Quo tendas anagogia.* This is the eschatological sense, that of the last things, the celestial realities which are no longer the symbol of something else. The classic, all-inclusive example is Jerusalem, which is (*a*) the historical city of the Jews, (*b*) the Church, (*c*) the Christian soul, and (*d*) the heavenly Jerusalem, the Church triumphant.

Of these four senses, De Lubac insists, neither the number nor the order (especially the latter) is a matter of indifference. He ranges through the various medieval ideas that apparently demanded four scriptural senses (e.g., the four rivers of Paradise) or three spiritual senses (e.g., the Trinity). He admits that these are *post factum* symbols, mental gymnastics; but he insists that the number and order are indispensable if we are to grasp the master intuition. It is simply a question of constructing the whole edifice of Christian thought, of extracting from the Bible the fulness of its "theology." We must begin by recalling the biblical facts, because on these facts the dogma rests; the moral application in its turn is based on the dogma; and the realization of our last end supposes this dogma lived in the morality.

But there is here not merely a necessary dependence of one sense on the other; there is a dynamic continuity. One sense begets the other. They are not just parts of a whole; it is always the selfsame reality seen under its successive aspects. The mystery is not only announced, prefigured, or vouched for by the facts; the facts themselves are already pregnant with the mystery. We do wrong, therefore, to oppose allegory to history; to the medieval mind the allegory is still the history, no longer merely recorded but "understood." In the same way the morality is not simply based on the dogma; it is the dogma, but lived. It sets forth the mystery of Christ and of the Church insofar as this mystery is really reproduced in the soul and life of the faithful; for Christ is interior to the Christian. Thus there is no true tropology save by way of allegory, or, as we would say, no authentic spirituality which is not an actuation of dogma; there is no mystery to believe which has not its translation in the soul. Tropology thus understood will be the spiritual sense par excellence. Finally, the consummation is not mere recompense; it is the reality of the dogma, no longer simply interiorized and lived, but fullblown and triumphant. Such is the essential datum of the distich: the mystery of Christ, prefigured or made present in the facts, interiorized in the individual soul, consummated in glory. That is why St. Thomas could say that the four senses are "de necessitate Scripturae." "By the doctrine which systematizes them something eternal has been aimed at and attained."

De Lubac recognizes that the above is a reconstitution; he does not pretend that each author studied is bearer of the full tradition; he is sensible of the havoc that could be played with his presentation by presenting all the authors in detail. But his aim has been, for fear of utter incomprehension, to cut across all that and "recapture the animating idea which alone explains so lengthy and so vigorous a flowering."

But, he asks, what relationship can such an idea claim with exegesis? The first problem is, how believe that to each detail of Scripture, once the literal sense has been established, there corresponds the triple stage of the other senses? His answer is, such is not the mind of the ancient tradition, despite excess in practice or even in theory. Augustine's metaphor, taken up again and again in the sweep of the centuries, represents the common conception: Scripture is full of Christ, yes; but Scripture is a harp, and though everything in the harp contributes to the sound, still not everything sounds. Even Gregory the Great had merely claimed: "Et fit *plerumque* ut . . . in una eademque sententia cuncta simul tria valeant inveniri."

In that case, one retorts, the affirmations of the distich hold for some texts, not for all. Undoubtedly, replies De Lubac. But he confesses to a qualm in replying to the objection posited that way. It supposes the viewpoint of the historian, who studies one text after another. But the believer's vision is synthetic; the Bible is one book, and of this one book he says globally: "Littera gesta docet. . . ." To him the Bible relates one history, that of salvation; this history has one sense, the spiritual or mystical sense, by turns allegorical, moral, anagogic. The individual "allegories" may be quite subjective, but the principle which they try to bring out, the tremendous "allegory" of Scripture—that is objective. De Lubac tries to show how, in this perspective, the reproaches ("imperfect," "inexact") hurled at our formula lose much, if not all, of their validity. He concludes that, all things considered, the formula does not seem so poorly fashioned. It evidences "a profound logic, which puts a unity of principle into sacred science. . . ."

De Lubac, very sensibly, does not propose a return to this tradition as a guide for contemporary exegesis and theology. He grants that it knew too long a vogue; perspectives have changed, for one thing; and the more the formula was systematized, the more it tended to the absurd.

The formula offers no help, he continues, to the present-day task of the exegete. It did, however, preserve the exegete's rights for the time when he could take flight. It even showed in principle the necessity for such work, by putting the examination of the "letter" at the root of all else. It was fatal only in the measure that exegesis, after having been the whole of theology, became a scientific specialty, and was imprisoned almost exclusively in the realm of the letter. The importance of the spiritual sense in its threefold tenor has not diminished in the Church, but—inevitable result of specialization—it is for others, and according to other methods, to restore its value.

—WALTER J. BURGHARDT, S.J., "On Early Christian Exegesis," *Theological Studies,* XI (1950), PP. 104-6.

II. The Literal Text as Foundation for all Exegesis

8. ST. AUGUSTINE

Medieval exegesis often appears arbitrary to us, and frequently it is, for the goal of all reading—charity—can be made to justify almost any spiritual interpretation. Nevertheless, as early as the patristic writers the dangers of arbitrary reading were recognized. St. Augustine's remarks in the *De Doctrina Christiana* are refreshing.

Whoever understands in the Sacred Scriptures something other than the writer had in mind is deceived, although they do not lie. Yet, as I began to say, if he is deceived in an interpretation by which, however, he builds up charity . . . he is deceived in the same way as is someone who leaves the road through error, but makes his way through the field to the place where the road also leads. Nevertheless, he must be corrected and must be shown how it is more advantageous not to leave the road, lest by a habit of deviating he may be drawn into a crossroad or even go the wrong way.

—St. Augustine, *Christian Instruction,*
translated by John J. Gavigan, O.S.A., in
The Fathers of the Church (New York,
1947), II, p. 57.

Similar sentiments were expressed by Gregory the Great in his prefatory epistle to the
Moralia (*Patrologia Latina*, LXXV, pp. 513-15)

St. Augustine also describes how one can avoid being deceived in his reading of the Bible. It is necessary to have a knowledge of languages and of reality—of words and things. On this foundation the critic should build his spiritual reading of the text.

A knowledge of languages is an efficacious cure for an ignorance of literal signs. Men who know the Latin language . . . have need of two others in order to understand the Sacred Scriptures. These are Hebrew and Greek, by which they may turn back to the originals if the infinite variances of Latin translators cause any uncertainty. . . .

Frequently, a translator who does not understand the sense very well is led astray by an obscure expression in the original language. He therefore translates it with a meaning which is utterly foreign to that of the writer. For example, some texts have: "Their feet are sharp to shed blood." *Oxus* in Greek means both "sharp" and "swift." So, he who translated as "Their feet are swift to shed blood," recognized the true meaning; the other drawn in the opposite direction by an equivocal term, made a mistake. Such translations are not ambiguous; they are erroneous, and there is a great difference between the two things. For we must be taught not how to understand such texts, but rather how to rectify them. . . .

However, in reference to figurative expressions, if, by chance, the reader is caused perplexity by any unknown signs, he must decipher them partly through a knowledge of languages, partly through a knowledge of things. . . . Some men, expert in that language [Hebrew], have rendered a truly valuable service to succeeding ages by having interpreted all these [Hebrew] words apart from the Scriptures and by having given the meanings for *Adam, Eve, Abraham,* and *Moses,* and also for the interpretation of the names of places like *Jerusalem, Sion, Jericho, Sinai, Lebanon, Jordan,* or whatever other names in that language are unknown to us. Because these have been revealed and translated, many figurative passages in the Scriptures are interpreted.

In addition, an imperfect knowledge of things causes figurative passages to be obscure; for example, when we do not recognize the nature of the animals, minerals, plants, or other things which are very often represented in the Scriptures for the sake of an analogy. It is well known that a serpent exposes its whole body, rather than its head, to those attacking it, and how clearly that explains the Lord's meaning when He directed us to be "wise as serpents." We should, therefore, expose our body to persecutors, rather than our head, which is Christ . . . There is also the belief that, having forced itself through a small opening in disposing of its old skin, the serpent gains renewed vigor. How well this agrees with imitating the wisdom of the serpent and stripping off the 'old man' that we may put on the new, as the Apostle expresses it; and we must strip it off passing through narrow places, since the Lord says: "Enter by the narrow gate." A knowledge of the nature of the serpent, therefore, explains many analogies which Holy Scripture habitually makes from that animal; so a lack of knowledge about other animals to which Scripture no less frequently alludes for comparisons hinders a reader very much. The same is true of an ignorance of minerals and plants. . . . Knowledge of the carbuncle, which glitters in darkness, also illumines many obscure passages of these books wherever it is proposed for the sake of comparison . . . Indeed, many, through an ignorance of hyssop—not knowing its potency, either for purifying the lungs or, as it is said, for penetrating rocks with its roots, although it is a little, unpretentious plant—cannot discover at all why it has been said: "Thou shalt sprinkle me with hyssop, and I shall be cleansed."

—*Ibid.*, II, 73, 75, 81-83.

In a similar way St. Augustine tells how a knowledge of "numbers" and the "elements of music" also help to clarify the meaning of passages in Scripture. Moreover, he indicates that the reader should have a full knowledge of history and philosophy to aid him in his studies. And finally, he encourages Christians to collect all sorts of information in encyclopedias for the benefit of readers, a request which medieval scholars fulfilled with a vengeance.

Now, some scholars have accomplished the task of interpreting, apart from their context, all the words and names in Hebrew, Syriac, Egyptian, or any other language found in the Sacred Scriptures which had been left there untranslated. Eusebius produced a history of past events because of the disputed points in the Sacred Books which demand its use. Consequently, just as these men, in matters of this kind, have made it unnecessary for a Christian to exert himself in many studies for a few facts, I believe the same thing could be done now, if there were someone capable who could be induced to devote a truly beneficial service to the advantage of his brethren. He could classify whatever unfamiliar places, animals, plants, trees, stones, metals, or other objects to which Scripture alludes. Then, after he has arranged them by classes, he should write down his explanations. He can do the same thing with regard to numbers . . . I do not know whether this could be done with the science of reasoning, but it seems impossible to me, because this is interwoven like strings through the whole text of the Scriptures.

—*Ibid.*, II, 111-112

9. ANONYMOUS (12TH CENTURY)

Now we may see how a medieval encyclopedist followed St. Augustine's advice. He discovers the potential symbolic meaning of the lion from the nature of the animal itself.

The name "Lion" (*leo*) has been turned into Latin from a Greek root, for it is called "*leon*" in Greek—but this is a muddled name, partly corrupted, since "*leon*" has also been translated as "king" from Greek into Latin, owing to the fact that he is Prince of All Animals. . . .

Scientists say that Leo has three principal characteristics.

His first feature is that he loves to saunter on the tops of mountains. Then, if he should happen to be pursued by hunting men, the smell of the hunters reaches up to him, and he disguises his spoor behind him with his tail. Thus the sportsmen cannot track him.

It was in this way that our Saviour (i.e. the Spiritual Lion of the Tribe of Judah . . .) once hid the spoor of his love in the high places, until, being sent by the Father, he came down into the womb of the Virgin Mary and saved the human race which had perished. . . .

The Lion's second feature is, that when he sleeps, he seems to keep his eyes open.

In this very way, Our Lord also, while sleeping in the body, was buried after being crucified—yet his Godhead was awake. As it is said in the *Song of Songs,* "I am asleep and my heart is awake," or, in the Psalm, "Behold, he that keepeth Israel shall neither slumber nor sleep."

The third feature is this, that when a lioness gives birth to her cubs, she brings them forth dead and lays them up lifeless for three days—until their father, coming on the third day, breathes in their faces and makes them alive.

Just so did the Father Omnipotent raise Our Lord Jesus Christ from the dead on the third day. Quoth Jacob: "He shall sleep like a lion, and the lion's whelp shall be raised."

So far as their relations with men are concerned, the nature of lions is that they do not get angry unless they are wounded. Etc.

> —*The Book of Beasts Being a Translation from a Latin Bestiary of the Twelfth Century,* TRANSLATED BY T. H. WHITE (LONDON, 1954), PP. 7-9. The multiplicity of meanings which this technique gave rise to can be illustrated by Alanus de Insulis' discussion of the lion (*Patrologia Latina,* CCX, 834-35), where *leo* is said to represent variously: Christ, the Tribe of Juda, powerful and rich men, the Devil, Antichrist, the just man, thieves and plunderers, and the Jewish people. Little attention has been given to the rationale which underlies such apparently dis-

parate interpretations; see D. W. Robertson Jr. and B. F. Huppé, *Piers Plowman and the Scriptural Tradition* (Princeton, 1951), pp. 5-6; M. W. Bloomfield, "Symbolism in Medieval Literature," *Modern Phiology*, LVI (1958), 76-77, 81; and item 16 below.

10. ST. BERNARD OF CLAIRVAUX

In his Sermons on the *Canticle of Canticles* St. Bernard of Clairvaux sometimes follows the studious principles of St. Augustine, but like many medieval writers he also belittles the literal text. In these passages he shows little concern for the intention of the author or for the meaning of the letter; he is intent on discovering a multiplicity of edifying spiritual meanings.

I know that I have explained this passage more fully and in another sense in my book upon the Love of God, and if it shall please any of you to read that, he can decide whether of the two is to be preferred. A prudent person will not, I think, condemn the giving of two senses to the same passage, provided that each appear to be grounded in truth, and that charity, which is the rule in interpreting Scripture, shall edify the more persons, inasmuch as there are a greater number of truthful senses, which each may apply to his own special need. For why should that be found faulty in the interpreting of Scripture, which we see is industriously practised in other things? To how many different bodily uses (only to take one thing for an example) do we put the element of water? In the same way a person is not to be blamed who gives divers senses, fitted to the various needs of souls, to a passage of Scripture. . . .

But I will, as far as I have received from the Lord, seek out the spirit and the life in the deep and mysterious meaning of the sacred text; this is the portion which belongs to me, as a believer in Jesus Christ. Why should I not extract the sweet and salutary nourishment of the Spirit from the barren and tasteless mass of the letter, as I separate grain from chaff, the kernel from its shell, or marrow from the bone? With this mere letter, which, when tasted, savours only of the flesh, and when swallowed, brings death, I do not desire to have anything to do, but only with that teaching from the Holy Ghost which is hidden in it.

—*Life and Works of Saint Bernard,* ED. DOM JOHN MABILLON AND TRANSLATED BY SAMUEL J. EALES (LONDON, 1896), IV, PP. 310 and 449.

11. STEPHEN LANGTON

A more disciplined critical technique, like that of the encyclopedist above, appears in the work of Stephen Langton.
His method is described here clearly, if unappreciatively.

In order to find the spiritual significance of any given text,
Langton will pick out several words. Of all their possible significations he selects those most suited to the context, sometimes ex-
plaining at length how they are reached. It is the combination of
the things symbolized by these words that determine the spiritual
sense of the passage. The skill of the commentator lies in judi-
cious choice and combination, and in discovering fresh symbolic
meanings for the words. He achieves his purpose by considering
the appearance, or qualities of the objects which they express.
Langton resembles his contemporaries in that his power of finding
points of similarity between unrelated things seems as endless as
it is tiresome. Yet there is method even here. The commentator
is not at liberty to make arbitrary comparisons, which do not rest
upon some basis of fact. It is essential that he have real knowledge of the object, or he cannot elaborate his exposition. We see
Langton hampered in this way when he comes to a text containing
an unfamiliar expression: e.g., "Erat autem Man quasi semen cori-
andri" (*Num.* XI, 7). He could dilate upon the topic at length,
he regretfully observes, if only the nature and quality of "corian-
der" were known to him.

> —BERYL SMALLEY, "STEPHEN LANGTON AND
> THE FOUR SENSES OF SCRIPTURE," *Speculum*,
> VI (1931), PP. 70-71.

12. DANTE

In a summary way Erich Auerbach describes the double-
effectiveness of medieval symbolism and Dante's in particular: how it achieves universal significances by means of the
particulars of reality. The method, he says, is figural realism.

In my essay "Figura" . . . I have shown—convincingly, I hope—
that the [Divine] Comedy is based on a figural view of things.
In the case of three of its most important characters—Cato of
Utica, Virgil, and Beatrice—I have attempted to demonstrate that
their appearance in the other world is a fulfillment of their appearance on earth, their earthly appearance a figure of their appearance in the other world. I stressed the fact that a figural
schema permits both its poles—the figure and its fulfillment—to

retain the characteristics of concrete historical reality, in contra-distinction to what obtains with symbolic or allegorical personifi-cations, so that figure and fulfillment—although the one "signifies" the other—have a significance which is not incompatible with their being real. An event taken as a figure preserves its literal and historical meaning. It remains an event, does not be-come a mere sign. The Church Fathers, especially Tertullian, Je-rome, and Augustine, had successfully defended figural realism, that is, the maintenance of the basic historical reality of figures, against all attempts at spiritually allegorical interpretation. Such attempts, which as it were undermine the reality of history and see in it only extrahistorical signs and significations, survived from late antiquity and passed into the Middle Ages. Medieval sym-bolism and allegorism are often, as we know, excessively abstract, and many traces of this are to be found in the Comedy itself. But far more prevalent in the Christian life of the High Middle Ages is the figural realism which can be observed in full bloom in ser-mons, the plastic arts, and mystery plays . . . and it is this figural realism which dominates Dante's view.

> —ERICH AUERBACH, *Mimesis: The Represen-tation of Reality in Western Literature,* TRANSLATED BY WILLARD R. TRASK (PRINCE-TON, N.J., 1953), PP. 195-96. Trask has also translated Ursula Brumm's "Symbolism and the Novel," *Partisan Review,* XXV (Summer 1958), PP. 329-42, which deals with the mod-ern novelist's and critic's emphasis on ar-bitrary, as opposed to realistic, symbolism.

13. BOCCACCIO

The importance of establishing a firm and authoritative historical basis for the development of analogical meanings is evident in Boccaccio's interpretation of Prometheus. The realism, the limitation, and the freedom of the analogical imagination are all working within the fourfold method.

Of the various interpretations which Boccaccio describes, he employs far oftenest the euhemeristic, the naturalistic, and the moral, and of these, perhaps the last two. His treatment of the legend of Prometheus, one of his most elaborate, is withal a fair illustration of his methods.

Historically, Prometheus must have been some distinguished teacher. So Pliny regards him, as do Eusebius, Augustine, Lactan-tius, Servius, and others. Lactantius guesses that he was the first to make mud images, and Pliny that he was the first to strike fire from a rock. Hence the legends of his creating men from mud and stealing fire from heaven. Boccaccio consults also Ovid, Horace, Claudian, Fulgentius, and Theodontius; and at second-hand cites Varro, Sappho, Hesiod, and Aeschylus, "a Pythagorean poet," who tells the story "in a rather long poem"!

Prometheus, then, was the eldest son of Iapetus, but forsook his inheritance in his youthful enthusiasm for study among the Chaldeans. At length he retired to the summit of the Caucasus to meditate and investigate the stars and the secrets of nature. In time he descended to teach the rude Assyrians astrology and meteorology until they became highly enlightened and civilized. Such, Boccaccio finds, is the literal, historical basis of the story.

Mystically, however, he sees in Prometheus as the creator of man, adumbrations of (1) God Omnipotent; or (2) of Nature producing each after its kind; or (3) of the natural man, perfect in Eden until the Fall. Then arises the second Prometheus, the learned man raising his fellows to civilization in morals, knowledge, and virtue—"so that some are mere children of nature, but others are newly created of doctrine." The fire which he stole from the wheel of the sun's chariot is but the gleam of heavenly truth proceeding from God's bosom, to light every man that cometh into the world. The wheel symbolizes its eternity, without beginning or end; and his furtive method hints that truth is not to be found in crowded cities, but only by meditation in silent solitudes. The tale of the gods' resentment and of the chaining to the Caucasus is but a concession of the poets to the vulgar notion, that the intense labor necessary to success in a laudable purpose is really a punishment inflicted by an angry God. As a matter of fact Prometheus visited Caucasus *before* he gave fire to men. Mercury, the gods' interpreter, led him thither and bound him, as the inspiring teacher lures one into solitary study and contemplation. The fetters are but self-imposed devotion to study, and the lacerations of the eagle but the pains of high meditation, healed at length by the joy of discovery.

Such lucubrations, usually less elaborate, accompany perhaps half of the myths recorded in the first thirteen books of the *Genealogy*.

—CHARLES G. OSGOOD, *Boccaccio on Poetry*
(PRINCETON, 1930), PP. xxiii-xxv.

III. CURRENT ATTITUDES
TOWARD MEDIEVAL EXEGESIS

14. B. SMALLEY

Miss Smalley's analysis of medieval exegesis is paradoxical. On one hand she considers it arbitrary spiritual reading which has no real reference to "the letter" or to reality.

On the other hand she says that two of the elementary tools for exegesis were etymologies and the characteristics of things. No matter how unscientific these methods may appear now, they brought the medieval critic as close to "the letter" and reality as his own sciences could bring him.

We then discover that what we should now call exegesis, which is based on the study of the text and of biblical history, in its widest sense, belongs to the "literal exposition." The 'spiritual exposition' generally consists of pious meditations or religious teaching for which the text is used merely as a convenient starting-point. It follows that so long as this conception of Bible studies holds good, we shall have many commentaries containing little exegesis.

'It is as though we were invited to focus our eyes not on the physical surface of the object, but on infinity as seen through the lattice . . . ; the object . . . exists—as it were —merely to define and detach a certain portion of infinite space, and make it manageable and apprehensible.'

This description of the "pierced technique" in early northern art is also an exact description of exegesis as understood by Claudius, if we substitute "text" for the "physical surface" of the artists' material, and "truth" for "infinite space." We are invited to look not at the text, but through it.

—BERYL SMALLEY, *The Study of the Bible in the Middle Ages* (OXFORD, 1952), P. 2.

Etymologies were more helpful even than numbers [in allegorical exegesis]. The conception went back to primitive word-magic. Hence Philo believes that a biblical name is a perfect description of the thing:

> . . . with Moses the names assigned are manifest images of the things, so that name and thing are inevitably the same from the first and the name and that to which the name is given differ not a whit. . . .

Then, closely connected with its etymology, is the description of the thing. Its special characteristics determine what it signifies. . . .

—Ibid., PP. 5-6.

Miss Smalley, then, assumes that literal meaning and spiritual interpretation are *opposed* to each other. Her assumption clouds an otherwise clear description of St. Augustine's critical position.

Insofar as he was a Neoplatonist, St. Augustine put the spiritual sense above the literal. His world was "a clear mirror where our thought sees in all things the reflection of God." The words of Scripture reflect their divine author, just as creation reflects its Creator. His world was a graded hierarchy where "all beings are necessarily superior or inferior one to another by the mere fact of their being different"; so with the senses of Scripture. He defines man as "a rational soul which uses a body," with the accent on the transcendence of the soul; so the spirit transcends the letter; their connection is tenuous and artificial, depending on the mechanical rules of allegory. As an original Christian thinker he gave the "letter" a concrete chronological reality which it had never had before. The narrative of Scripture is fitted into a philosophy of history based on the Incarnation. St. Augustine accepted the historical truth of the letter more wholeheartedly than St. Jerome. We must believe in the fact; then and then only may we seek its spiritual meaning.

The only case where the fact, as related by the sacred writer, may be doubted is when it does not conduce to charity. St. Augustine stressed charity where the Alexandrians had stressed wisdom. The whole end of Bible study is to increase our love for God and our neighbor: 'We must meditate on what we read till an interpretation be found that tends to establish the reign of charity.' Since charity implies purity and faith, 'whatever there is in the word of God that cannot when taken literally be referred either to purity of life or soundness of doctrine you may set down as figurative.'

In his exegesis St. Augustine tries to steer a middle course between literal and allegorical exposition. He gives the literal sense a wide meaning, taking it to include metaphor. He prefers to give both a literal and a spiritual interpretation to the same text, the one signifying or prefiguring the other. He very seldom sacrifices the literal sense to a subjective spiritual interpretation.

—*Ibid.*, PP. 23-24.

15. W. TROY

Here William Troy calls for a reshaping, in current terms, of the fourfold method for modern criticism; the method is useful because of the universal values which it incorporates.

What is possibly most in order at the moment is a thorough-going refurbishment of the medieval four-fold method of interpretation, which was first developed, it will be recalled, for just such a purpose—to make at least partially available to the reason that complex of human problems which are embedded, deep and imponderable, in the Myth.

> Littera *gesta docet, quae credas* Allegoria,
> Moralis *quid agas, quo tendas* Anagogia.

Of these four levels of meaning, surely the most important for us today is the last, the *anagogical,* which teaches us "whither we may turn ourselves." For it should be implicit in this footnote that if we are to be saved, which also assumes that we wish to be saved, it can only be through some reintegration of the Myth in terms of the heartbreaking concerns of the times.

—WILLIAM TROY, "MYTH, METHOD, AND THE FUTURE," *Chimera*, IV (SPRING 1946), PP. 83.

16. D. W. ROBERTSON, JR.

More recently D. W. Robertson, Jr. has said that critics of medieval literature should become better acquainted with the exegetical methods and traditional biblical symbols of the Middle Ages. He calls attention to the traditional connotations of words and things which modern critics of medieval literature have often ignored, and he calls for a reconsideration of the distinction which has been made between medieval Christianity and medieval "secular" literature.

Since the Bible was also a model and source book for literature [in the Middle Ages], it is necessary for the historical critic of medieval literature to familiarize himself with the conventions of Scriptural exegesis. A few of the elementary principles may be examined here. In the first place, the Bible was said to teach nothing but charity and to condemn nothing but cupidity. But large portions of the Bible, especially the Old Testament, express the message of charity in an obscure way. When this message is not apparent on the surface, it was thought necessary to resort to interpretation. For the purposes of this task, various techniques were employed, some of them verbal and some of them physical. Names might be interpreted to imply a kind of word play. Thus, "Jerusalem" was said to consist of two elements meaning "City of Peace." Most of the names, both of persons and of places, which appear in the Bible were interpreted in this way, and in addition all the machinery of classical rhetoric was brought to bear on the text. The physical techniques are a little more difficult for us to understand. Numbers were thought to be signs of abstract concepts. Thus, "three" and "nine" are signs of the Trinity; "seven" is the number of life on earth or of the church; "eight" indicates the Resurrection of Christ. Many of the things mentioned in the Bible were thought of as signs of other things. Thus, a lion, not the word "lion," is a sign either of Christ or of Satan. As in this instance, such signs frequently embrace two opposites. A sign, as opposed to a verbal figure, might have tropological, allegorical, or anagogical values—sometimes one of these, sometimes two, and sometimes all three. In other words, a principle stated in signs or implied by a sign might apply to the individual, to society or the church, and to the after life. This procedure is not quite so "mystical" as it sounds. All that is meant by it ultimately is that a given precept or principle may apply equally well within man, within society, or within Heaven or Hell. A good example is afforded by "Jerusalem." Verbally, it means "City of Peace." *But since Jerusalem is an actual city as well as a word, it is also a sign.** As a sign it indicates the highest kind of human satisfaction, whether in the individual, in society, or in Heaven. The values of a given sign might be numerous. In the first place, a sign may have four levels of meaning. If we include the opposites, there are eight. And some signs might have several basic meanings, so they imply several sets of eight somewhat different values. Theoretically an object may have as many meanings as it has characteristics in common with other objects in the universe, but practically the better known signs are limited by the contexts in which they appear in Scripture. For purposes of clarity, I shall speak of verbal symbols as "figures" and of physical symbols as "signs." The importance attached to this kind of analysis in the Middle Ages is

* Italics mine.

attested by the fact that the *trivium* was devoted to the analysis of figures and the *quadrivium* to the analysis of signs. Medieval encyclopedias, the *De universo* of Rabanus Maurus, for example, are largely devoted to the exegetical meanings of figures and signs. And in the twelfth century, a number of exegetical dictionaries were published, giving the most common values for figures and signs in the Bible. One of these was written by a poet, Alanus de Insulis. . . .

The analogy between Scriptural techniques and poetic techniques was observed at a very early period [in the Middle Ages]. Scotus, for example, makes a direct comparison of the two. Christian thinkers were for the most part loth to part with their heritage of Classical literature, especially Latin literature. Since, however, it could not be enjoyed in itself, but was to be used for purposes of furthering charity, it was necessary to interpret it much in the same way that it was necessary to interpret the Old Testament. But in the interpretation of pagan literature only verbal techniques could be employed. Pagan authors might be capable of rhetoric and word play, but they could not be expected to understand the signs whose meanings are revealed only under the direct inspiration of the Holy Spirit. *Moreover, pagan poetic narratives are not accounts of actual events.** The *Aeneid* is not a history, but a lying fable. Beneath the lying cortex, however, diligent study may reveal a nucleus useful to the faith. The words "cortex" and "nucleus," together with a variety of synonyms for them, became popular literary terms as well as exegetical terms in the course of the Middle Ages. . . . A medieval Christian poem was like a pagan poem in that the external narrative was a lie. The poet combined things not found combined in nature so as to form an artificial "pictura." . . . But a medieval Christian poem differs from a pagan poem in that the author might employ signs as they are used in the Bible as well as figures. Thus, any of the multitude of Scriptural signs may appear in a medieval poem, and since these signs are things, the new poetic combination of them may not resemble verbally any passage in Scripture. For example, a Christian poem may contain a description of a garden based on signs taken from both Genesis and the Canticum and dressed up to suit the literary tastes of the poet's own audience. The result is a *pictura* which is fundamentally Biblical, but which does not resemble any Biblical scene and does not contain any Biblical phrases.

—D. W. ROBERTSON, JR., "HISTORICAL CRITICISM," *English Institute Essays 1950,* ED. ALAN S. DOWNER (NEW YORK, 1951), PP. 9-11, 12-13.

* Italics mine.

17. H. GARDNER

It is possible that in emphasizing something long neglected Professor Robertson may not have sufficiently called attention to the "real and literal" as the basis of medieval symbolism. He refers to interpretation as though it were an unusual technique to which the critic has recourse when certain occasions arise. His observations sometimes sound like Miss Smalley's when she remarks that in medieval exegesis, "One finds, as did Alice, a country governed by queer laws which the inhabitants oddly regard as rational. In order to understand medieval Bible study one must live there long enough to slip into their ways and appreciate the logic of their strict, elaborately fantastic conventions." (*The Study of the Bible,* p. 5.) Such a view does not fairly account for the best in medieval exegesis and does not explain the assumptions with regard to the literal level made by some of the laconic and apparently cryptic exegetes. An incomplete application of the techniques of Biblical exegesis to current literary criticism may lead to an approach which, Helen Gardner says, passes over the actuality of the literary text and its particular and human character.

I cannot feel satisfied with a literary criticism which substitutes for the conception of the writer as "a man speaking to men," the conception of the writer as an imagination weaving symbolic patterns to be teased out by the intellect, and in its concentration on the work by itself ends by finding significance in what the work suggests rather than in what it says, and directs our imaginations towards types and figures rather than towards their actualization. As literary criticism I cannot regard the new symbolical or typological approach to the Gospels as satisfactory. It does not explain a prime historic fact; that for centuries Christian emotion directed towards the historic person of Jesus Christ, true God and true Man, has found in the Gospels the strength of its own conviction that "Christ walked on this earth." I feel the same kind of dissatisfaction with the results of these methods applied to the interpretation of poetry. I am not happy at the assumption that there is a royal road by which we can get at "meaning," and I am particularly suspicious when the critic buttresses the claim that he has found the "meaning" with the statement that this was the meaning the work must have had for men of its own age, since we know how men of this age thought. To borrow the words of Dr. Muir, "Things truly made preserve themselves through time in the first freshness of their nature." It is the first responsibility of an interpreter that he should neither disregard nor damage that first freshness with which things made by long-dead men speak directly to the mind and heart. . . .

It is argued that we must revive within ourselves the capacity to recognize hidden senses, and learn to read these hieroglyphs and forgotten symbols if we are to read the poets of this period [before Milton] with a full imaginative sympathy and be aware of the meanings which the author would have expected his readers to be sensible of and to respond to. He, like his readers, was a child of his age and we must learn its way of thought. . . . It is impossible not to feel after reading much modern interpretative criticism that the author and his work have disappeared and that it is the interpreter's insistent company which we are left alone with. . . .

Our own preoccupation with myth, metaphor, allegory, and symbol as related methods of expressing the imagination's sense of the unity of its experience has led to a concentration on the "spiritual senses" of works which has made the literal sense something to be brushed aside as soon as possible. It is claimed that in so doing we are finding the true historical sense, since this was a continuing habit of mind which endured from the Middle Ages through the Renaissance into the seventeenth century and, to our impoverishment, was lost when at the close of the century the old "medieval world picture" was replaced by the modern scientific one. This view, which is here stated in its crudest form, might be called, with no impoliteness intended, the myth behind much modern criticism of the poetry of the Elizabethan and Jacobean period. It embodies, as do all strongly held myths, some elements of truth; but it tells us more, I think, about those who framed it and hold it than about the sixteenth and seventeenth centuries, and reflects the preoccupations of the critic more than those of the author. . . .

The unhistorical nature of this whole approach, in spite of its insistence that we must not read our own ideas into the past, lies in its lack of interest in anything but ideas, its ignoring of events and circumstances, and its consequent reduction of individual writers, who are historical persons, to habits of mind, and of works of art, which are historical objects, to *exempla* of these habits of mind and repositories of ideas. For all its respect for the past it is, in fact, contemptuous of it. It substitutes for historical reality a kind of Golden Age of the Mind, when the difficulties which we feel as historical beings were not felt, when faith was easy, and man, knowing his place in an ordered system of things, happily saw correspondences everywhere, only slightly disturbed by the possibility that the universe might not be geocentric. . . .

Against the view that the power to see "the spirit in the letter" is the secret of the greatness of the greatest period in English literature, it would be equally possible—I think myself it would be truer—to claim that the growing sense from the twelfth century onwards of the importance of the letter and of the spiritual nourishment to be drawn from it was at the root of the greatness of much late medieval art, and that the insistence of Protestantism on the reading of the whole Bible, and on the primacy of the literal sense of the Scriptures, is not unconnected with the flowering of our literature in the reign of Elizabeth. . . .

It has been said that the Middle Ages lacked two essentials for a sound exegesis: "une science philologique et surtout le sens historique." But medieval literature and art testify everywhere to the response of the human imagination to historical reality. There is continuity here, as well as in the survival of allegory. There is also a rich development. . . .

Many literary critics, like the typological critics of the New Testament, impress on their readers the necessity of trying to think in this [typological] way. Both, rather unaccountably, assume that this is very difficult for "modern" man. They ought, possibly, to be warning us instead to be on our guard against its obvious attractiveness to many modern minds. To the aesthetic sensibility of today the symbolic presentation of Christ seems more expressive and more congenial than the attempt to picture him in his humanity. . . . The theologian of today may rightly concentrate on whatever image best illuminates his present concern; but the literary critic cannot disregard the other images. Much of the literary criticism of the Gospels in the nineteenth century may be justly charged with sentimentality. Its authors might well retort upon some of their successors the countercharge of inhumanity. It is a charge which can be brought against much of the art and literature of this age.

> HELEN GARDNER, *The Limits of Literary Criticism* (LONDON, 1956), PP. 39, 43-44, 45-47, 55, 61-63. This work has recently been reprinted in *The Business of Criticism* (Oxford, 1959).
>
> *The Business of Criticism* (OXFORD, 1959), pp. 125-26, 131, 133-136, 147, 155, 157. This material originally formed part of the Riddell Lectures for the University of Durham, 1956.

18. M. W. BLOOMFIELD

Professor Bloomfield also outlines some objections against symbolist interpretations for neglecting the particular, the literal and the human in a literary work.

The first objection, then, to the symbolic approach is not that it finds a Christian *sententia* in medieval literature but that it assumes that this symbolic method is unique to the period and that there is no essential difference between literary works and theological or pastoral works. It misunderstands the nature of meaning and of literature. It neglects the concrete for the universal and assumes that the concrete exists only for the universal in a work of art, which is not true even of the Bible. It is as if one were to love a woman because she represented eternal beauty or eternal good. Her particularity—her figure, face, skin, and personality—is submerged in her "meaning." She is what Professor Wimsatt would call a "sign," not an icon. There is no "concrete universal" in the world of the symbolists, only the universal.

The second objection is that the emphasis on the symbolic as opposed to the literal approach to the Bible is not characteristic of the later Middle Ages, except perhaps in sermons, which are conservative and must, of necessity, stress the moral. Although there are warnings earlier against neglect of the literal or historical sense of Scripture, beginning in the twelfth century the symbolic method as applied to biblical exegesis underwent strong attacks, and in the later Middle Ages, except for certain standard interpretations dealing mainly with the prediction of Jesus in the Old Testament and the normal interpretation of any tale or event, the literal sense was the one which received the major attention. In other words, at the time of the rise of the great vernacular literatures, we find a corresponding decline in the emphasis put on the symbolic method in biblical interpretation.* . . .

Third, even in the period of its greatest use the symbolic method with its three- or fourfold levels was never mechanically or completely applied to Scripture. These levels should rather be viewed as possible ways of interpreting the manifold meanings in the Bible. All meaning at any time is multiple. The cross, for instance, can stand today for Jesus' sufferings, for Christianity, for the church, for the truth, for good as opposed to evil, and so forth. To attempt to systematize various possible meanings, without understanding what is involved, can lead only to a debased and mechanical interpretation of the highest mysteries. Such attempts reveal a profound misunderstanding of all historical study and, even though the Middle Ages loved system theoretically, medieval history in particular. Besides, in effect, no one can consist-

---

* While this may be true of biblical interpretation, just the opposite is the case with the interpretation of classical mythology. Early medieval works which deal with mythology are generally literalistic and naturalistic, with some scattering of moral exegesis; but from the twelfth century to the fifteenth century the interpretations generally become more elaborately symbolic. The present writer is preparing a study of the development of mythological interpretation through the Middle Ages.

ently apply the fourfold criterion except to a few hackneyed
terms like Jerusalem.

> M. W. BLOOMFIELD, "SYMBOLISM IN MEDIE-
> VAL LITERATURE," *Modern Philology,* LVI
> (1958), PP. 75-76.

19. R. P. BLACKMUR

From these observations Professor Bloomfield moves on to
others which tend to be exclusively literalistic. For example,
he seems to argue that the fourfold method is reserved for
biblical interpretation only, as though it was not, or should
not have been adapted by poets and critics to suit the needs
of secular literature. We would suggest, with R. P. Blackmur
and the critics already cited, that many problems are involved in medieval symbolism and the fourfold method, and
that the solution of these problems provides a challenge to
the modern critic to discover some of the riches in poetic
technique that were available to poets of the past.

It [the poetry of *Divine Comedy*] is the language of a poet
who is free to make full use of his inspiration, certain that *by one
mode or another* he will be able to set it forth *to one degree or
another*. . . .
There is a sentence in the letter to Can Grande which could hardly have been fresher the day it was written . . . "The form or
method of treatment is poetic, fictive, descriptive, digressive, tran-
sumptive; and likewise proceeding by definition, division, proof,
refutation, and setting forth the examples." . . .
He [Dante] favored pretty much the use of the whole mind—all
the way from its light-shot sanity to the steam of its most drunken
night-bog—in the particular medium of poetry. . . . To him the
whole mind illustrated as near as possible the whole of human behavior. . . . Dante loved music perhaps for secondary reasons;
poetry he loved for its own sake, and like any good lover found
some form of everything else he loved somehow in the poetry.
There was even, as we know from the *Convivio,* a hankering in
him to find the actual lady he loved housing in her body of poetry
both the lady of philosophy and the lady of theology; which is to
say, really, and in his defence, that though the ladies differ in
the embrace all love is the same. . . .
In the *Convivio* he examined three of his odes to see what lay
behind the letter, which, so to speak, may not have been in his
mind at the time of composition—or at any rate not consciously

in his mind—but which, under scholastic examination, is seen to have transpired there. What was passionate love in earthly flesh *transpires* now as contemplative love of Lady Philosophy; and it is of both that it may be said *La Donna mia porta negli occhi amore.* At any rate, so we say at best, and so Dante was later able to say of the eyes of Beatrice when he meets her in the Terrestrial Paradise at the end of the Purgatory. But when he was making his prose argument in the *Convivio,* Dante tended to insist—as if truth were a matter of equivocation rather than equivalence—on the allegorical phase of his poem as its only true content, and to insist that the odes had been addressed to Lady Philosophy exclusively in the first place. Thought finds it hard to assent to its own behavior.

. . . Dante learned a great deal about poetry by trying to put everything into it and what he learned he could summarize—in our ten terms—without comment. We can only say that all four aspects of his theory as here put together depend on the active, conscious, deliberate presence of extremely highly developed skills in composition and understanding: a rich lore in the use of the mind available to Dante not only consciously but also to his very finger tips.

Not all finger tips resume the consciousness. Boccaccio, whose life overlapped Dante's, and who wrote his Life, did not have this skill or lore. Neither have the scholars had it, if my messengers tell me right. Only in the last twenty years or so has scholarship begun to recover understanding of the skill, and scholarship remains dubious, not of the skill, but of our knowledge of it. The disappearance of such skill is as hard to account for as the disappearance during the Dark Ages of the skill of making good bread. The guess may be hazarded that the secularization of literature destroyed the usefulness of the conceptual and imaginative aspects of the technique of scriptural interpretation and rhetorical executive techniques. What had been deeply useful in the understanding of life became a mere special competence and the competence became ornamental, and the ornamental became artificial with no longer any grasp on actuality. To get at a riddle is one thing, to solve a puzzle, though as laborious, another.

It is for us to recover the skill and resume the lore for our own purposes, if we can but find what they are.

—*Kenyon Review,* XIV (SPRING 1952), PP. 300, 286-87, 287-88, 291-92, 295.

20. C. CHARLIER

Finally, Dom Célestin Charlier offers a valuable series of comparisons which help to make medieval exegesis more understandable; it is not as strange as it has been made to seem. At the same time the dangers of undisciplined spiritual reading are clear. Much of what is said here about the symbolic interpretation of the Bible applies equally well to the symbolic interpretation of secular literature, especially that of the Middle Ages.

Surely we may conclude by stressing the notable agreement of fundamental attitudes which inspired the patristic method [of exegesis] and those which characterize the new orientations of the historic method, despite their different point of departure and their development proper to epochs which separate them by more than a thousand years.

First of all both agree by considering history a vital phenomenon and, more particularly, Sacred History a transcendental evolution the intimate development of which is only perceptible to the faithful, in a true and total union.

Both also agree by recognizing in words a depth which human reflection—reacting to exterior circumstances at the same time as obeying its interior inspiration—is capable of extracting throughout a progressive evolution.

Likewise, both agree again by establishing as an essential principle of all spiritual exegesis the recognition of internal bonds which unite the Old Testament to the New. At the same time these bonds apply to the continuity of the divine designs which are expressed in the supernatural logic of facts, and also apply to the organic belief in revelation. Act and Word, at this point, are intimately and inseparably joined and must be grasped in their unity. The modern idea of "thème" expresses, for all practical purposes, what the Fathers called "type." The study of these themes is the basis of all spiritual reading of the Scriptures.

Finally both agree by subordinating typology in its truest sense to this basic study. Typology should not be a means of eluding the problems which the Old Testament poses, but instead should bring out a recognition of its undeniable message as it brings out a recognition of the unbreakable bond which unites the Old to the New Testament.

Typology itself has no value; still less can it be superimposed on the actual significance of the texts; thus, neither does it provide any divine teaching extrinsic to the literal sense nor does it correspond to any purpose superadded by the Holy Spirit. It is not an epiphenomenon, but rather an expression in some way spontaneous and natural—in the external appearance of events or in the style of writers—of a continuity which is underlying and more profound, living and objective. Typology, then, has interest only insofar as it stresses the recurrence of an essential theme. In order for typology to exist it is not sufficient that a relation of figure to reality be discernible; this relation must also be bound by an objective link which establishes the historical preparation of the figure, just as much as the ideal prefiguration, of the reality which it stresses.

We shall give here a single example which has often been invoked in the recent controversies: the scarlet ribbon suspended by the courtesan Rahab from the wall of besieged Jericho. The scarlet ribbon has no other connection with the blood of Christ than its color and a functional similarity which is completely external: it saved Rahab, and the blood of Christ saves the Christian. But is this sufficient for affirming that the Holy Spirit has hidden a prefiguration of one under the other? No internal bond unites the red ribbon and the redeeming blood. One did not take rise from the other; faith in the second did not spring from the contemplation of the first. It is completely different, for example, with the Paschal Lamb, or with the blood which Moses sprinkled on the people, in order to consecrate the Alliance, at the foot of Sinai; these rites efficaciously gave start, in the religious conscience of Israel, to an opening movement subject to the revelation of the sense of the Passion, on the day of the New Alliance, and they efficaciously prepared, in the history of the People of God, the objective germination of the event.

A conception of Inspiration is at stake here. If scriptural inspiration is the projection of divine ideas based entirely on the formulation of human ideas, the Bible is a written cipher, and we can rightly demand of the exegete only one science: that of cipher, and this cipher is the figurative relation. Human sense and the terrestrial event can only link the divine idea to the earth and to time; they are not the temporal incarnation of it. In this hypothesis divine thought not only springs from the thought of the sacred writer, divine thought is superadded to his thought. And as the blood of Christ cannot have been placed, neither explicitly nor implicitly, nor embryonically in the scarlet ribbon by the writer of the account of Josue, we are obliged, in order to discover it there, to dissociate the spiritual sense from the literal sense. But such a twofold division of the Bible can only endanger the intimate sense of the Incarnation, of which the mystery of the two Testaments is only a form.

The plenary significance of the Bible is written in the profound cohesion of its internal evolution. This evolution fluctuates between two terms which are called the literal sense and the spiritual sense. Doubtless it would be more exact and more simple to speak of the "initial" and of the "plénier" sense, as of two moments which mark the extreme limits of one and the same temporal development at the interior of one and the same significance and one and the same single reality.

It is not difficult to initiate the Christian progressively to the living comprehension of this movement. It is enough to teach him to read the Bible in its historic perspective, to instruct him in some of the rudimentary techniques, and especially to introduce him to the particular mentality of the biblical world. The danger of typological exegesis is precisely this: it separates the Christian from an effort of adaption by offering him methods which dispense with it. These methods satisfy his immediate need for clear notions and for adequate distinctions; they even hold him an instant by the charm of their ingenious constructions, but they leave unsatisfied his thirst for a living and profound contact. The soul is not nourished deeply by sentiments nor by ready-made ideas, but by past and present truth. The soul waits for the impact of a thought converted into experience. But this is the very definition of the Bible, if one considers it simply as the witness and the progressive incarnation of the living Thought of God.

—DOM CÉLESTIN CHARLIER, "MÉTHODE HISTORIQUE ET LECTURE SPIRITUELLE DES ÉSCRITURES," *Bible et Vie Chrétienne*, No. 18 (JUNE/AUGUST, 1957), PP. 23-26. The translation is my own.

**Addressed to YOU
as a book reader
by Edward R. Murrow**
Director, United States Information Agency

Hardly a day passes that someone somewhere in the world does not make inquiry about these United States. If it be true that in only some places are we the object of affection, it is equally true that in every place we are the object of curiosity.

In this ever-changing world in which many peoples in one generation seek to accomplish the changes of centuries, this country has a great role to fill. We are, if we choose, to carry on a great dialogue between man and that better part of himself known as knowledge. <u>The world is hungry to know and to learn.</u> We must satisfy that hunger. Our Information Agency seeks to satisfy it through Voice of America broadcasts, libraries, film and television showings, exhibits and lectures in more than 100 countries overseas.

The desire for knowledge remains great. Books are knowledge. They are the tools of truth and freedom. A book is the heart of a child and the hope of a man.

But millions of people around our globe—both children and men—have no books. Students in many countries undertake their lessons—but without books to read. Theirs is the legacy of the uninformed. The task is the challenge of the unavailable.

It is to meet this unavailability that, with the New American Library of World Literature, our Agency has joined in this campaign. A packet of representative BOOKS USA will go abroad to service the burning desire to know that is so much of this modern world. We urge your support.

Director, U.S. Information Agency

The world wants to know more about the U.S.
HERE'S HOW YOU CAN HELP

You can bring the knowledge and enlightenment of fine literature to thousands of individuals in a country of your choice. Outstanding books, sent in your name to areas where the need is greatest, will be read, re-read, absorbed and discussed by persons who want to know more about the United States. Here's how the BOOKS USA plan operates:

The New American Library of World Literature is providing on a non-profit basis a library packet of eight representative American books which sell retail for $5.15. To send them, you pay only $3.00 plus $1.00 to cover the delivery to the country you specify, a total of $4.00. The packet will be distributed by the U.S. Information Agency to a library, school, or other center where thousands will read these outstanding books.

Join this drive to spread knowledge through fine literature. Your gift will be acknowledged directly to you by the recipient overseas. The readers of your books will, in turn, inspire others to new goals of enlightenment, freedom, and decency among men.

20th CENTURY LITERATURE

THE MENTOR BOOK OF MAJOR AMERICAN POETS
      edited by Oscar Williams and Edwin Honig MQ436
APPOINTMENT IN SAMARRA by John O'Hara   D1895
THE APPRENTICESHIP OF ERNEST HEMINGWAY
      by Charles A. Fenton   MP385
THE CATCHER IN THE RYE by J. D. Salinger   D1667
ARROWSMITH by Sinclair Lewis   CT92
THE AGE OF INNOCENCE by Edith Wharton   CT106
THE TROLL GARDEN, by Willa Cather   CD31
PALE HORSE, PALE RIDER
      by Katherine Anne Porter   CP137

Simply fill out this coupon and mail with your check or money order.

To: New American Library, P.O. Box 2310
     Grand Central Station, New York 17, New York

Send (one or more) BOOKS USA library packets containing the 8 books listed above, in my name, to the country (or countries) checked below. Here's my check (or M.O.) for $............. (for........packets at $4.00 each).

☐ ARGENTINA ☐ GHANA ☐ KENYA ☐ NIGERIA ☐ TANGANYIKA
☐ BRAZIL ☐ INDIA ☐ KOREA ☐ PAKISTAN ☐ THAILAND
☐ CEYLON ☐ INDONESIA ☐ LIBERIA ☐ PHILIPPINES ☐ TRINIDAD &
☐ CHILE ☐ JAPAN ☐ MALAYA ☐ RHODESIA WEST INDIES
☐ FINLAND ☐ JORDAN ☐ MEXICO ☐ SUDAN ☐ UGANDA

NAME ....

STREET .... CITY............... STATE..........
Since this coupon goes to us for order fulfillment and the books must be freighted abroad by the U. S. Information Agency to the country of your choice, allow at least four months for acknowledgment. This offer is good until Sept. 30, 1963.